Put It in Writing

Put It in Writing

Learn How to Write
Clearly, Quickly, and Persuasively

ALBERT JOSEPH

New and Updated Edition

McGraw-Hill

New York   San Francisco   Washington, D.C.   Auckland   Bogotá
Caracas   Lisbon   London   Madrid   Mexico City   Milan
Montreal   New Delhi   San Juan   Singapore
Sydney   Tokyo   Toronto

Library of Congress Cataloging-in-Publication Data

Joseph, Albert.
    Put it in writing : learn how to write clearly, quickly, and
persuasively / Albert Joseph.
      p. cm.
   ISBN 0-07-039308-7
   1. Business writing. 2. Report writing. I. Title.
HF5719.J67 1998
808'.0665—dc21   97-52954
                                                    CIP

McGraw-Hill

*A Division of The **McGraw·Hill** Companies*

1 2 3 4 5 6 7 8 9 0 FGR/FGR 9 0 3 2 1 0 9 8

ISBN 0-07-039308-7

*The sponsoring editor for this book was Betsy Brown, the editing supervisor was
Scott Amerman, and the production supervisor was Pamela Pelton. It was set in
Baskerville by North Market Street Graphics.*

Printed and bound by Quebecor/Fairfield.

*This book has previously been published by the International Writing Institute; fourth
edition copyright © 1989 by The International Writing Institute.*

*McGraw-Hill books are available at special quantity discounts to use as premiums and
sales promotions. For more information, please write to Director of Special Sales, McGraw-
Hill, 11 West 19th Street, New York, NY 10011. Or contact your local bookstore.*

 This book is printed on recycled, acid-free paper containing a
minimum of 50% recycled, de-inked fiber.

To Dylene, as always,
for having to put up with a writer all these years.

Special thanks to Zarina Hock, National Council of
Teachers of English, for research on difficult points.

Thanks also to the men and women of the United States
Navy Fleet and Mine Warfare Training Center, Charleston,
South Carolina, who tested the grammar section of
this book (Part Three) in classrooms before it was published.

Contents

PART 1 ON CLARITY — 1

Chapter 1: The Things Every Writer Wants — 3

What Style of Clothing Should Our Writing Wear? — 4
Clarity, the Major Challenge — 4
Writing Quickly and Productively — 6
The Image Writers Create — 6
How These Unnatural Writing Styles Developed — 7

Chapter 2: Five Principles of Clear Writing — 11

Principle 1: Prefer Clear, Familiar Words — 12
Principle 2: Keep Most Sentences Short and Simple — 18
The Devil's Advocacy — 26
  Closer Look: Word Sense — 28
  Sentence Sense — 30

To the Prudent Student — 32

Chapter 3: Five Principles of Clear Writing (continued) — 35

Principle 3: Prefer Active Voice Verbs; Avoid Passives — 36
Principle 4: Use Conversational Style as a Guide — 39
Principle 5: Revise, Revise, . . . and Revise Again — 40
Further Advice for the World of Work: Allow People into the Paragraphs and Pages — 42
The Devil's Advocacy — 43
  Closer Look: Prefer Active Voice Verbs — 46
  Use Conversational Style — 48

Chapter 4: Changing Some Old Attitudes   51

The Importance of Connectives   51
The Three Taboos   52
Two Other Things We Should Not Have Been Told   57
How Important Is Brevity?   58
The Devil's Advocacy   59
    Closer Look: Connectives Build Bridges   61

Chapter 5: Measuring the Ease of Reading   65

The Reading Process   66
How the Experts Measure   68
Customized Guidance for the Writer   70
About Legal Writing   75
About Scientific Writing   76
About Academic Writing   77
The Devil's Advocacy   78
    Closer Look: What Makes Something Readable?   81

Chapter 6: Guidelines for Nonsexist Writing   83

The Infamous Generic *He*   84
Other "Man" Words   84
Job Descriptions   85
Male Bosses and Female Subordinates?   86
About *Ms.*   87
The Devil's Advocacy   87
    Closer Look: Nonsexism Is Easy   88
    More Examples   89

Chapter 7: Commonly Misused Words   91

Chapter 8: New Writing in the Computer Age   99

You Still Do the Hard Part   99
Spelling, Proofreading, Grammar, and Readability   100

Exceptional Help for Large Documents   102
The Major Question Remains   103

PART 2 ON ORGANIZING   105

Chapter 9: Power to the Reader   107

Understanding Readers   108
Leading the Reader to the Path   110
The Inverted Pyramid Structure   110
The Five *Ws* of Journalism   111
The Corned Beef Sandwich Writing Lesson   115
The Inverted Pyramid's One Disadvantage   118
A Recommended Format for Reports   120
A Checklist for Organizing   123
The Devil's Advocacy   124
    Closer Look: The "Inverted Pyramid"   127

Chapter 10: Sense and Nonsense about Planning   129

Beating the Deadline   130
Making the Breakthrough Happen   131
The Blissful "False Start"   131
The Sleek and Modern Outline   132
Mind Mapping Techniques   134
The Devil's Advocacy   135
    Closer Look: The Blissful "False Start"   137
    A Case Study: The Sleek and Modern Outline   137

Chapter 11: The Elegant Finishing Touches   141

Headings: Joy to Readers *and the Writer*   141
The Power of White Space   142
Why the Mystery about Paragraphs?   143
The Treatment of Graphic Information   146
Bullets, Symbols, and Special Typefaces   148
Fact and Fancy about Letters   149

Chapter 12: When Writers Become Speakers   **153**

When Readers Become Listeners   153
Write the Speech?   154
Memorize, and Deliver It from Memory?   155
Butterfly Repellent   156
The Three "Tell Them" Parts of a Speech   157
That Person at the Lectern   157
Visual Aids   158
The Speaker's Voice Skills   159

Chapter 13: Managing the Writing of Others   **161**

The Trouble with Evaluating Writing Skills   162
When and How to Give Help   163

PART 3 ON GRAMMAR   **165**

Chapter 14: What Is Grammar?   **167**

How Do We Learn It?   167
What Makes Grammar Correct?   168
Who Decides What Is "Standard"?   168
Why Does It Matter as Long as People Understand You?   169

Chapter 15: About English   **171**

Its Remarkable History (and the French Connection)   171
Latin's Influence   177
Its Characteristics   178

Chapter 16: Words (the Parts of Speech)   **181**

Adjectives, Verbs . . . and Everything in Between   182
Closer Look: Grammar Basics   184

Chapter 17: Phrases and Clauses—from Words to Ideas   **189**

A Phrase Is . . .   190
A Clause Is . . .   191
Closer Look: Self-Test on Phrases and Clauses   194

Chapter 18: The Noble English Sentence 197

The Simple Sentence 197
Compound, Complex, and Compound/Complex Sentences 199
More about Objects 200
Syntax: The Art of Making Sentences Behave 202
Closer Look: The Simple Sentence 205
Compound Sentences 206
Complex 206
Compound/Complex Sentences 207

Chapter 19: What a Difference Punctuation Makes 209

The Bread and Butter Marks—The Period and Comma 210
The Elegant Punctuation Marks 214
Closer Look: Count the Punctuation Errors 219
The Bogie Errors 219
The Correctly Punctuated Passage 219

Chapter 20: The Five Most Common Mistakes 221

Dangling Participle 222
Subject-Verb Disagreement 223
Noun-Pronoun Disagreement 224
False Series 227
The Missing Second Comma 228
Closer Look: Dangling Participle 229
Subject-Verb Agreement 229
Noun-Pronoun Agreement 230
False Series 230
The Missing Second Comma 231

Glossary of Grammar Terms 233

Preface

The two commandments of writing, I believe, must be: *Think clearly* and *write clearly.* If there must be a third, it should be: Neither of these is very useful without the other. Beyond these, if the creator of writing commandments were to grace us with a fourth, it almost certainly should be: Make reading an important part of your life; good habits will rub off on you.

Careful thinking and sensible language usage, then, are the essential ingredients of good writing. They are the fundamentals of the writing process.

This book deals with the latter of the two, the *language arts* part of writing.

What is a writer? Not just novelists and journalists need writing skills. Anyone who sits down to write something is a writer—whether it is a report, or advice to a friend, or a letter to a department store that charged you for a life-size statue of Pocahontas you did not buy. Although language usage skills alone will probably not win the day (you must first have a message worth stating), making your point convincingly will empower your position. The opposite is also true; poor expression makes it easy for others to reject or ignore your position, even when you are right. The power of the pen—or word processor— *is* mighty. That surprises most students and many professional men and women, but it is true. Ask the people who have been where you hope to be.

It is often said, "Some people are born writers." Well, perhaps. Some people might be born with that rare imaginative mind which allows them to *create* stories, or plotlines, that grip us and hold us spellbound. This writing talent we call *creativity,* and it is a rare gift. But the writer's tool for expressing that creativity is language, and using it skillfully is the other half of the writing process, the *language arts* half. Learning to use the English language skillfully is neither mysterious nor very difficult, but the learner must first think of language as the *carrier* of the creative half, the *message*.

I most certainly take issue with the cliché, attributed [wrongly] to scholar and author Marshall McLuhan, "The medium is the message."* They are quite separate; writers must deal separately with the message *and* the words and sentences that will convey it, and, although usually not aware of it, so must readers.

In the classrooms I have often advised would-be professional writers: Don't try to say things brilliantly; *try to say brilliant things*. It is the message that matters first. Of *Moby Dick*, Herman Melville said, "To produce a mighty book you must produce a mighty theme." Those who go to New York City relying on writing style alone end up in other professions.

This book contains little that is new about writing. It deals with the ordinary language arts tasks writers face: choosing the right words, building them into a smooth flow of readable sentences, and organizing expository information in the order that best helps the reader. These are the challenges writers *and readers* must deal with if ideas are to be communicated successfully from "senderbrain" to "receiverbrain." Writers *encode* (send); readers *decode* (receive). To a large extent, the sender determines how well the reader will read.

Dare we define language as a tool for transporting information? If not, for what other purpose do cultures create language? Beauty? Of course. No other beauty, however, can outshine that of bringing the light of knowledge to people everywhere—conveying as much information as possible, as accurately and clearly as possible, to as many people as possible. We can have this gift, fortunately, with no sacrifice of the other wondrous beauties of language.

May writing contribute to the fullness of your life.

* The book title is *The Medium Is the Massage* (not *Message*). McLuhan and coauthor Quentin Fiore observed that societies have always been influenced more by the technology of the medium than by the content of its message.

Introduction

The first writing was business writing. Stone tablets found at archeological digs in ancient Samaria and Egypt, carved some 5000 years ago, were records of the transfer of property and goods.

Spoken language is much older, probably as old as human society. Many linguists and anthropologists believe, in fact, that human society began as our prehistoric ancestors learned to transmit their feelings and thoughts by making simple sounds. Grunts became words, then sentences, and the species we call "people" rose above all other species and dominated the surface of the earth. Gradually people learned to tell stories and to carve illustrated records of their activities on cave walls. Much later, alphabets were invented, and now permanent records could be carved in stone and were portable.

Still later, societies learned how to create a flat, flexible material from fibers of certain plants, and paper replaced stone tablets and became the vehicle of knowledge and enlightenment that it is today. Writing of religious and civil laws came first, followed by writing to inform, and last, to entertain.

This book is for people who are nonwriters (that is, who are not professional writers) but who must write, or who want to write to tell their story *clearly and accurately* to others. It may also help those who want to write more quickly—without wasting time fumbling over false starts and rewrites—and to present their valuable ideas in a tone that pleases the reader and presents a pleasant, dignified image of the writer.

Well-written ideas also reflect the beauty of language, for those who care about that, because the same language characteristics that make paragraphs and pages clear also give them beauty. In addition, these principles should help most people become better readers, speakers, and listeners. Especially reading skill may improve, because knowing how to recognize the most common writing weaknesses will help readers to notice those weaknesses and overcome them.

THE INFORMATION IS DIVIDED INTO THREE PARTS

Part One is on clarity. This part discusses five widely respected principles of language usage followed by writers through the ages. Following these, Part One takes aim at some widespread superstitions—bad advice about words, sentences, and paragraphs that most people encounter some-where along the road of life. Nonsexist language, an important and relatively new consideration, is also discussed in detail. Part One also introduces a simple way to measure how easy (or difficult) the para-graphs and pages are to read.

Part Two is on organizing. This part describes ways of arranging infor-mation in the order that best helps the reader to receive and under-stand. The goal is to convey as much information as possible, as accurately as possible, as quickly and easily as possible. *Always the reader.* Part Two also presents new (and surprisingly effective) outlining strate-gies that take advantage of, rather than oppose, the functions of the brain as it tries to construct logical flow during the *reading* process. It also deals with ways of arranging information on the pages in formats that best help the reader.

Again, always the reader. *He or she is the only reason we write.*

Part Three is on grammar—a user-friendly brushup or an in-depth study, from the basic to the exotic, depending on the need.

Put It in Writing

PART 1

On Clarity

CHAPTER 1

The Things Every Writer Wants

The chief virtue that language can have is clearness, and nothing distracts from it so much as the use of unfamiliar words.

—Hippocrates

Every writer wants to succeed, whether creating a letter or a great book, and to succeed anyone who writes needs to understand this:

In any communication the principal characters are a sender and a receiver. The ideas being communicated exist in the sender's brain as electrochemical neuron systems, not words, and if communication succeeds those exact ideas (or close) will end up in the receiver's brain, also as electrical energy. But we cannot transmit them that way, so we convert the ideas to words and sentences instead. (Linguists call this process *encoding*.) These black marks on pages (or sounds spoken into a microphone) are easy to transport, but the marks or sounds exist just for the transportation. The receiver's brain, of course, must convert the black marks, or bits of sound, back to electrical impulses. (Reading experts call this process *decoding*.) Comprehension follows.

Success as a writer, then, depends on the ability to use language in ways that will cause readers to receive exactly the message the writer intended—accurately and clearly.

The French philosopher René Descartes (pronounced "Day-*cart*") is best known for expressing, in a few simple words, this profound abstract thought: "*I think, therefore I am.*" (In Latin that is: "*Cogito, ergo sum.*") A scholar today might have written: "*The cognitive process presupposes the existence of the cognitive source.*" And no one would ever hear of it again. The writer's inartistic use of language often deprives readers of the message.

WHAT STYLE OF CLOTHING SHOULD OUR WRITING WEAR?

Compare writing styles to the styles of clothing we wear. We may own tuxedos or formal gowns, and at the other extreme tank tops and jeans. But in everyday activities most of us wear something between those; in normal, everyday activities either of those extremes would hurt our image. Likewise, there can be extremes in the language style we use to convey our thoughts to others, and these extremes may hurt our image.

Street talk and slang, the linguistic equivalents of tank tops and jeans, are helpful to most of us—and personally satisfying if we use them at the right time and in the right place. So too, extremely formal and scholarly language should be used with enthusiasm in environments where and when that is expected. But in most writing situations neither of those extremes is helpful—and either one may be harmful. As with clothing, moderate style will open most doors.

CLARITY, THE MAJOR CHALLENGE

The first thing we ask of the language is *clarity*—that language transport our ideas clearly, accurately, and efficiently—so that the message received is the one the sender intended. Of course, we can also paint beautiful word pictures with language. Or we can skillfully create moods. But these and similar artistic goals identified by linguists are secondary. The only purpose for which cultures *create* language is to transport ideas. It is this simple, then: A society cannot function very well with a transportation system that damages its cargo in transit. *The writer has done the job fully,* as sender in the communicating process, only when the ideas are so clearly presented that the reader (receiver) cannot possibly misunderstand them.

Most adults, when they write, have a tendency to overcomplicate. Perhaps because they do not really know (in many cases no one ever taught them) exactly how to write or, more specifically, what they are trying to achieve when writing. Lacking better advice, they may try to sound as scholarly as possible. (Classroom discussions with successful, profes-

Whose English Is Better?

Dare we ask? The British generally consider American English barbaric. Most Americans concede the point without argument and consider anyone with a British accent to be a literary giant; we suffer a national inferiority complex about language. But should we? There are no major differences between British and American English—except, of course, pronunciation.

Grammar. Only two differences are found in ordinary usage, and they are minor. British say, "British Leyland Motors *have* introduced *their* new . . ." (collective nouns take plural verbs and pronouns). Americans say, "General Motors *has* introduced *its* new . . ." (collective nouns take singular verbs and pronouns). British say, "When everyone had *got* there." Americans say, "When everyone had *gotten* there." *But note:* Our pilgrim ancestors (along with all other English-speaking people of the seventeenth century) said *gotten.* Americans, then, use the Elizabethan English form.

Vocabulary. In formal usage, few words change. (One interesting exception: the *period* at the end of an American sentence is called a *full stop* across the Atlantic Ocean.) Most differences are in idiom or slang: British *tubes* are American *subways;* British shoppers *queue up* while American shoppers *stand in line* (except in New York City, where they stand *on* line); British *ring up Mum,* but Americans *phone Mom.* Such

(continued on following page)

sional adults reveal a thought process something like this: "*I'm an adult. Children use small words and short sentences and express themselves in simple terms, so I should do the opposite.*") In doing so, the adults may prevent their valuable ideas from reaching their destination.

Here is an example of what can go wrong, an example of what we mean when we say readers have trouble receiving ideas accurately when writers use needlessly complicated style. This is an actual policy statement from the files of a government agency:

Needlessly complicated:

Technical assistance to institutional administrative staffs is authorized in determination of the availability and appropriate utilization of federal or state entitlements designating assistance in resolution of problems occasioned by requirements of handicapped children. (33 words)

In plain English:

We can help your staff determine if federal or state funds are available to help meet the needs of handicapped children. We can also help you plan how best to use those funds. (33 words)

It seems unlikely, however, anyone reading the first version would receive that message, no matter how hard he or she tries. The transportation system has delivered its cargo in unrecognizable condition. The original passage may sound dazzling, but it does not communicate; an important idea is broadcast but not received.

And that is not enough. Communication does not take place until the idea has been broadcast *and received*—and, furthermore, received *accurately*—and our job as writers is to do whatever is necessary to *be* received accurately.

But caution: Oversimplifying is equally damaging. This happens when writers leave out important information or when simple words make a statement inaccurate or cause it to sound childish.

Oversimplified:

We can help you get government money, and we can help you spend it. (14 words)

Whether needlessly complicated or oversimplified, when we use language badly the reader may receive some message other than the one we believe we are sending. Enlightened writers are constantly aware this can happen, and they work hard to prevent it.

(continued from the previous page)

differences are frequent; they cause no communication problems and create interesting conversation between colonists and royal subjects.

Spelling. British use: colour, honour; Americans use: color, honor. British use: centre, fibre; Americans use: center, fiber. British use: minimise, organise; Americans use: minimize, organize.

Pronunciation. Ah, here is where the British cast their spell. The American says "Half of the staff laugh at the photograph"—with the *a* as in *cat*. The Oxford scholar says "Hahlf of the stah-ff lauh-gh at the photograh-ph"—with the *a* as in *far*. (But not all the English attend Oxford, and many have very different pronunciation patterns.)

Americans are usually surprised to learn that our way is the way Shakespeare and Queen Elizabeth would have pronounced those words. After crossing the Atlantic to the New World, the colonists kept (and still use) the pronunciation of the original mother tongue; it is the mother tongue that changed. The broad *a* (hah-lf), today the mark of the cultured, educated English, is of Cockney origin and was considered undignified until the mid-nineteenth century.

Note, incidentally, the four different ways of spelling the *f* sound in the sentence "Half of the staff laugh at the photograph"; such spelling inconsistencies are more common in English than in any other major language.

WRITING QUICKLY AND PRODUCTIVELY

Does anyone ever have enough time? The second benefit of healthy writing habits is *speed*—the writer's productivity. Unsure writers often waste surprising amounts of time trying to get started, struggling to plan the order of the ideas, and the key to productive organizing is the subject of Part Two of this book. But needlessly complicated style is often a more notorious time waster. Examine this passage from a company memo:

Wasted time:

Management has become cognizant of the necessity for the elimination of undesirable vegetation surrounding the periphery of our facility. (19 words)

The message the writer had in mind is easier to write:

Please kill the weeds around the building. (7 words)

Although this example is exaggerated, unnecessarily complicated language often uses twice as many words as necessary—sometimes even more. This means twice as many words to put on paper. Whether they are written longhand, dictated, typed, or entered into a computer, twice as many words means twice as long encoding them. Then consider this: The words "*Management has become cognizant of the necessity for the elimination of undesirable vegetation surrounding the periphery of our facility*" do not come naturally; the writer must sit and wrestle with clumsy word choices and with the sentences he or she will construct of them.

But again, that meant "*Please kill the weeds around the building.*" Those words come naturally and quickly; they are easy to write.

For those two reasons—the search for unfamiliar words and the extra time it takes to structure them into complicated, difficult sentences—language slows down the writing process for the writer who shuns simplicity. The one, by comparison, who can express his or her thoughts in plain English has the distinct advantage of finishing quickly and going on to other things. This is the second gain that sensible language usage promises those who embrace it. Another reason we should remind ourselves of often: *When all else fails, try English.*

THE IMAGE WRITERS CREATE

The final bonus sensible language offers sensible writers is the intangible we call *image*. Whether they should or not, people judge us all our lives by the way we use our language, just as they judge us by the clothing we wear. More and more today our contact with others is through writing. To influence others we must first have worthwhile things to say. But that itself is not enough; how we express those ideas will have much to do with whether our reader accepts them with confidence.

And so writing skill is an important aspect of *leadership,* or *persuasion.* Career advancement is at stake. It is not by accident that the outstanding leaders in business and industry, government, the arts—in fact in all fields—are excellent communicators. That is how important writing is to everyone's career. It is probably every person's second most important skill, regardless of his or her profession. Every person, adult or student, may reasonably assume that several times in his or her life the ability—or inability—to write will make (or has made) a difference in career advancement.

How These Unnatural Writing Styles Developed

Almost all of us know how to use clear, uncluttered language; in the formative years we relied on it totally, and we still rely on it in casual situations.

What, then, causes intelligent adults so often to write in the needlessly complicated style we have described? What can go through their minds that would cause them to reject a language usage style that is easy to write, easy to read, and beautiful, and choose instead one that is hard to write, hard to read, and abrasive to mind and ear? Classroom discussions with professional men and women are revealing.

Honestly misguided. The most common explanation is an innocent one: *Most people who try deliberately to write elaborate and overstuffed words and sentences do so because they think that is the style the world expects of them.* Who can blame them? They see it around them on the job and in textbooks, professional journals, and even, sometimes, in editorial pages.

Lazy thinking. Almost as common, classroom analysis reveals, is this explanation: *The writer has not thought through his or her ideas clearly enough.* Remember, the writing process—whether for a great novel or a business letter—consists of *creating* the ideas *and expressing* them.

Every person's writing is the end result of his or her *thinking,* on paper. But if we accept this, we must also accept that the paragraphs and pages cannot possibly be any clearer than the thinking that went into creating the ideas they contain.

Unfortunately, some writers use complication as a substitute for clear thinking. For anyone with good command of vocabulary and grammar skills, it is possible and may be quicker to present ideas that are only half thought out, yet in a way that sounds dazzling and profound. The *reader* who does not already know the information (and readers usually do not) may think it too complex to understand, when in fact the complexity may be in the language used to convey it. (That thought process goes something like this: "*I can't understand a word of this, so it must be for geniuses only.*" [The alternative would be: "I can't understand a word of this, so there must be something wrong with me." Given those choices, the result is predictable.]) Always be aware while writing, because this point is so basic and important, that *we cannot express our ideas in ultimate clarity until we have thought them out in ultimate clarity.* And if the reader does not understand, the writer failed in his or her goal as a communicator, which is to broadcast a message in such a way that it is received fully and accurately. Nothing less will do.

The writer is a teacher. He or she knows something the reader does not know; that is the reason one is the writer and the other is the reader. It is not enough to say: "*Here it is if you're good enough.*"

This is not to say readers, too, should not participate in the thinking process. If we write with wisdom and skill, we may open new windows in the reader's mind, for further thought or wonder. But no reader should ever wonder: "*What does this say?*"

Satisfying the ego—trying to impress others.   Pity the person who overcomplicates to impress. This person is likely to be a bit unsure of his or her ideas or of what readers may think of his or her skills. This person is begging through the written word: "Please, won't someone notice how intelligent I am?"

Impress with our writing? By all means. But writers in search of style should look to the great writers through the ages—or to their favorite writers of today. Successful writers impress with the virtue and value of *what* they write, not the scholarly sound of *how* they write it. Let the impressiveness, the dignity, the beauty in your paragraphs and pages come from the *ideas,* not the *words and sentences* used to express them. Create valuable thoughts, then deliver them in a language style that raises them to a pedestal for all to see and admire. *This* is the way to impress. We are, after all, past that point in life when we could impress people with the size of our words.

Concealing weak material.   *Resist the temptation to make weak material seem better than it really is.* It does not work. The writer who tries this hopes to conceal that the substance is weak and hopes that if the work can be made to sound so complicated no one can understand it, no one will recognize it has said very little. The snow job.

How English Changes

One of the best-known passages in world literature is Shakespeare's "O Romeo, Romeo! Wherefore art thou Romeo?" Yet, most people misinterpret it. Juliet is not asking, "Where are you, Romeo?" She is asking: "Why are you Romeo?" (Why couldn't you be someone else, so we could marry? The next lines are: *Deny thy father, and refuse thy name; Or, if thou wilt not, be but sworn my love, And I'll no longer be a Capulet.*)

That passage is an example of the changes that have constantly taken place as English passed through history. In Elizabethan England, *wherefore* was the common word for *why.* We cannot possibly know that (and other changes like it) as we read Shakespeare unless someone tells us, and so we rely on a specialist (usually an English teacher). Yes, unedited Shakespeare is hard to read today; without help readers will almost invariably misunderstand many passages. This is not their fault—or Shakespeare's. He wrote for the common people of his time; that is why he wrote plays. He simply had no way of predicting the language changes that would come.

Unfortunately, writers often succeed with this kind of deception; large words and twisty-winding sentences often *do* conceal that the ideas are not thought out very precisely. Furthermore, most readers have profound respect for scholarly-sounding things they cannot understand; these readers would be embarrassed to admit they are unable to understand them.

Sometimes it seems the entire world is playing a sort of literary version of "The Emperor's New Clothes." Few people can understand much of what is written, but no one will admit it.

Five Principles of Clear Writing

*Words are like leaves, and where they most abound, much
fruit of sense beneath is rarely found.*

—*Alexander Pope*

These principles have guided authors through the centuries for writing of all kinds (except poetry). They would be equally appropriate
whether for a college term paper, a business letter, or a great novel.

Advisors often begin with *know your reader*. This wisdom has to do more,
however, with planning *what* to say than with *how* to say it. Be wise. Think
clearly *before* beginning the language arts part of the job: What purpose
should this writing serve—what effect should it have, and what needs
to be said to achieve that effect? Here, more than in the words-and-
sentences part of writing, people who write are most likely to determine
how well the paragraphs and pages will succeed, because no amount of
good writing *style* can win the day if the message is not the right one for
the situation. No books or form letters can tell us what to say in any given
situation. (We can, however, be certain of this: *The thoughtful writer resists
telling things in greater detail than necessary just to show how well informed he or
she is on the subject.*)

We help ourselves by trying to picture the reader's viewpoint. We may
not *agree* with that viewpoint, but if we understand the obstacles we need
to overcome, we will surely be better able to overcome them.

Realistically, however, and unfortunately, writers cannot always know their reader or his or her viewpoints. Still, we know important things about readers in general—and about the reading *process*—that can guide us in using language skills to write (*encode* information) in ways that can best help those who read (*decode* it). The *five principles of clear writing* are:

- Prefer clear, familiar words
- Keep most sentences short and simple
- Prefer active voice verbs; avoid passives
- Use conversational style as a guide
- Revise, revise, and revise again

This chapter examines the first two principles in detail.

The source of bad writing is the desire to be more than a person of sense—to be thought a genius. If people would only say what they have to say in plain terms, how much more eloquent they would be.

—Samuel Taylor Coleridge

PRINCIPLE 1: PREFER CLEAR, FAMILIAR WORDS

Word Management

Anyone serious about writing needs a clear understanding of the basic tools. *What is the purpose of the large collection of words we call "vocabulary"?* Our objectives in choosing words should be *precision* and *clarity*.

In English, small words are usually the clearest and easiest to understand. This is easy to prove statistically; as far back as the 1930s linguists and educators conducted research on the relationship of word size and readability.* (For broader but quicker proof, just examine any dictionary.) Research also reveals—and this surprises novice writers—that

---

* Leading research in this field was by Edgar Dale and Jean Chall, The Ohio State University.

small words are generally more precise than larger ones. (*Box* is more precise than *container.*) Caution, however. When we say writers should prefer clear, familiar words, this does *not* mean avoid using large words. Rather, avoid using an uncommon word if exactly the same thing can be said with a familiar one. When writers use words harder to understand than necessary, they build communications barriers between sender and receiver. Thoughtful writers will not do anything, knowingly, to create unnecessary barriers.

Therefore, thoughtful writers do not use *facilitate* when they could use *help.* They do not write *utilize* when they could write *use,* or *endeavor* when they could use *try,* or *sufficient* when they could write *enough.*

They do not use a word such as *subsequently* when they could say . . . well, what? *Subsequently* demonstrates the way large words can make a statement imprecise and create misunderstanding. When asked what it means, people are likely to respond: *next, later,* or *therefore. Subsequently* can be *next* or *later.* (But even these have important differences.) And even though they are wrong, many writers use the word to mean *therefore,* and many readers read it that way. (The correct matching word would be *consequently.*) Of course, the writer knows which of those three meanings he or she intends, but readers are unlikely to notice they have three choices here (including an incorrect one), and those who do notice would have no way of knowing which meaning the writer intended. Imprecision is introduced by a word larger than necessary.

Another such word is *indicated*—a favorite in business and academic writing. Does the writer mean *proved* or *suggested?* Readers have no way of knowing and probably do not realize they have two choices. Remember, readers are paper readers, not mind readers.

Or consider the word *parameters*—a complex mathematical term important to engineers and scientists. Even dictionaries disagree what it means, and most people who use it intend it to mean *limits*—a strange misuse, probably derived through the word *perimeters.*

Or, consider *paradigms*—a favorite of educators. All of us could live full lives and never need this word. Worse is *paradigmatically.*

Granted, *sufficient* is not much more difficult than *enough.* But it is an unnecessary overload, no matter how slight. If the writer's attitude is to choose words more difficult than needed, he or she may do so a few times every sentence—perhaps 15 or 20 times on a page. The collective overload this kind of writer delivers to readers is devastating, even in a sentence as short as this one:

Needlessly complicated:

Solicit the employee's assistance in achieving resolution of the problem.

A Misunderstanding That Had to Happen

If Shakespeare's language (early modern English) is hard to read today, Chaucer's (middle English) is even harder and the language of *Beowolf* (early English) impossible. Throughout the history of English, then, the greatest literature has been challenging to read. Gradually, as a result, it was almost inevitable the attitude would develop (especially among the educated): *Good writing has always been hard to read and understand; therefore, so should mine be.* That attitude is fairly common today among people who are not trained as writers but must write anyhow.

Those people have missed an important point: Shakespeare's works were not hard to understand at the time he wrote them. They are difficult today simply because the language has changed so much since then. So often it is the *writing style*, not the *content*, that gives readers trouble. That is certainly true of early literature—for reasons easy to explain. But it would be impossible to justify writing deliberately today in a style that is hard to understand—unless the writer wants to be unclear or is trying to impress others with his or her language skills.

A more sensible attitude: Impress with the *ideas*, not the *words and sentences* used to convey them. Indeed, the more complex the ideas, the greater the need for clear, simple language so others can understand them fully.

In plain English:

Ask the employee's help in solving the problem.

Imagine the burden of reading sentence after sentence, paragraph after paragraph, written in the needlessly heavy style of the first example above. Readers would have little hope of receiving much information. Readers would collapse into whimpering heaps of nerves.

Short words are usually more specific. Winston Churchill advised, *"Short words are the best, and the old words when short are the best of all."**

Many people are surprised to learn that large words, usually held in such high esteem, are often less precise. Does *vegetation* bring to the computer screen of the reader's mind the image of *rose bushes* or *trees?* Does *undesirable vegetation* mean *weeds?* Or does the writer using that phrase intend it to mean (or might a reader think it means) *calla lilies growing where you want tomatoes?* Does *emotional reaction* mean *smiling* or *punching someone?* Is a *utensil* a *fork* or a *frying pan?* (Similar examples can be seen often in this book.) It is difficult to be vague in small words.

Remember, the writer's goal is to be precise and clear—at the receiving end.

Certainly we need the larger, less specific words when we want to make broad and general statements. (In a magazine article about all the items in a kitchen used for cooking, serving, or eating, *utensils* is the collective word.) But when our goal is to be specific, the words we turn to are usually small: *pot, bowl, knife and fork.* If we write *the utensil,* the reader might not see the one intended. That is how English works.

The exception: professional terms, or jargon. When new concepts come into our culture and require new words, more often than not these end up large words. The reason is that cultures find it convenient to create new words by combining existing ones and (in English) adding Greek or Latin prefixes and suffixes. In many cases words are created in that manner for specialized fields—words such as *multisensory, demographics, recidivism.* Words such as these serve as a highly specialized form of shorthand for specialized professions; readers in those professions understand them, and writers would need far more words to express

---

* Winston Churchill, prime minister of England during World War II, author of many books and a master of satire, called the needless use of large, difficult words "*terminological inexactitude.*" Among his most respected works: the five-volume "*A History of the English-Speaking Peoples.*"

those same concepts in commonly known words. A chemist, for example, needs words such as *polymerization.* An engineer needs *magnetohydrodynamics;* do not bother searching for a smaller synonym. An accountant needs *liquidation, depreciable, profitability.* But even though sometimes necessary, words such as these, often called *jargon,* carry with them an important disadvantage. They are a private language—"shop talk"; they exclude outsiders, and the thoughtful engineer, economist, or other specialist does not use them outside the shop, when writing or speaking to people who do not know them.

Even such specialized professional terms are not always necessary, however; sometimes smaller synonyms *are* available. *Oviposition* is a scientific term for *laying eggs*—nothing more, nothing less. Here, the jargon complicates and excludes most people needlessly; it brings the disadvantage without the advantage. Likewise, an *epistaxis* is a *nosebleed,* and that is what doctors should call it; and *prenatal* is Latin for *before birth.* What could be wrong with English?

Human nature, it seems, tempts people of all kinds to create special language that sets them apart from others. Did your friends and you speak "pig Latin" in your childhood? *"Ids-kay at-thay ould-cay eak-spay ike-lay is-thay ere-way ecial-spay."** Everywhere, it seems, there are people who enjoy using private language to announce: "Behold! My thoughts are so special that ordinary mortals could not possibly understand them." Any words readers cannot understand are private language.

Develop a large vocabulary, by all means. But use it graciously; do not show off with it. We should have the large words available when we need them, but most of us should need them more as readers than as writers.

Remember, even though a writer may know the large words, his or her reader may not. Remember also, the writer's job is not just to broadcast but *to be received,* and to be successful the broadcaster must do whatever is necessary to be received *accurately.* Anything less would be intellectually snobbish, and unrealistic.

Short words add beauty.   Another misguided argument is that *beauty* in writing comes from large words. No, no. The larger words may sometimes allow us to say something complicated that could not be expressed in small ones, but they are usually the ones that *take away* the beauty from language.

In words, the factors that contribute most to beauty are imagery and rhythm. Surely imagery is greater in small words: *joy in the eyes of a child . . . the smell of fresh cut grass. . . .*

---

* "Kids that could speak like this were special."

Examine how William Maxwell, a respected American author spanning more than half of the twentieth century, creates images—the way most good storytellers do: with small, vivid words. In this scene from his short story, "The Fisherman Who Had Nobody to Go Out in His Boat with Him," we can almost see and hear the climax unfolding, as though we were there. We can certainly *feel* it:

One evening, the fisherman didn't come home at the usual time. His wife could not hear the wind or the shutters banging, but when the wind blew puffs of smoke down the chimney, she knew that a storm had come up. She put on her cloak, and wrapped a heavy scarf around her head, and started for the strand, to see if the boats were drawn up there. Instead, she found the other women waiting with their faces all stamped with the same frightened look. Usually the seabirds circled above the beach, waiting for the fishing boats to come in and the fishermen to cut open their fish and throw them the guts, but this evening there were no gulls or cormorants. The air was empty. The wind had blown them all inland, just as, by a freak, it had blown the boats all together, out on the water, so close that it took great skill to keep them from knocking against each other and capsizing in the dark. The fishermen called back and forth for a time, and then they fell silent. The wind had grown higher and higher, and the words were blown right out of their mouths, and they could not even hear themselves what they were saying. The wind was so high and the sound so loud that it was like a silence, and out of this silence, suddenly, came the sound of singing. Being poor ignorant fishermen, they did the first thing that occurred to them—they fell on their knees and prayed. The singing went on and on, in a voice that none of them had ever heard, and so powerful and rich and deep it seemed to come from the same place that the storm came from. A flash of lightning revealed that it was not an angel, as they thought, but the fisherman who was married to the deaf-mute. He was standing in his boat, with his head bared, singing, and in their minds this was no stranger or less miraculous than an angel would have been. They crossed themselves and went on praying, and the fisherman went on singing, and in a little while the waves began to grow smaller and the wind to abate, and the storm, which should have taken days to blow itself out, suddenly turned into an intense calm. As suddenly as it had begun, the singing stopped. The boats drew apart as in one boat after another the men took up their oars again, and in a silvery brightness, all in a cluster, the fishing fleet came safely in to shore.

William Maxwell, *All the Days and Nights*, Alfred A. Knopf

How wondrous, that tiny black lines and curlicues on a white sheet can invoke such feelings. Of the 443 words, only 19 (4 percent) contain more than two syllables. Of those, six are the word *fisherman*. Only one word (*miraculous*) is larger.

Rhythm, too, is far easier to control with small words. Note how Edgar Allan Poe used small words to build a rhythmic beat that creates (deliberately) a distant, almost monotonous tone, reminiscent of a tom-tom beat:

> <u>On</u>ce upon a <u>mid</u>night dreary, <u>while</u> I pondered, <u>weak</u> and weary,
> <u>o</u>ver many a <u>quaint</u> and curious <u>vol</u>ume of for<u>got</u>ten lore. . . .
>
> Edgar Allan Poe, "The Raven," Doubleday

That rhythmic pattern is called *trochaic* (each measure, or foot, is one accented syllable followed by [in this case] three unaccented) *tetrameter* (four measures to a line). The pattern may sound familiar; it is the same rhythm a Walt Disney film gave us a century later in a popular movie and song:

> <u>Su</u>percala<u>fra</u>gilistic<u>ex</u>piala<u>do</u>cious.
>
> *Mary Poppins*, Walt Disney Studios

The greatest writer of all, William Shakespeare, for centuries has enthralled readers with the power and wisdom of his plays and charmed us by composing them with long passages of formal poetic rhythm. The words in the famous passage below are the common words used in everyday life at the time he wrote; with the exception of *thou*, they are still the common ones used everyday today. The rhythm of each line is: da DA, da DA, da DA, da DA, da DA:

> But <u>soft</u>! What <u>light</u> from <u>yon</u>der <u>win</u>dow <u>breaks</u>?*
> It <u>is</u> the <u>east</u>, and <u>Jul</u>iet <u>is</u> the <u>sun</u>.
> A<u>rise</u>, fair <u>sun</u>, and <u>kill</u> the <u>en</u>vious <u>moon</u>,
> Who <u>is</u> al<u>rea</u>dy <u>sick</u> and <u>pale</u> with <u>grief</u>
> That <u>thou</u>, her <u>maid</u>, are <u>far</u> more <u>fair</u> than <u>she</u>.
>
> William Shakespeare, *Romeo and Juliet*

That rhythm is called *iambic* (each measure is one unaccented beat followed by one accented) *pentameter* (five measures to a line).

---

* We have trouble, though, with the verb at the end of the sentence in line 1. The late Middle English of Shakespeare's time still carried many of the Old English traits of its Teutonic (Germanic) ancestry.

SOME COMMONLY USED WORDS THAT ARE MORE DIFFICULT THAN NECESSARY, AND SIMPLER SUBSTITUTES.

Do Not Use	When You Could Say:	Do Not Use	When You Could Say:
accordingly	therefore; so	indebtedness	debt
aforementioned	these	indicate	show
applicable	apply to	in order to	to
assistance	aid; help	in the event that	if
attributable to	caused by	in the near future	soon
by means of	by	prior to	before
compensate	pay	provided that	if
consequently	so	purchase	buy
considerable	much	terminate	end
correspondence	letter	transmit	send
facilitate	help; ease	utilize	use
the foregoing	this; these	visualize	see
for the purpose of	to	whether or not	whether
inasmuch as	because	with regard to	about

Memorable sentences are memorable on account of some single memorable thought.

—Alexander Smith

PRINCIPLE 2: KEEP MOST SENTENCES SHORT AND SIMPLE

Sentence Management

Examining the styles of respected authors is one of the best ways to improve one's own style. Successful writers know the importance of sentence-building skills. Dividing thoughts into information clusters of reasonable size is a key to readable writing, but sentence control is important also for artistic reasons: Sentences, as much as words, control the *mood* created as the ideas flow by the reader's mind. This is true of nonfiction as well as fiction, although readers are more likely to be aware of such things in reading for pleasure.

In most successful writing for adults the sentences usually average between 15 and 20 words in length. Most students average fewer than 15 words per sentence (too low, unless they are writing for children), and most business men and women average between the low- and upper-20s range (too high, regardless the audience). The developing writer should examine closely: if his or her average sentence length is in that under-15 range, the writer should look for opportunities to smooth the flow by combining some of those very short sentences. Readers will be grateful. If the average is over 20 words per sentence, lowering it is usually easy, but not always; look for opportunities to divide some very long ones.*† This, too, will bring joy to readers. (This paragraph and the one above it contain 236 words divided into 13 sentences. The longest is 40 words, the shortest is 4, and the average is 18.2 words per sentence.)

Information clusters should be of reasonable size.   Remember, the advice is to *average* between 15 and 20 words per sentence. A pleasing mixture is desirable. The shortest possible sentence in the English language is two words: subject and verb‡; there is no maximum. Skilled authors rarely settle into a style in which all sentences are of medium length; the result would be a monotonous style inviting readers to go to something else. The sample passage on chickadee letterhead (see page 20) demonstrates the way writers can effectively control readability and mood by controlling the lengths of sentences.

Long sentences can be readable, but with the exception of professional writers, most people cannot construct extremely long ones very well; doing so requires exceptional grammar skills and keen sensitivity for balancing the emphasis of major and subordinate ideas. Most adults risk trouble at about 30 or 35 words, and as a sentence gets longer it is

---

* Some writers, deliberately or without being aware, create sentences with *embedded* ideas—that is, one or several ideas sandwiched between parts of a sentence belonging to another (major) idea. The embedded parts can be single words, phrases, complete clauses, or all these. Writers need superb skills to keep these readable, and once written such sentences are not easy to unravel and rewrite, but often that is exactly what is needed. (See "Syntax," Chapter 18.)

† The semicolon after *always* serves here as a semiperiod, as opposed to a super-comma (see page 214) and is treated as a period in counting sentence length.

‡ The first two-word sentence in this book appears on page 11.

Good writing almost always averages between 15 and 20 words per sentence. Do not write all sentences within these limits, however, because doing so would create a style so dull it would bore the average reader. Mix them up. Although probably unaware of it, readers feel comfortable with the changing pace, changing mood, they experience when the sentences are occasionally as short as 3 or 4 words or as long as 30 or 35.

There are reasons your favorite authors are your favorites. Skilled writers do many things with language to create exactly the mood they want, and one of the most effective of these is control of sentence lengths.

Short sentences give emphasis; the shorter they are, the harder they hit. They also create the feeling of action. This is because shorter sentences mean more sentences and therefore more verbs. Verbs are the action words, and so skilled writers deliberately use short sentences to create the tense, fast-moving mood appropriate for action passages.

Long sentences, however, slow down the pace and are generally useful for the mood necessary in descriptive passages, as important for proper balance as the action. They meander along, like peaceful stretches of a river, at the relaxed speed best suited for detailed viewing, slowly, deliberately unfolding information about the people, places, and things that provide the background for the actions. Although an important part of most writing, these passages tend to subordinate the ideas they contain and therefore are generally ineffective for important information.

It is the combination of these two artistic techniques that causes readers to say, "I couldn't put this book down." (The shortest sentence in this passage is 3 words, and the two longest are 35; the average length is 17 words per sentence. The total number of words is 237.)

more likely to contain a confusing grammatical mistake or an important idea that goes unnoticed.

Most very long sentences are hard to read.   Like unnecessarily hard words, very long sentences increase the communication line resistance between sender and receiver. Even if the writer can write long sentences repeatedly and keep their grammar correct, he or she is likely to do a poor job transmitting the ideas. Readers may get tangled, unable to follow all the ideas from beginning to end. Of course, those twisty-winding sentences will almost always look clear to the writer. But unsure writers should always remind themselves that the writer has one major advantage no reader will ever have: The writer knows what he or she is trying to say and is not relying on those little black lines and curlicues on the page to find out.

Put one major idea into a sentence. Long sentences often contain two or more important ideas, and that challenges the second half of principle 2: Keep most sentences short *and simple*. By *simple* we mean each sentence should be devoted to only one major idea; let the size and shape of that idea determine the size and shape of the sentence. And in so doing the writer is likely to end up with a rich variety of sentences averaging between 15 and 20 words in length.

When writers put two major ideas into one sentence, as is likely in long sentences, they risk grammatical errors. Examine this sentence:

> Early results of the KittyCare survey show clearly that voters support the plan of the children who worked so hard, quite different from the County Commissioners' recommended plan, which I have learned will cause the trustees of the Doggie Brigade a lot of trouble.
> We do not think the Council of Churches and Synagogues would. . . .

The first paragraph (above) is one long sentence—43 words. Trouble is often buried in sentences that long; even if the writer can keep the grammar straight, readers are likely to have difficulty following the ideas. This writer did not quite keep the grammar straight; there is certainly a problem in that KittyCare sentence. Will *the children's plan* or *the County Commissioners' plan* cause the Doggie Brigade trouble? Rules of grammar or punctuation guide readers at a subconscious level, but they can also misguide if writers are careless. (Realistically, readers may not read carefully enough to notice that two very different meanings are possible; most would be likely to react subconsciously, thinking either the children's plan or the commissioners' plan will trouble the Doggie Brigade trustees, unaware the statement could be read either way.)

If, as readers examine the passage above, they think *the Commissioners' plan* will trouble the Doggie Brigade, they are probably reacting subconsciously to a rule of grammar most of us first encountered in eighth or ninth grade—*the rule of pronoun antecedents*. This tells us a pronoun will try to stand for the last noun before it. The pronoun is *which,* and what noun appears before it? Grammar, then, tells us *the Commissioners' recommended plan* will trouble the Doggie Brigade.

But readers who think *the children's plan* would invite trouble have grammar on their side too—*the rule of nonrestrictive clauses and phrases.* This one tells us we can lift out the part between the commas and read the sentence without it. Then it reads: *Early results of the Kittycare survey show clearly that voters support the plan of the children who worked so hard, which I have learned will cause the trustees of the Doggie Brigade a lot of trouble.*

And so grammar tells us either meaning can be correct. A reader's response to that sentence would depend on which rule of grammar he or she happens to react to subconsciously.

The writer created that blind spot because the two major ideas did not quite fit into the sentence's grammatical structure. This is a common mistake. Again, the longer the sentence, the more likely the writer will send some grammatical error to readers.

A remedy to the troublesome sentence above? Separate sentences:

Early results of the KittyCare survey show clearly that voters support the plan of the children who worked so hard, quite different from the County Commissioners' recommendation. I have learned that (?) will cause. . . .

Short sentences are hard hitting.   The shorter the sentence, the harder it hits, and for that reason skilled writers often pack their most important ideas into sentences of very few words. But use these with reason and care; too many short sentences will sound weak and childish and will quickly drive readers away.

Short sentences are easier to write.   Almost all writers find themselves, occasionally at least, stuck while writing—knowing what they want to say but unable to put it on paper. They are not stuck getting started; that is an organizing problem and will be examined in Part 2. Rather, they are stuck somewhere in the middle of the writing.

Most writers find they are tangled and unable to untangle the ideas *in the middle of a complicated sentence.* We can always start one; finishing some sentences, however, may give us fits. The reason is often that the grammatical structure is wrong for the ideas. Too much may be squeezed between the capital letter and the hoped-for period, and the grammar or punctuation (or both) will not fit them all—pushing the sentence in a direction we do not wish to go.

Poor writer. The would-be sentence has become an obstacle course. How to get unstuck in such a situation? Inexperienced writers stagger desperately toward the next period to get out of that mess. (A grammar maven can tell, because the obstacle course is left behind for the reader to deal with.) When stuck in the middle of a sentence, resist the temptation to stagger on. Experienced writers know this is a time to retreat to the last period and start again. Separate that long sentence into two, three, or sometimes even four short ones. The obstacle course will vanish.

Sentence sense saves time.   Just by dividing ideas into sentences easily *and naturally*, most inexperienced writers can write considerably faster than they do. Those long, awkward sentences are the ones that use up so much time.

Instant Help: The Meat Cleaver Technique

This is another working tool of professional writers, an important and relatively easy one. Even novice writers can often help a long sentence greatly by simply chopping it into two shorter ones.

This kind of help is handy when the sentence contains two or more major ideas, one after the other, and the reader's brain is forced to drag an increasingly heavy load as it plods toward, hoping for, the next period. Chop the long sentence neatly in two. Sometimes doing so is as easy as changing a comma to a period and beginning the second half with a capital letter. Other times it may be necessary to stitch the wound—change a few words to restore proper grammar in both parts after the chop.

The writer need not always divide separate ideas into separate statements. If the two major ideas are short they will not overburden the reader as one sentence:

> The GoldWing motorcycle caravan raised $12,000 for the clinic, and the biking couples have already announced they will make the trip again next spring. (24 words)

But if it gets very long, more than 30 or 35 words, the sentence may overburden the reader, and if over 40 words it almost certainly will unless the writer has far better than average writing skills. Most writers should consider chopping those very long ones in two*; this is probably the easiest and most immediate way inexperienced writers can improve their sentence skills—and save time:

> The Fifth Engineering District has requested the installation of a satellite downlink terminal at the River Road Station, where the digital converters will

---

* Another useful sentence divider is the semicolon, as above. (See Chapter 19.)

be located, for the purpose of providing all cities in the district access to flood terrain data from the Army Corps of Engineers. (46 words)

Here is the logical breaking point:

The Fifth Engineering District has requested the installation of a satellite downlink terminal at the River Road Station, where the digital converters will be located, ✗ for the purpose of providing all cities in the district access to flood terrain data from the Army Corps of Engineers.

Here is what the *meat cleaver technique* can do. Notice that in this example it was necessary to do a little rewording at the chop, to keep the grammar correct in both parts:

The Fifth Engineering District has requested the installation of a satellite downlink terminal at the River Road station, where the digital converters will be located. This will provide all cities in the region access to flood terrain data from the Army Corps of Engineers. (44 words, 22 words per sentence, perfectly respectable for a short passage if the average of the *entire* writing is between 15 and 20)

Long sentences may bury ideas. Limiting sentences to one major idea does not mean ruling out subordinate clauses. Rather, use subordinate clauses in most cases for subordinate (*less important*) ideas. Avoid putting *major* ideas in the same sentence unless both ideas are very short; otherwise, even if the writer can keep the grammar straight, buried ideas result. They are likely to compete with each other for emphasis, for the reader's attention, and, when this happens, one wins and the other loses. Or they share equally, and neither idea gets the full attention it deserves.

Here is an example of a major idea buried as a subordinate clause. The buried part is between the arrows:

If *Goobly Dogs'* gig to rock halftime at the Super Bowl is all but locked up and delivered, ➡ as Jennie Frisina, HBA's eastern manager, is telling everyone, ⬅ they will become the first all-female Hispanic group to score really big time before a worldwide TV audience. (44 words)

In plain English:

Jennie Frisina, HBA's eastern manager, is telling everyone *Goobly Dogs'* gig to rock halftime at the Super Bowl is all but locked up and delivered. If it is, they will become the first all-female Hispanic group to score really big time before a worldwide TV audience. (45 words, average 22.5 words per sentence)

The period is the noblest punctuation mark of them all—and the one that can solve the most problems for writers *and readers*. Generally, we can assume safely: The more the writer concentrates on using periods correctly, the clearer and more enjoyable the paragraphs and pages will be.

But again, caution. Although an occasional sentence as short as a few words can be remarkably effective, *too many* short sentences make the writer's work sound childish. Worse, they create problems for readers by causing all ideas to sound equally important (because they do not allow the use of many subordinate [less important] phrases or clauses):

The new software works perfectly. I learned how to use it by attending the Bentleyville seminar. This was included in the purchase price. We should now be able to send out food distribution reports before noon every Tuesday. That has been our experience so far. The review committee has been requesting we do this. The reports are shorter than in the past. Color graphics make the usage and cost data easier to read. We no longer need to transfer database information. The first week, some of the continuous report forms jammed in the feeder. The Bentleyville group corrected this malfunction. It had nothing to do with the software.

Only 108 words, but they were divided into 12 sentences averaging 9 words in length. The result is extremely hard to follow and not very likely to inspire confidence. The longest sentence was 15 words, the shortest, 5. Readers cannot receive information that way very long. Did you want to scream?

Try combining some short sentences if that average is under 15 words per sentence. In doing this writers are not just manipulating numbers; we are changing the grammatical (and logical) relationships between ideas to make them easier to follow. Not all ideas are equally important in the things we write about; some need more—or less—attention than others, and the writer's skill in dividing ideas into sentences determines how much attention each one gets. We can give one idea a loud voice and another a soft one; that is why languages give us subordinate phrases and clauses. Or, when we feel two very short ideas are equally important, we can give them equal emphasis by placing one after the other in the same sentence, then combine them with a connective (conjunction) such as *and* or *but*. Remember, readers cannot *feel* the relationships between ideas the way you, the writer, can. Readers are paper readers, not mind readers. They need to *see* those relationships, and writers must help them do so:

> The new software works perfectly, and I learned to use it by attending the Bentleyville seminar included in the purchase price. Based on our experience so far, we should now be able to send out food distribution reports by noon every Tuesday, as the review committee has been requesting. The new reports are shorter, and the color graphics make the usage and cost data easier to read. Another advantage is that we no longer need to transfer database information. The first week, some of the continuous report forms jammed in the feeder, but the Bentleyville support group has corrected this malfunction. It had nothing to do with the software.

This time 109 words, comprising 6 sentences that average a respectable 18.2 words per sentence. The longest is 28 words, the shortest, 8.

THE DEVIL'S ADVOCACY

DEVIL'S ADVOCATE

Going back to choice of words, I understand what you're saying, but I'm a little puzzled. Why should a person enlarge his or her vocabulary if not to use some of those esoteric and recondite words?

GURU

Of course we should all continue enlarging our vocabularies. As long as writers continue to use little-known words, and as long as libraries contain books by those writers, you should keep developing your vocabulary as a *reader*. Otherwise you'll miss information you might want to know.

DEVIL'S ADVOCATE

From poor writers!

GURU

No, from writers who wrote in a time when attitudes on language differed from ours today. Or, even if the writers were . . . let's say . . . misguided on language usage, they might still be saying things you want or need to know. Be tolerant. Tolerance is good for your well-being, and useful information is useful even if the writer makes you work hard for it. You don't think I know what *esoteric* and *recondite* mean, do you?

DEVIL'S ADVOCATE

I can also write long sentences and keep the grammar correct. Why shouldn't I?

GURU

Go ahead. But only if you're willing to say, "It's okay if my readers don't get my message; that's their problem; I did my job." But did you? Grammatically correct doesn't mean clear.

DEVIL'S ADVOCATE

Don't short sentences sound choppy: "Run, Spot, run. See Spot run"? Is this the image writers want to send?

GURU

But that was three words per sentence. We said average between 15 and 20, and if you do there will be many longer ones to balance any very short ones. You're right, however; short sentences can produce choppy passages, and skillful writers are constantly snooping around for choppiness and know how to prevent it. That's why *connectives* are so useful; they bridge the logic gap between the end of the last idea and the beginning of the next one.

DEVIL'S ADVOCATE

This new attitude about short sentences is intriguing—that impact is inversely proportional to length.

GURU

Oh, don't do this to me. Of course you mean: the shorter the sentence, the harder it hits. Listen, go back and reread Chapter 2—carefully this time, and please don't come back until you have a better attitude about words.

DEVIL'S ADVOCATE

Well, . . .

GURU

Just do it. Trust me; I'm your friend.

About Sentence Fragments

Even the strictest grammarians allow occasional sentences that are not grammatically complete. When we use them, however, two rules are important: (1) Do not use them very often. (2) Keep them short, so the reader will know the incomplete form is deliberate. Used this way, a sentence fragment can be an effective rhetorical device. Sometimes, anyhow. The first sentence fragment in this book is in the Preface (paragraph five); it has no subject or verb.

DEVIL'S ADVOCATE

Okay, but look. You're advocating a way of writing that's pretty new and different. In real life, supposing the *reader*—who may be my manager, or the instructor in a course I'm taking—believes the opposite about words and sentences and *wants* the writing to sound scholarly? You said that's a common misconception.

GURU

Yes, and you raise a thoughtful point. Your manager or instructor may indeed believe that; lots of very capable and very nice people do. If he or she insists, you may be forced to use words larger than necessary, or complex sentences, or both. But writing in a particular style, in a particular situation, for a particular reason, is far different from writing that way all the time because you believe it's the only correct way.

DEVIL'S ADVOCATE

If every writer uses easy words and sentences, won't we all sound alike? Wouldn't that sameness destroy style?

GURU

Au contraire, mes amis. Quite the contrary, my friends. It's that preconceived notion that language needs to be complicated which destroys individual style. All writers who practice that style sound like all the others, and they all sound like a government report on the price of cabbages. Shedding that notion grants you the freedom to sound like yourself.

However, you may in some particular situation *want* to sound colorless, without style. The point is, at all times you should know how to control the characteristics of your paragraphs and pages.

CHAPTER 2 CLOSER LOOK: WORD SENSE

Words larger than necessary often make paragraphs and pages unclear. By obscuring ideas, they sometimes fail to communicate, as in this example:

> Our inability to approve your application for credit is based on insufficient down payment. We are concerned with the potential inability to meet repayment obligations as scheduled, due to inadequate income.

> **In plain English:** We're sorry, but we are unable to approve your loan application with the down payment you wish to make. The high monthly pay-

ments that would be required are often too heavy a burden for borrowers at your present income level.

Although the original passage may sound dazzling, it fails to get its message across to most readers. Remember, communication has not taken place until the ideas have been broadcast *and received*.

Some people might feel the clearly worded message is insulting. If so, it is the content that insults, not the words used to convey it. Try as we may, sometimes we cannot avoid telling people things we know will anger or offend them, but organizations dealing with the public know that cold, formal language does not make bad news any more pleasant. Conversely, warm, friendly language may make readers feel a little better about the company, bank, or government agency that had to refuse their request. We would like to think, furthermore, that anyone responsible enough to write letters such as this one would be thoughtful enough to include some goodwill statement. Opening the passage with "We're sorry" seems so natural one wonders how any writer could overlook such an important comment.

Large Words Often Make Writing Sound Impersonal and the Writer Stuffy.

Erin addressed the May staff meeting of the Classical Music Division to explain the new system. Attendees were duly impressed with the multitudinous tasks involved in the accumulation of relevant, pertinent recording data and the methodology by which these tasks are implemented by the MCS staff.

In warm, personal words: Erin explained the new system at the Classical Music Division's May staff meeting. All of us who attended were impressed by the amount of work involved in collecting recording data, and by the methods the MCS staff uses to collect it.

Multitudinous tasks? Oh come, now. Most readers would laugh at that, and should. Or consider *relative, pertinent data*. Would anyone try to collect any other kind? Was this writer trying to impress with the size of his or her vocabulary rather than with valuable and dignified ideas? We are past the time in life when that would succeed. In the real world, writers choose words to get things done—whether to help design an airplane, comfort a friend, raise funds for a community theater, or explain how to use a computer program.

A comma between *data* and *and?* Strictly speaking, no. But the rules of punctuation say it is proper to provide a pause between groups of words if readers might otherwise misread the passage.

SENTENCE SENSE

The words in this passage are reasonable for the message, but the six very short sentences create a choppy, childish tone.

> We like this company's work. The wooden forms needed for pouring concrete are always accurate. And delivery is usually on time. They have been late only once since we started using them. That was during the railroad strike last year. Unfortunately, their price for this job is too high.

> **In longer sentences:**   We like this company's work. The wooden forms needed for pouring concrete are always accurate, and delivery is usually on time. They have been late only once since we started using them, but that was during the railroad strike. Unfortunately, their price for this job is too high.

The original version averages 8.2 words per sentence; some very easy sentence combining brings that up to 12.5, and the result is a more mature, thoughtful tone.

Even 12.5 words per sentence, however, is generally too low. It may be fine for occasional short passages, but for sustained adult reading—especially for expository information—readers want the information to flow in clusters averaging between 15 and 20 words per sentence. Remember to mix them up, however. Not all sentences should be between 15 and 20 words; readers would get bored.

If a Sentence Contains Too Many Important Ideas They Will Compete with One Another for Emphasis, for the Reader's Attention.

> Roman, who throws a 95-mph fastball and has a change-up and good slider, suffered his worst defeat since he was named rookie of the year two seasons ago, allowing a one-out single by Rod Brewer in the first then walking three straight batters, throwing ten consecutive balls at one point.

> **In shorter sentences:**   Roman, who throws a 95-mph fastball and has a change-up and good slider, suffered his worst defeat since he was named rookie of the year two seasons ago. He allowed a one-out single by Rod Brewer in the first, then walked three straight batters, throwing ten consecutive balls at one point.

The meat cleaver technique in action. The original passage was fairly clear, but the rewrite makes an important improvement. Separated into two sentences, both major ideas get the attention they deserve.

But Note: Some writers might prefer this as three sentences, further chopping the first one into two: "Roman throws a 95-mph fastball and has a change-up and a good slider. He suffered his worst . . ." Or, chopping the second sentence: ". . . *three straight batters. He threw ten consecutive* . . ." (But not both; four sentences here would be overchopping.) An important point is demonstrated here: Even within the limit of 15 to 20 words (average) per sentence, writers have all the freedom of style anyone needs.

Readers Suffer Greatly When Vocabulary and Sentence Structure Are Both Burdensome.

> This kind of study should be formal and direct, involving thorough analysis of all pertinent factors and presentation of a wide range of specific alternatives such that each individual Grand Worthington board member merely has to choose from a wide array of facts which by their mere presence instills confidence and assurance that GW children are getting the best secondary education program that is available.

(Is the grammatical error in that sentence obvious? Breakdowns of this kind become more common as the sentence gets longer.)

> **In plain English (easy words and sentences of reasonable length):** This kind of study should be formal and direct, examining all related factors and presenting a wide range of choices. Grand Worthington board members will then have confidence that GW children are getting the best secondary education program available.

(Grammatical error: *instills* should be *instill,* to agree with the plural noun *facts.* (If the verb *instills* is intended to agree with the singular noun *array,* then the pronoun *their* must be *its.* But the sentence sounds awkward that way.)

The original passage contained far too many ideas for one sentence, and as a result a grammatical error crept in that would hurt the writer's image and the image of his or company. How ironic that it appears in a sentence about confidence! The passage also burdens readers unnecessarily with complex words when simple ones can say exactly the same thing. (Example: *Alternatives* instead of *choices.*) The writer who tries to impress with language risks embarrassment in the eyes of those people he or she is trying to impress.

TO THE PRUDENT STUDENT . . .
. . . ESPECIALLY IF YOU HAVE
JUST ENTERED COLLEGE

More will be expected of you as you move up the education ladder, and you will often be judged by your writing (because it is so visible). How, then, should you write? You may or may not receive useful advice in your academic classes.

When writing becomes an important part of our lives, in college or in the world of work, educated adults often go through a subconscious thought process something like this: "I'm an educated adult, and I'm expected to sound like one." But then: "How do educated adults sound?" Lacking specific guidance and left to themselves to develop a writing style, people seem to be pulled toward the attitude: "The educated adult writer should be exactly the opposite of the child writer."

Children, when they start becoming able to develop language arts skills, invariably express their thoughts in small words and short sentences. Therefore, later in life: "The way to write like an educated person is to use large words and long sentences." Not so. It is just not that simple.

The way to write like an educated person is to *be informed* and then use language effectively to convey your information accurately, efficiently, and clearly to others.

What if a teacher or professor prefers students' reports in complex language? Some educators do, especially as you advance in higher education. Some believe in a style called *the language of academia,* a vague phrase with no precise definition, and in extreme cases they may give lower grades to report not written that way. Although we may disagree with their attitude toward language usage, we certainly cannot judge them as educators on that basis.

The prudent student should find out what is expected—especially in postgraduate study. When a professor assigns a report, ask whether he or she has a preference: lay English or academic style?

For academic style, simply reverse the advice on word choice and sentence structure (principles 1 and 2) in this chapter; prefer the complex word to the simple, and average between 25 and 30 words per sentence (with some considerably longer).

But, as you do, remember: Writing in a particular style, in a particular situation, for a particular reason, is far different from writing that way all the time because you think it is the correct way.

Oh yes, about letters home: They (the family) really do expect you to sound different (more grown up) the first time you write home. They expect more than just computer clutter. Please them instantly by averaging between 15 and 20 words per sentence (see principle 2, page 18). For most students this means lengthening some sentences; for most businesspeople it would mean shortening some.

Instead of:

Aunt Dee is so sweet. I miss her. I really appreciate all she's done for me. Part of the reason I want to succeed is so I can repay her. And Uncle Bert, too, of course.

Try:

Aunt Dee is so sweet. I miss her and really appreciate all she's done for me, and part of the reason I want to succeed is so I can repay Uncle Bert and her.

Welcome to the language of the real world, Student.

Five Principles of Clear Writing (Continued)

The first human being who hurled a curse instead of a weapon against his adversary was the founder of civilization.

—Sigmund Freud

Approach each writing task with this attitude: Proper use of language gives us the power to express even our most difficult ideas clearly and simply, *with no sacrifice of accuracy.*

Writers who have achieved this gift of language power enjoy an exhilarating level of satisfaction when the thoughts and the words come together just the right way. Artistry is part of their writing, and a kind of dignity is evident to readers—the dignity that is part of, and comes from, the message.

Chapter 2 discussed the two most important principles of clarity: familiar words and smooth-flowing sentences. The other three of the five principles of clear writing are:

- Prefer active voice verbs; avoid passives
- Use a conversational style as a guide
- Revise, revise, and revise again

These principles are followed by this added advice for writers in the world of work:

- Allow people into the paragraphs and pages.

PRINCIPLE 3: PREFER ACTIVE VOICE VERBS; AVOID PASSIVES

Verb Management

Recall the school year spent learning the parts of speech and the basics of sentence structure? The English teacher introduced the roomful of small people to a sentence such as "The dog buried the bone," and we began learning those basic terms: subject—transitive verb—direct object (*dog—buried—bone*).

That sentence structure is the backbone of English language usage. It is in the *active* voice. The same thing in the passive voice would be "The bone was buried by the dog."

An Invitation to Misunderstanding

A committee member writes: "The village council changed our design for planting wildflowers along the riverbed." Notice this is the same structure as "The dog buried the bone": subject, transitive verb, direct object (*council, changed, designs*). Winston Churchill called this structure "the noble English sentence."

In the passive voice that statement would be: "Our design . . . was changed by the village council." Notice that in the passive version the subject is *design*. The verb is still *changed,* but it has picked up the auxiliary (helping verb) *was.* And the object is now *council.* Subject and object have traded places.

In the active voice, which is the more natural way, the subject performs the action described by the verb (the role of the subject is active), and the object receives it. In the passive, instead of performing the action the subject *receives* the action of the verb. (The role of the subject is passive.) Because it has taken on that little helping verb, a passive is a *complete* verb, not transitive. This means the sentence is grammatically complete at that point. It does not need a direct object; its object hangs there, still useful, but as the object of the preposition *by.* However, the entire prepositional phrase, *by the village council,* is an unnecessary part of the grammar, and, because these *by-whom* prepositional phrases hang there awkwardly, writers are tempted to pay them scant attention and drop them out. Then our sentence reads: "*The design was* (or *has been*) *changed.*"

Now the sentence does not tell *by whom*. And, more often than many writers realize, *by whom* is an important part of the information. The writer knows who did what but may not notice that the sentence does not share this information with the reader. The reader, too, may be unaware some information is missing and, in filling the gap intuitively, may assume wrongly. The writer's mind sees: "The village council changed the design . . . ," but the reader's mind may see: "The bank that owns the land changed . . . ," or, "Smedley changed the design . . . he messes up everything." Or even: "The state Environmental Protection Agency. . . ." Thoughtful writers do not give readers such choices.

These two samples show the importance of the *by whom* information:

The following procedure is recommended:

When the red light goes on, the instrument *should be shut* down, and all settings *should be checked.* It *should be turned* on again only when it *is confirmed* that all pressures are within tolerances.

Notice how much more information the active voice conveys:

The union recommends the following procedure:

When the red light goes on, *the operator* should shut the instrument down, and *the supervisor* should check all settings. *The lab assistant* should turn it on again only when *the research manager* confirms that all pressures are within tolerances.

At no time is a passive more risky than in the writing of procedures or other written instructions. Do not write, *Sonny Babcock should be met at the airport at 3:15 p.m.* It might not get done. The writer is saying something must be done but not who must do it; the reader may not realize he or she is supposed to do it, and Sonny ends up taking a cab from the airport—not a good way to treat a customer. Rather, write: *You* (or whoever else) *should meet Sonny Babcock at. . . .* Notice the difference? The active voice is clearer and more emphatic, and therefore the instructions are more likely to be followed.

The passive is not always dangerous, however. Sometimes *by whom* is obvious or not important. For example, in a research report a scientist is usually describing his or her own work. *By whom* is obvious, and if he or she were to report the various stages of that work in the active voice the subject would repeatedly be *I*. That would be awkward and inappropriate, and in this case the passive would probably be better. (*But note* that special care would be needed if part of the activities reported were performed by someone else.)

Or, *by whom* may be unimportant: *The tension* was broken *only when the last of the missing paintings* was recovered.

In addition to withholding information, passive voice verbs make the paragraphs and pages dull. For both those reasons, careful writers should use them sparingly.

Metaphor: For Color and Description

A metaphor is a group of words that implies a comparison to something else, usually to create a vivid or colorful image (*Melissa is a tiger at the bridge table*). Different from simile, in which the comparison is direct. (See page 163.) Though colorful, metaphors are generally imprecise, leaving the reader to decide exactly what the writer means.

Mixed metaphor happens when two metaphors are used that contradict each other or for some other reason are not appropriate when used together (*she climbed the ladder of success with both feet planted firmly on the ground*). The writer guilty of such thoughtless expression invites ridicule—and deserves it.

Compare:

Boudreau and Hall described those events in detail, and now Carrabini realized that the three young officers had fooled everyone.

With:

Those events were described in detail by Boudreau and Hall, and it was now realized by Carrabini that everyone had been fooled by the three young officers.

Caution: *Passive* and *past* are not the same. They sound somewhat alike only by accident, and passive voice verbs occur in all tenses. We could say: *The plans were approved* . . . , *The plans* are *being approved* . . . , or *The plans will be approved*. There we have past, present, and future tenses, but they are all passive and equally weak for the same reason.

Recognizing passives is easy. They always have some form of the verb *to be* (that helping verb) in front of the main verb. *The design* was *changed. Sonny Babcock* should be *met. Everyone* had been *fooled*. Once the verb is recognized as passive, turning it active is simple. Just ask, *by whom?* The answer to that question reveals the subject needed for an active voice sentence.

It is recommended *that we wait until the World Series is over before advertising on TV*. By whom? The sales manager *recommends that we wait* . . . , or, The budget committee recommends . . . , Or, *I recommend* . . . ?

Mary *is loved*. By whom? John? Gregorio? Everyone who knows her? *By whom* can make a great difference to the reader.

But note: Not all forms of the verb *to be* are passive. This may sound complicated, but it is really quite easy to understand. If verbs such as *was, is, are, will be,* and so on stand alone, not as part of another verb, they themselves are "complete" verbs, in the active voice: Mary *is* lovely. In examples such as this one, *was, is,* and *will be* are not helping verbs in front of another verb; they are the whole verb. Like passives, these verbs do not need an object. (A not-very-important-for-most-people fact: In the example above, *lovely* is a predicate adjective.)

Compare:

All-star Rachel Leibert-Weiss *was named* the team's player of the year last season. She *is described* as the WNBA's best shooting guard and almost certainly *will be voted* most valuable player if her numbers continue at this pace. (All three verbs are passive voice.)

With:

Sports fans in the Tulsa area *named* all-star Rachel Leibert-Weiss player of the year last season. Opposing players *describe* her as the WNBA's best shooting guard, and *Cybersport* readers almost certainly *will vote* her the league's most valuable player if her numbers continue at this pace.

PRINCIPLE 4: USE CONVERSATIONAL STYLE AS A GUIDE

Style Management

Most of us are far better talkers than writers. For adults with reasonable (not necessarily stellar) vocabulary and grammar skills, spoken language gently coaxes us toward expressing things the way they should be expressed. (The reason: In all cultures, spoken language developed long before writing appeared [about 5000 years ago]. Language usage patterns, therefore—and vocabulary—were well established before our earliest ancestors began to think about such things as alphabets and writing.)

The advice, "use conversational style," however, does not suggest we should write in slang or in careless ways. Writing should be more precise than conversation, because the writer has more time to choose words and build sentences carefully—and the reader has more time to examine carefully for meaning and to notice faults; he or she will usually ignore a little carelessness in casual conversation but will not forgive that same carelessness on our pages.

In addition to the historical fact that spoken language came much earlier than writing, there are two practical reasons most people communicate more effectively when they are speaking. First, we have had more practice speaking than writing; we have done it every day since approximately age 2. Second, the situation itself is more likely to improve the transfer of information. Most of our speaking in our life-times is in conversation, and so we get instant feedback—chances to cor-rect any mistakes. Face to face with the receiver, we have many ways of knowing if we are failing to make ourselves understood—a questioning look on the other person's face, or sometimes the blunt statement, "I don't understand." Even though we may not have been aware it was hap-pening, that instant feedback has helped us improve our speaking skills since the years when we were just beginning to construct language pat-terns in our minds; we have benefitted from instant correction service.

As a result, people often have two very different language usage *styles* when they communicate. The difference is so pronounced there seems almost to be a switch in the back of the head—one position for speech, the other for writing. Most writers when they sit down to write should remind themselves to turn that switch to the *speaking* position. But doing so may not be easy.

Another important suggestion: When the mind just refuses to help us find the right way to express an idea in writing (and we all have those times), think: "How would I say this to a loved one or friend at dinner?" It may not be easy, but the words that would express that idea to some-one in relaxed conversation, in a casual surrounding, are likely to be an effective way of writing it. Another version of the same technique: How would your favorite radio or TV newscaster say it?

Again the warning, however. Most of us use language a bit carelessly in conversation; we must be more careful to choose the right words, and to be grammatically correct, in writing than in talking. The *listener* will for-give small amounts of casual carelessness; the *reader* will not. But that should not be very challenging. Most writers should have no trouble using correct grammar if they try to avoid dangerously long and compli-cated sentences. The true principle 4 should probably be: "Use a con-versational style—well, sort of, anyhow."

PRINCIPLE 5: REVISE, REVISE, . . . AND REVISE AGAIN

Quality Management

No letter or report, no great book, was ever written (except through Divine guidance) that could not have been made better if the writer had had one more chance to read and revise.

I call, at this point, upon the author's privilege to address the reader in the first person. The principles presented in this book have served me well as a writer and teacher. But applying them has not always been quick or easy. Our paragraphs and pages should always be easy to read, but our readers may never know the difficulty—the anguish—we sometimes go through to get them that way. *Thinking* exactly what we want to say, then *saying* it with reasonable language usage skill, may sometimes be sublimely simple or at other times so difficult we may doubt our ability to do it in a particular passage, and when we succeed we usually know it, and the satisfaction makes the effort worthwhile. Even so, I find it unthinkable that the *first version* of any writing could not be made better. It just doesn't happen that way.

Why revise if you have already done your best? Well, let us say you have done your best *so far.* We all have blind spots, and to find and correct them we need to separate ourselves from our work. Only then, *we* can see our work as our *readers* see it. The further (longer) this separation, the more weaknesses we are able to see and correct.

Little lines and curlicues:　Blind spots are idea gaps—passages, large or small, that did not quite say what we intended, or perhaps how we intended, but we cannot see the gap. (Neither, if the writing *seems* clear, can the reader.) All of us have occasionally revisited something we wrote earlier and wondered: "Could I have written that?"

This trouble is inherent in the nature of language and the brain. Our thoughts exist as neural (electrochemical) impulses, not words. But we cannot transmit them that way. Writers (or speakers) convert their information from those impulses to words *just for the transmission,* and readers (or listeners) convert them back. Picture the writer sitting there during the writing process. We monitor our work as we write—almost as though standing over our own shoulder, looking down as a typical reader would, and constantly asking: "How am I doing?" Too often it answers: "Just fine; keep it up." The trouble comes because too often our brain betrays us. The trouble comes because each of us is the *least* typical reader of our own paragraphs and pages. We know what we are trying to say; we are not relying on those little lines and curlicues on the page to find out. No other reader can have that privilege. And so, if a passage comes close but does not say exactly what we intended, or says it a little awkwardly, we tend to see not what we wrote but what we *intended.* An idea gap exists, but the "writerbrain" fills in the missing information involuntarily. No "readerbrain" can do that; readers are paper readers, not mind readers. The reader may have trouble understanding, may dislike something we wrote awkwardly, or may not be aware he or she is missing anything.

Later, when we are no longer so close to that work, we *can* see our paragraphs and pages as a typical reader would. Then we notice our gaps in logic, or our awkward phrases, and can correct them.

And that is the final part of the writing process.

FURTHER ADVICE FOR THE WORLD OF WORK: ALLOW PEOPLE INTO THE PARAGRAPHS AND PAGES

Tone Management

This advice is closely related to principle 3 (active voice verbs), because when we reword sentences from passive to active, people find their way in (often as subjects of transitive verbs).

A widespread myth holds that expository writing should be impersonal whenever possible. Misguided writers have even coined a name for the style that avoids references to people: "Third person," they call it. But people who believe this baseless advice usually mean "no person."

In grammar, *third person* refers only to pronouns, and it means *he, she,* or *it* (and their various forms [cases]). Should we really limit ourselves only to *it*? Avoiding references to human beings does not seem to serve any sensible purpose. People who encourage third-person writing style should define much more precisely what they mean, and why; writers trying to follow rules would then have better guidance.

Because that term is used so loosely, it has become a cliché, and like most clichés it has no specific definition; it means different things to different people. But even in very formal writing *third-person style* certainly cannot mean that prudent writers must avoid referring to people.

What tempts anyone to write, or advise others to write, in this impersonal style? The answer usually given is: "We've always done it that way." An inadequate explanation. People are often, if not usually, an important part of what we write about. Why try to hide them? Writers of business reports should feel free to refer to others whenever their presence will improve the paragraphs and pages.

This does not mean dragging people in without purpose, however. Rather, writers need not feel timid about referring to people when doing so seems useful or natural.

Yes, writers may call themselves "I." Not one of the respected style manuals places a restriction against this—but there is a sensible limitation: English teachers probably advised most people, "Don't repeat *I, I, I,* over and over again." They advised well, but the reason has more to do with clear thinking and accurate reporting than with good manners. It is simply this: People who look around and constantly observe themselves to be the center of all important activities are probably not observing very accurately. Still, an occasional *I* is entirely proper—even in the most serious and dignified writing.

Does tone have anything to do with objectivity?   Why would it? Somehow, many people believe that impersonal tone (without references to people) is a sign the writer treated the subject objectively. When we stop and think about it, however, why would tone have anything to do with critical thinking? Tone can be deceptive. One can imagine a written work shamefully prejudiced and biased, yet seeming (to casual readers) to be objective because a cold and scholarly tone creates the *impression* of objectivity. The opposite can also be true and equally misleading; a warm, personal tone can be equally deceptive, creating a false impression of sympathy, or humility, when the *content* of the writing may be the exact opposite. Language arts skills can give writers that kind of power—the power to deceive. There is simply no relationship between the tone of the writing and the objectivity of the writer.

But Caution: Careful writers do not use *I* and *we* interchangeably. Traditionally, only kings call themselves *we;* this reference is to the partnership between God and king (and is the origin of the term *divine right.*) If there is doubt, *we* is probably appropriate.

Interestingly, writers who want to express personal opinion often turn, in many cases without being aware, to the passive voice verb form, "It is believed . . . ," rather than "I believe. . . ." That may sound impersonal, but it is also dangerously vague—and sometimes timid.

Again, this is not to say writers should *search* for ways to bring people into their paragraphs and pages; they should simply not feel they need to avoid doing so. Generally, referring to people will make the paragraphs and pages sound more *courteous* and pleasant. More important, statements will become more informative and precise.

THE DEVIL'S ADVOCACY

DEVIL'S ADVOCATE

Suppose . . . this is concerning passive voice verbs . . . a person makes a mistake—let's say, in figuring the cost of an important project. Wouldn't it be smarter to say, "The cost was figured incorrectly. . . ." than "I figured the . . ."?

GURU

(Sigh.) It had to come up, didn't it? It always does. This is not a language usage question; it's a judgment question. Yes, deception is one of the recognized uses of language, so your question is reasonable, and in this case the passive voice does conceal some troublesome information. But look, even if that's what you want to do, the more important and practical question may be: *How well does it conceal it?* Sooner or later, it seems, you are going to end up in the active voice, because it's likely someone will ask the dreaded *by whom?* question. Is this little deception cool, then?

DEVIL'S ADVOCATE

Clarify something else, please. That example at the beginning of this chapter, "The village council changed our design. . . ." Suppose that said, ". . . has changed our design. . . ." Now there's a form of *to be* in front of the main verb, but it isn't passive.

GURU

Ah, good question. You're right; it's in the active voice, not passive, because the subject (council) is performing the action (changed). And that's the only fully accurate way of recognizing whether a verb is active or passive. *Has changed* is the verb form called "past tense," active voice. Its subject is performing the action. It is passive when the subject is *receiving* the action; that would be, "has been changed."

Here's another thing about passives: The two parts of the verb *are* sometimes (as here) *separated*. "The angry customer *was* quickly and firmly *escorted* outside by two security guards." Nothing changed in the basic structure of the sentence.

DEVIL'S ADVOCATE

Is it true that once the writing is started in the active or passive voice you should stay with it—you can't switch from one to the other . . . or maybe, not until the next paragraph?

GURU

Who dreamed that one up? Of course you may. (You just used both, in the perfectly natural wording of your question.) It would be impossible to write very long, sticking to just one or the other. Maybe you were told you shouldn't change verb *tenses*, but that advice is also wrong and would also be impossible to follow.

DEVIL'S ADVOCATE

Referring to people in formal writing seems a little pushy. We were always told it's in poor taste . . . bad manners . . . unless you're writing a personal letter or a novel or short story.

GURU

It's not a matter of etiquette; it's a matter of reporting accurately, and people are often (usually?) an important part of the things we write about, especially in the world after academia. Why try to pretend they do not exist?

DEVIL'S ADVOCATE

How about *the undersigned?*

GURU

Oh, come off it. That creates the image of a 1920s office, and you wearing a green eyeshade and sleeve garters, sitting under a bare light bulb that hangs from a single wire. How odd that anyone would sneer at *I* but profoundly respect *the undersigned;* their meanings are identical today, so they must be equally proper or improper. Once, *the undersigned* was a respected term. It became fashionable when people of high rank had secretaries and clerks who were good at composition (and penmanship) write their letters for them. Everyone knew that the person who signed the letter hadn't written it; the phrase became a mark of the very important and privileged person. As that happened, people of lower rank began using the phrase—a little deception to elevate oneself in the eyes of other people. People would write things like, "The undersigned holds you dear to his heart." How very odd.

DEVIL'S ADVOCATE

You're convincing me, but who will convince my boss? The five principles may be okay here, but they're not the way things are done in my company. My boss won't buy into this way of writing.

GURU

Don't be sure. But also, don't get fired. The thing is, managers are usually eager for better ways of doing things, but often people use the excuse: "Oh, the boss will never allow that," without ever finding out.

Still, it may be true occasionally that a manager believes, like so many other people, that good writing should sound scholarly and cold. In that case, talk to each other. Try to convince him or her of the advantages of plain English. Usually you can, if you can be convincing about two basic points: First, that the *content* doesn't change; you're still the same person, using the same judgment, in deciding *what* a letter or report should or shouldn't say. They pay you for that. And second, that the new style, though maybe more relaxed, is still dignified and probably more courteous. If the boss remains unconvinced, then of course you write the way he or she wants. But, again, writing in a particular style, in a particular situation, for a particular reason, is far different from writing that way regularly because you think it's the only correct way.

DEVIL'S ADVOCATE

About rewriting . . .

GURU

Let's not even discuss it, except to say: *You need to rewrite, and the more important the document, the more times you should rewrite and rewrite again.* Trust me; I'm your friend. Nor does this need diminish as we become more experienced writers. Quod erat demonstrandum.

DEVIL'S ADVOCATE

What?

GURU

Thus it has been demonstrated.

CHAPTER 3: CLOSER LOOK: PREFER ACTIVE VOICE VERBS

Each of the sentences below is in the passive voice, followed immediately by the exact same message in the active voice. Notice that each of the passive voice verbs begins with some form of *to be*—and in each of the passive sentences except the last one, a prepositional phrase (beginning with *by*) tells readers the source of the action. In the last sentence there is no *by whom* phrase, and so readers are left to themselves to fill in that missing information. Sometimes *by whom* is obvious, but misunderstandings or serious mistakes can happen if it is not.

Passive: This idea *will be killed* by the entertainment committee in a New York minute.

Active: The entertainment committee *will kill* this idea in a New York minute.

Passive:　Should these forms *be completed* by part-time employees?

Active:　Should part-time employees *complete* these forms?

Passive:　Small gifts *were exchanged* by the delegates, and it *was pledged* they would meet again when the crisis is over.

Active:　The delegates *exchanged* small gifts, and they *pledged* they would meet again when the crisis is over.

Passive:　It *will be argued* by the defense lawyers that most of the DNA evidence is inadmissible.

Active:　The defense lawyers *will argue* that most of the DNA evidence is inadmissible.

Passive:　Our children *are* usually *taught* that most adults are intelligent and kind.

Active:　We (or *Our schools,* or *Walt Disney movies,* or *Adults*) usually *teach* our children that most adults are intelligent and kind.

How Information Robbery Happens

The next sample passage further shows how passive voice verbs can rob the paragraphs and pages of precision by failing to tell *by whom.* The writer knows who did (or will do) what but cannot see that he or she is withholding this valuable information from the reader:

> It *is recommended* that digital embedding *be used,* and it *is believed* that this *can be done* easily.

A harmless sentence? An uninformed reader would have no way of knowing that the writer is reporting an important finding of a research project conducted for his or her company by Purdue University, and is expressing the opinion of Dr. Hajime Sato. In the active voice that information is presented clearly:

> Purdue University recommends we use digital embedding, and Dr. Hajime Sato believes we can do this easily.

The original passage is a misunderstanding waiting to happen. Four passive voice verbs in one sentence, and none told *by whom;* in all four the writer left out the prepositional phrase that would contain this information. No reader could possibly supply those answers. Of course, the meaning looked perfectly clear to the *writer*. But remember, readers are paper readers, not mind readers.

Sometimes *by whom* is obvious or unimportant; then the passive may be appropriate:

> After the storm, victims *were aided* by police and volunteers. The rainfall *is believed* to be the heaviest of any 24-hour period in the city's history.

Turn it active? The paragraph would then read:

> After the storm, police and volunteers *aided* the victims. U.S. weather officials *believe* the rainfall was the heaviest of any 24-hour period in the city's history.

The question here is where the emphasis should be. The subject of a sentence usually stands out, and in the first (passive) version that would be *victims*. In the active voice version it would be *police and volunteers*. Inappropriate. In this case the passive voice is desirable; it places the emphasis where it should be. No information is missing, because the prepositional phrase tells *by whom*.

Consider the second sentence, however. "It *is believed* . . ." By whom? U.S. weather officials believe . . . ? A 102-year-old resident believes . . . ? The difference is important, and only the writer could fill in the information hidden by a passive voice verb.

USE CONVERSATIONAL STYLE

It can be a guide to the best way of writing most things. It can save us time in finding the best way of expressing a difficult idea, and it will often make the paragraphs and pages clearer and more gracious. This passage is from the personnel department of a large hospital, but the principles of writing are the same regardless of the subject or the organization:

> **Unthinkable:**　Acknowledgment is made of your recent correspondence regarding employment opportunities available in this institution.
>
> 　Additional information is requested for proper evaluation of your credentials and career objectives. In this regard, an application for employment is enclosed together with a self-addressed envelope for your convenience. Upon receipt of the completed application, it will be reviewed and consideration will be based on openings relative to your qualifications.

Should an opening compatible with those qualifications be available, you will be notified.

Some people really do write that way.

In plain English: Thank you for inquiring about job opportunities at our hospital.

To evaluate your skills properly, we would like to know more about your background and goals. I have enclosed a job application and self-addressed envelope for your convenience. When we receive your completed application, we will review it carefully and notify you if we have an opening that fits your qualifications.

Notice that rewriting did not cause even the slightest sacrifice or change in *content*. Likewise in any writing, if the writer feels simplicity and warmth would help readers, the principles of clear writing do not require even the slightest compromise of the accuracy, value, or dignity of the writer's ideas. That would be a bad trade, and it is never necessary.

Missing information—Dogs that lick babies' faces: Earliest known records of the canine species Samoyed describe a Russo-Alaskan work dog, a starkly white species abounding in strength and demonstrating exceptional comaraderie. So pronounced is the latter trait that its disposition and frequent acts of affection toward the young have produced surprising stories among owners. Conversely, although the animal generally possesses a high degree of intelligence it is noted for its resistance to behavior modification.

In plain English: The earliest records of the Samoyed describe a very strong, all-white sled dog in Russia and Alaska. It was, and its descendants still are, loyal and affectionate, and exceptionally playful with children. (This year's champion likes to lick babies' faces.) On the other hand, although generally an intelligent animal this dog is unusually hard to train.

The first version reminds us of a hard-to-study and hard-to-stay-awake textbook passage (although it was from a magazine article). The rewrite is more like the way most of us would *say* the same thing. Imagine reading anything written in the style of the original passage, on any subject, for very long periods. Most readers would fall asleep. The rewrite is closer to the way most of us would *say* the same thing; it conveys the same information far more effectively. But there is another message here: The conversational version *tells more*, and the added information is particularly enlightening and vivid. Writers who feel the need for a more formal style are often tempted to leave out interesting but informal information. They may feel that some abstract phrasing (in this case *disposition and demonstrations of affection toward the young*) expresses the thought fully, or they may feel the informality would be out of place. Either way, readers are deprived. (In the original, they cannot even know that *the young* are children, not puppies.)

Changing Some Old Attitudes

My method is to take the utmost trouble to find the right thing to say, and then to say it with the utmost of levity.

—*George Bernard Shaw*

Languages change. Especially, the language of the United States and the British Commonwealth changes to suit the needs of the cultures it serves, as those cultures change. Languages also pick up strange, hard-to-explain traits, and people often have intense feelings about what is correct or incorrect usage in the language of their nurture.

THE IMPORTANCE OF CONNECTIVES

Writers are mind readers—of their own minds, that is. (What they have written always looks clear to them or they would not have written it that way.) But readers are paper readers; they rely on those little black lines and curlicues on the pages to receive information from the writer's mind.

The principles of clear writing in the last two chapters have guided readers for centuries, but those principles alone do not create *fluent* writing, information that *flows* logically and smoothly from sentence to sentence, paragraph to paragraph. We need to pay attention as well to the invisible information in the spaces between sentences, and between paragraphs. Experienced writers know that writers can fall into an abyss at some of those spaces unless a bridge is provided to fill the gap. This is likely to be a very small but important gap in logic; the reader needs help to understand the relationship between the end of the last idea and the beginning of the next one—a relationship the writer can *feel*.

We call the words that bridge these gaps *connectives*. But here, a conflict often arises.

Throughout their educations most students in U.S. schools and universities spend more time studying English than any other subject. Once past the early years, however, most of that time is spent studying *literature* and very little on developing language arts skills. We read. We study the writing of others. But do we study their language arts techniques, so we might develop our own? Might the designers and guardians of this system have thought that somehow we would learn to write by reading? It does not happen that way—any more than we learn to cook by eating. Most students passing through our education system receive very little specific advice on language usage and writing skills. (We see signs the emphasis is shifting in recent years, however, with more teaching devoted to composition.)

THE THREE TABOOS

Our language (British and American) has changed drastically since much of the great English literature was written. Gradually, as the language and cultures continued to change through the centuries, much of great literature and scholarly writing became so difficult to read and understand that English teachers became specialists at explaining it. By the mid-1980s teaching attitudes began shifting, with more emphasis on teaching composition. Still today, however, most English teachers are literature specialists, untrained to teach composition. And many hold up literary or scholarly style as the model for writing today.

All of us, however, received at least some exposure to the important rules of English language usage as we passed through our education system. Unfortunately, many also receive some well-intentioned but questionable "rules-that-are-not-really-rules" along the way. These are usually negative—things we were told prudent writers just do not do.

Taboo 1: We May Not Begin Sentences with And or But.

Of course we may. In fact, there are times we should (and most good writers do). Here is why: These small but mighty words are called *conjunctions*, or *connectives*. What do they connect? Our ideas. And (oops!)

The Illogic of English

Is *illogic* a word? English commonly creates an adjective by adding the suffix *al* to a noun (logic, logic*al*). Why, then, not the opposite—create a noun by removing the *al* from an adjective (illogic*al*, illogic)? But this does not always work.

Prefixes also give us that kind of inconsistency—and fun. When uncouth people attend finishing school, do they become *couth*? If a disgruntled person's troubles go away, may he or she be called *gruntled*? If you are disheveled and clean up, do you become *sheveled* (or *heveled*)? English is full of such inconsistencies. They prove little, but they make interesting cocktail conversation.

what is the basic vehicle of the idea? *The sentence.* When someone advises us, then, that we may not begin sentences with *And* or *But,* we are deprived of the two most useful rhetorical devices for connecting the flow of logic from one sentence to the next. Two choices remain: We may have the smooth flow of the connective *or* the clarity and efficiency of short sentences, but we may not have both.

But (oops!) good writers refuse to make that choice. What can be wrong with short, smooth sentences? *Connectives allow us smooth, logical flow* and *the clarity and impact of short sentences.*

Writers should not deliberately seek opportunities to begin sentences with *And* or *But.* Rather, there is no need to back off from these helpful words when using them seems the natural thing to do. Here is an example in which a respected writer felt beginning sentences with *And* and *But* was natural and desirable. *The Wall Street Journal* is regularly one of the best written publications in the United States:

> Alabama earmarks the ~~highest~~
> Kentucky the least.
>   But the report warns that earmarking generally "constitutes a constraint on budgeting, with few if any advantages for state revenue and budgetary management." Earmarking also "diminishes legislators' and governors' budgetary control by making comprehensive budgeting more difficult."
>
>   **NEW YORK TRIES to keep more residents from fleeing to lower-tax states.**
>   Many wealthy people literally don't want to be caught dead in New York because of the state's high estate taxes. That's one reason some move elsewhere, such as to Florida. A provision in a recently enacted New York law cuts estate taxes for many people, but lawyers predict it won't keep many from thinking about leaving.
>   In essence, the new law allows a deduction of up to $250,000 for the value of a New Yorker's principal home in computing the taxable estate. But that won't help renters, and many wealthy homeowners would still ~~be better off fin~~ ~~~~ to
>
> change "buy" to "hold" or ~~speculative~~ hold," instead of the blunter "sell." It's still a sure sign to institutional investors to head for the exits. But less savvy investors, who depend on research reports to decide what to buy and sell in the marketplace, may have little idea the stock could be headed for a dive.
>   "There's a game out here," says Peter Siris, a former analyst at UBS Securities Inc. "Most people aren't fooled by what analysts have to say . . . because they know in a lot of cases they're shills. But those poor [small] investors — somebody ought to tell them."
>   The pressure to avoid negative reviews is more intense than ever, in large part because analysts have become more expendable amid the Wall Street layoffs of recent years. And the pressure is coming from more than just the companies whose securities are involved. Some institutional buyers berate or penalize brokerage firms for issuing negative research on stocks they hold. Aft~~er~~ ~~~~

—*The Wall Street Journal* (Dow Jones & Company, Inc., publisher)

The timid may argue that respected publications such as *The Wall Street Journal* have literary freedom to bend the rules of grammar. The editors of that publication would certainly not agree; skilled writers do not bend or ignore rules—not even slightly. There has never been a rule against beginning sentences with *And* or *But.* Witness this editorial passage from the (unabridged) *Oxford English Dictionary,* acknowledged by scholars worldwide as the foremost authority on English usage:

GENERAL EXPLANATIONS.

THE VOCABULARY.

THE Vocabulary of a widely-diffused and highly-cultivated living language is not a fixed quantity circumscribed by definite limits. That vast aggregate of words and phrases which constitutes the Vocabulary of English-speaking men presents, to the mind that endeavours to grasp it as a definite whole, the aspect of one of those nebulous masses familiar to the astronomer, in which a clear and unmistakable nucleus shades off on all sides, through zones of decreasing brightness, to a dim marginal film that seems to end nowhere, but to lose itself imperceptibly in the surrounding darkness. In its constitution it may be compared to one of those natural groups of the zoologist or botanist, wherein typical species forming the characteristic nucleus of the order, are linked on every side to other species, in which the typical character is less and less distinctly apparent, till it fades away in an outer fringe of aberrant forms, which merge imperceptibly in various surrounding orders, and whose own position is ambiguous and uncertain. For the convenience of classification, the naturalist may draw the line, which bounds a class or order, outside or inside of a particular form; but Nature has drawn it nowhere. So the English Vocabulary contains a nucleus or central mass of many thousand words whose 'Anglicity' is unquestioned; some of them only literary, some of them only colloquial, the great majority at once literary and colloquial,—they are the *Common Words* of the language. But they are linked on every side with other words which are less and less entitled to this appellation, and which pertain ever more and more distinctly to the domain of local dialect, of the slang and cant of 'sets' and classes, of the peculiar technicalities of trades and processes, of the scientific terminology common to all civilized nations, of the actual languages of other lands and peoples. And there is absolutely no defining line in any direction: the circle of the English language has a well-defined centre but no discernible circumference*. Yet practical utility has some bounds, and a Dictionary has definite limits: The lexicographer must, like the naturalist, 'draw the li͡   ͡ewhere', in each diverging di͡ection. He͡

—Oxford English Dictionary *(Oxford University Press, publisher)*

The curious thing about this taboo is that all of us who read observe sentences every day beginning with *And* or *But.* But most readers probably never notice them. And that, incidentally, should be a powerful suggestion: If writers searching for style use these little tools of grammar intelligently, their readers will not notice.

If improving style by shortening sentences occasionally (see Chapter 2) seems uncomfortable to beginning writers, they will soon understand why connectives are so important a part of writing; these mighty little words serve as bridges between ideas, carrying the reader safely and logically from the end of one to the beginning of the next. True, they add nothing to the grammar. But they add important *flow.* There is a logical meaning imparted by *And: FLASH*—the next idea is related to and agrees with the last. Still a different logical meaning is imparted by *But: FLASH*—the next idea is related to but somehow conflicts with the last. Other connectives are equally important; look for opportunities to begin sentences with words such as *Therefore, Next, Still, Furthermore,* and many others.* Do not deprive yourself of these important bridges from thought to thought. In some cases they alone can make the difference between a shaky and a skilled writer.†

* These, however, are conjunctive adverbs; writers can do more things with them than with conjunctions.

† This example of linguistic purity (conjunctions) from The Holy Scriptures: The first two sentences of *Genesis.1* do not begin with "And;" the next 32 sentences do.

The first sentence beginning with *And* or *But* in this book is on page 14.

Taboo 2: We May Not End a Sentence with a Preposition.

Again, of course, we may; the alternative is often an awkward, unnatural sentence. Prepositions are weak words and, therefore, a sentence that ends with one tends to dribble to a close, like a bouncing ping-pong ball, rather than ending crisply. Still, that is sometimes a better choice than taking the long way around.

Probably the best known illustration of this point is a famous Winston Churchill story. Allegedly, while the great man was prime minister of England, a junior officer criticized him for ending a sentence with a preposition in one of his inspirational speeches during World War II, when the future of England seemed in doubt. The great man shot back with sarcastic wit:

> *"This is the type of arrant pedantry up with which I will not put."*

If this story is true, Churchill (hero of wartime England and author of the five-volume *A History of the English-Speaking Peoples*) would end this sentence with two prepositions.

The prejudice against ending sentences with prepositions seems to come, in some fuzzy way, from Latin (having to do with the word <u>pre</u>posi-tion"). Fuzzy because Latin has no such restriction. (In fact, one of the most widely written or spoken Latin phrases in the history of Western civilization is the liturgical *Dominus vobiscum.* That is *God be with you,* and notice where the *cum* [*with*] is positioned.)

Even if Latin had such a restriction, to proclaim that it must therefore apply to English would be a remarkable nonsequitur. Ours is not one of the Romance (Latin-based) languages, and Latin rules simply do not fit the Anglo-Saxon mold.

The first sentence ending with a preposition in this book ("*from*") appears on page 16.

Taboo 3: We May Not Repeat Words.

This taboo is probably the most restrictive of all. (We call this belief "The Elongated Yellow Fruit Syndrome," named for writers who can never bring themselves to use the word *banana* to refer to a banana the second time. A squirrel becomes a *bushy-tailed rodent;* snow becomes *that fleecy white stuff.*) You may have been advised, "Use a word once. If you need it again, or at least if you need it very soon, that's too bad; you've used it up. Use a synonym instead." This is truly damaging advice.

The issue here is *first-choice words*. When an intelligent adult selects a particular word—either intuitively or after careful thought to keep a sentence clear—that selection is probably a reasonable endorsement; this particular word, and no other, was the first-choice word for expressing that particular thought in that particular situation.

We are told to seek a different word for variety. But our objectives are *clarity and precision*—not variety. Consider the implication: If our first-choice word was the correct one, but now we must use something else to express that same thought, we go to a second-, third-, or fourth-choice word. Rather, reuse the first-choice one. Enlightened writers usually attain all the variety readers need through the changing flow of information in the subjects and the situations they write about.

Again our literary giant for the defense is Winston Churchill. In the early years of World War II, when English cities were flattened by aerial bombing and invasion by powerful German armies seemed only days away, he electrified the world, and lifted the spirits of the suffering British people and strengthened their resolve to fight, in a radio speech that can still be heard today. The words were:

> *"We shall not flag or fail. We shall go on to the end. We shall fight on the seas and oceans, we shall fight with growing confidence and growing strength in the air, we shall defend our island whatever the cost may be. We shall fight them on the beaches, we shall fight them on the landing grounds, we shall fight them in the fields and in the streets, we shall fight in the hills; we shall never surrender."*

Few exact synonyms are found in English; writers searching for them usually go from specific to abstract as they substitute, and the abstract word may offer a choice of several specific meanings. Therefore, the paragraphs and pages become less precise.

Another danger is that the writer may mislead the reader by switching words. That person at the receiving end, staring at the little lines and curlicues on the page, may not realize the person at the sending end intended the original and the synonym to mean the same thing. For example, suppose an engineer is discussing a car's timing belt. Ah, me. English gives no synonyms for either *timing* or *belt*. If that sender cannot use those words again, he or she might refer to the *component* the second time. That could mean almost any part of a car. The computer that controls the suspension system? The rearview mirror? And the third time the writer might refer to the timing belt as the *device*. Other parts of the car receive similar vocabulary treatment, and eventually, inevitably, the receiver comes to *the unit*. Which one? Now the writer has switched signals hopelessly without warning the reader. Or consider the word *microscope.* If it is called the *instrument* the second time, that could mean almost anything. A voltmeter? A violin? Little irregularities such as these can derail the flow of information as it travels from the writer's brain to the reader's.

Unit, incidentally, is surely one of the most awkwardly used words in the English language. Enlightened writers use it only when referring to units of measure, such as *unit price* or *unit package.* Used as a universal synonym for all nouns, a unit is an industrial "whatchamacallit."

Repeat first-choice words. Remember, the objectives when we are choosing words should be clarity and precision—not variety. *When writers use second-, third-, or fourth-choice words they are hurting their reader by blurring images.*

What about your thesaurus? It seems unlikely that Monsieur Roget wrote his magnificent work to help us weaken our statements. More likely he had in mind helping us find the first-choice word when the one we have is not quite right.

To avoid *too much* repetition, the language gives us pronouns. We may refer to the timing belt as *it,* or to two or more as *they.* (Every writer must take care, however, that the link between the pronoun and the word it stands for is obvious. Putting that grammatically, pronouns need antecedents, and the relationship between them must be obvious or the sentence can become an obstacle course.) Use pronouns as naturally in your paragraphs and pages as you would in conversation.

This important point about grammar is repeated, to prevent misunderstanding. Correct usage is essential—as important today as it has ever been. (Part 3 of this book is a grammar guide and reference manual.) But our language should not inhibit us, and above all its rules should not deprive us of valuable tools. Good writing is easy to read and sounds natural, and style should not call attention to itself; language does its job best by staying in the background, holding our ideas up for all to see. When any writer feels that beginning a sentence with a connective, or ending with a preposition, or repeating a good word seems natural or desirable, probably the most sensible thing is to go ahead and do so. In these cases the ideas will flow so smoothly that readers are unlikely to notice a few things some of them may have learned are wrong.

TWO OTHER THINGS WE SHOULD NOT HAVE BEEN TOLD

Mixing Verb Tenses

Consider yourself lucky if no one ever advised you that *you may not mix verb tenses.* Posh and piffle! (Perhaps *pshaw!*) How else could we say:

The Wandering *Only*

The attendant on an international flight announced, "During the flight you may only smoke while in your seat." Wow! The airline would (we hope) allow passengers to do many other things while in their seats. If nothing else, they ought to be permitted to breathe. For decades, language purists have complained that large numbers of writers put *only* in the wrong place when it is an adverb, as here. (It can also be an adjective: the *only* person.) They are right, but their argument is a bit weak because the error is unlikely to change the meaning or create awkwardness. If it did either, careful writers would probably notice and correct it.

Remind yourself that *only,* by definition, limits the word it modifies to *one* of something (*one-ly*). Be sure it is the right thing. "During the flight you may *only.* . . ." Stop there, and think. Because *may* is the beginning of some verb, what follows *only* is the rest of that verb, and that (*smoke*) is what is limited (*you may only smoke*). The trouble is, it shouldn't be; passengers may do several other things while in their seats. The intended statement, of course, was: "*During the flight you may smoke only while in your seat.*

Best advice: Place *only* as close as possible after the word or phrase it limits. You will do that anyhow, if you are skilled in the art of syntax (see page 202).

Jaroslav Casik <u>called</u> (past tense) from Metro Hospital this morning and <u>is wondering</u> (present) when the equipment they <u>ordered</u> (past) <u>will be delivered</u> (future).

A Cluster of One?

Nor should writers listen seriously when someone argues that *a paragraph must contain at least two sentences.* The rationale here is questionable and inflexible: that a paragraph is a cluster of related sentences and there cannot be a cluster of one. Writing usually does not thrive too well in an environment of that kind of inflexible thinking.

A single sentence, especially a very short one, can be a marvelously effective paragraph. *Pow!* It can attract attention; it draws the reader's eye because it stands out from the longer blocks of text that surround it.

True, a paragraph is generally a cluster of related sentences. But we must be able, occasionally anyhow, to accommodate a cluster of one.

Resist the temptation to use this rhetorical device often, however; if most paragraphs are very short the effect is lost. Smooth, logical flow of ideas will be broken as the pages of text take on the appearance of an outline, and the occasional long paragraphs will be the only ones that get attention.

HOW IMPORTANT IS BREVITY?

Almost all developing writers have heard, perhaps repeatedly, that good writing should be as brief as possible. This advice may be risky.

Abraham Lincoln once said (we are told) that a man's legs should be just long enough to reach the ground. Is "Grand Lincolnian logic" a reasonable guide to how long, or short, a written piece should be? Just long enough to say what needs to be said? There is more to it than that.

Although brevity is desirable—especially in expository writing—conveying the message and the mood accurately and clearly to readers is far more important. It is the reason we write. The enlightened writer understands that, although readers are not likely to be aware consciously, reading *comfort* is more important to them than the length of the piece, and good writing provides that comfort, and if readers do concern themselves with length they measure it in time, not number of pages. To the reader, then, brevity is more a function of clear expression and sensible organizing than of total length. (Part 2 of this book discusses organizing.)

Fortunately, in most cases the same characteristics that make writing clear also make it brief. The advice on brevity, then, is: *Seek clarity, and the brevity will come.* But if a writer seeks deliberately to be as brief as possible, two things may go wrong. First, he or she may leave out important information in that zeal. Second, the paragraphs and pages may end up sounding blunt because they are stripped of descriptive passages or of the courtesy words that create an image of a thoughtful and open-minded person. The writer becomes less *persuasive,* and the paragraphs and pages less *assuring,* as a result.

Still, there is the question . . .

Too Little or Too Much?   Repetition or review of important points can sometimes be useful. What if the writer is unsure whether certain information may or may not be important and is concerned the piece may be getting too long? Include that information? Omit it? When unsure, the wiser course seems to be to include it. If all the information is properly organized, readers can pick and choose intelligently, reading everything or just the parts they think are important to them; a little too much information will not hurt. A safe maxim: *Think about it. Then if in doubt, leave it in.* Better for readers to have it and not need it than to need it and not have it.

THE DEVIL'S ADVOCACY:

DEVIL'S ADVOCATE

Setting up conflicts with readers isn't my idea of what writers should want to do. Okay, let's say the enlightened reader knows that the three taboos are just misunderstandings, not rules. But other people might think—and you agreed there's this danger—that it's wrong to begin sentences with conjunctions, or end with prepositions. I'm going to look like a jerk in their eyes.

GURU

Do this to convince doubters and to make yourself feel good: Ask the doubter to open any book *by a professional writer,* to any page at random, then bet an ice cream cone you'll find at least one sentence beginning with *And* or *But* on that page. You'll almost always win. The point is, that person has been reading similar sentences every day of his or her life *but hasn't noticed them because they're so natural.* Why, then, are you worried people will notice yours? Bet someone an expensive dinner on any given day that you will find at least five sentences beginning with *And* or *But* on page 1 of that day's *Wall Street Journal.* You can have a free dinner with someone new every night.

DEVIL'S ADVOCATE

But I'm not going to . . .

GURU

Wait! Stop! See?* You just did it!

DEVIL'S ADVOCATE

(Sigh.) But I'm not going to be there to do that bet with my readers.

GURU

Well, test *The Wall Street Journal* and buy yourself that expensive dinner. You can't lose, and you'll learn a lot. The point is, if *you* haven't noticed these things as a reader, can't you relax and assume your readers don't notice them either? But you raise a thoughtful point: Don't go out of your way to exercise this new freedom with *but*. Use it too often and your reader certainly may notice and think less of you.

DEVIL'S ADVOCATE

Why not begin sentences with *Also* and *However* when connectives are needed, instead of *And* or *But?*

GURU

You can, and most of us do without worrying about it. These are actually conjunctive adverbs, not pure conjunctions. Because they're adverbs, they modify the verb, and so the writer gets the choice of placing them at the beginning of the sentence (*However, they soon realized this was unsafe . . .*), in the middle next to the verb (*They soon realized, however, this was unsafe . . .*), or at the end (*They soon realized this was unsafe, however . . .*). You can't do that with conjunctions; that's the big advantage of conjunctive adverbs. My favorite is *therefore*.

DEVIL'S ADVOCATE

Why?

Infamous Quotation 1

Immediately after his inauguration in 1977, President Jimmy Carter issued an executive order requiring all federal regulations in plain English. The implications were awesome, and there were strong reactions (mostly negative) throughout the government. A few months later at the Brookings Institution, a group of legal scholars, writing experts, and government executives met to discuss the implications of the President's order. At this meeting, a dean of the Columbia University School of Law said: *"I'm not sure I'm comfortable with the idea of legal writing in plain English. The whole thing seems sort of anti-intellectual to me."* A quarter of a century later, that attitude still prevails among legal scholars.

(Also see: "About Legal Writing," page 75. Also see: "Infamous Quotation 2," page 183.)

---

* See "The Interrobang" (page 122).

GURU

Because it announces *causal relationship* between the ideas it connects, and in my opinion that's the most useful concept for logical thought. Teach the children to understand the difference between cause and effect, and you've given them an invaluable foundation. I also like little connective phrases, such as *Even so . . .* and *In fact. . . .* There are many others that provide that *smooth flow* readers like so much and need so much.

DEVIL'S ADVOCATE

Please clarify about repeating first-choice words. If writers shouldn't use synonyms instead, what's the point of Roget's *Thesaurus?*

GURU

Poor Monsieur Roget. He must look down from the halls of that great SFFCW (Society of the Friends of First Choice Words) in the sky and wonder how it came about that so many people misunderstand his great work. Again: When you look for synonyms because you have already written the word you wanted and feel you must now use something else, you're moving from first choice words to second, third, and sometimes fourth choice. You're going backward, and why would you? The odd thing about this is that synonym hunters never hesitate to reuse little ordinary words such as *the, in,* or *for.* They deprive themselves only of key words. How strange. Use a thesaurus to find a first-choice word when you know the one you have isn't quite it.

CHAPTER 4   CLOSER LOOK: CONNECTIVES BUILD BRIDGES

This 131-word sentence, from a church newsletter, is complex and needs improvement. In addition to several major ideas presented one after another, at several points it contains a major idea *embedded* in another:

> Penny Goldman, the choir's soprano soloist, mentioned to me while we were chatting during the refreshment hospitality after the Requiem Concert last week that with the exception of one uncle who escaped to Israel, became a successful farmer, and now manages an Arab/Israeli agricultural research center there, all of her parents' relatives living in Hungary at the outbreak of World War II were taken to the German death camp at Treblinka and exterminated in the gas chambers a week before the war ended, and this survivor visits her family in Richmond every few years, and lo and behold, although

he is hearing impaired and could not distinguish the musical notes very well, here he was, very old, sitting in the audience with us to hear Penny sing Mozart that very night. An inspiring story.*

Not many writers can construct a 131-word sentence and keep the grammar flawless, but this one could and did. Perfect grammar, however, does not necessarily mean clear writing, and that terribly long sentence needs help. Thank goodness for the three-word sentence that ends the story; it provides exhausted, struggling readers some much-needed relief at the end. Further help is needed. The sentence needs to be unwoven, chopped, and reworded:

> Penny Goldman, the choir's soprano soloist, told me an inspiring story after the Requiem Concert last week, while we were chatting during the refreshment hospitality. All of her parents' relatives living in Hungary at the outbreak of World War II were taken to the German death camp at Treblinka, to be exterminated in the gas chambers there. This was just one week before Germany surrendered. Only one escaped, an uncle, who made his way to Israel and became a successful farmer. Now he manages an Arab/Israeli agricultural research center there, and he visits Penny's family in Richmond every few years. And lo and behold, here he was, very old, sitting in the audience with us to hear Penny sing Mozart that very night. But he is hearing impaired and could not distinguish the musical notes very well.

The same information, almost exactly the same length (138 words) becomes eminently readable. Those words are divided into six sentences, allowing the ideas to be separated skillfully; average sentence length is 19.7 words. Statistics such as these make an important difference to readers.

The one-sentence passage below badly needs breaks in the ideas; without them the writer lost control of grammar. It then needs connectives to provide readers both the clarity and impact of short sentences *and* the smooth logical flow of the connective:

> Formerly, the miniature dinosaur assemblies could be installed in their frames immediately if they matched current specifications, including the newest one for controlling humidity, until some eastern museums started developing different requirements, sometimes without notice, causing delays and complaints, and we still have not gotten over the funding cut and the changes it

---

* "An inspiring story" is not a sentence; it has no subject or verb. Such structures are called *sentence fragments,* and they are totally acceptable (sometimes even refreshing) in all but the most formal writing. Because they provide readers the same kind of break as sentences, they should be counted as sentences in the figuring of average sentence length.

requires, almost an everyday happening, as if that weren't enough, the new color coding, though it seemed like an excellent idea when we approved it, requiring retraining some employees.

Of course that sentence packs far too many ideas between a capital letter and a period. The writer struggled with 82 words, and those 82 words are trying hard to convey four major ideas and six slightly less important (subordinate) ones. Unfortunately, they do not get the job done. The writer lost control; grammar breaks down half way through, as it does so often in sentences that long. Readers deserve better treatment. Applying the "meat cleaver technique" (see page 23) to this passage is remarkably effective. The chopping points are not all obvious, but keeping the relationships correct is possible when we deal with the ideas in more manageable word groups.

However, would inexperienced writers allow one or more of the newly created sentences to begin with conjunctions? They should, because these small but mighty sentence openers serve a mighty purpose: providing smooth, logical flow from the end of one idea to the beginning of the next. They also add breathing places—resting places where readers can regroup their thoughts. If, however, hesitant writers cannot bring themselves to begin sentences with conjunctions, *conjunctive adverbs* can achieve similar results. Furthermore, because they are adverbs they can fit comfortably and perform their job nicely at more than one location in a sentence; they need not be the first word:

> Formerly, the miniature dinosaur assemblies could be installed in their frames immediately if they matched current specifications, including the newest one for controlling humidity. Now, *however,* several eastern museums are developing different requirements, sometimes without notice, causing delays and complaints. *Furthermore,* we still haven't gotten over the funding cut, and the changes it requires are almost an everyday happening. As if that weren't enough the new color coding, though it seemed like an excellent idea when we approved it, requires retraining some employees.

The statistics are now: 83 words, 4 sentences, 20.8 words per sentence.

Seeking Synonyms . . .

. . . rather than repeating first-choice words, may cause imprecision. English has few *exact* synonyms;* a second-choice word is usually more

---

* But more than most other major languages. This is because of England's early history; the British Isles were repeatedly conquered and occupied by foreign armies, and words remain from their many languages. (See Chapter 15.)

general. Even if an exact synonym is available, using two different words to describe the same thing may mislead readers; they may think the writer is referring to two different things. Read this carefully:

What really happened near the Roswell (New Mexico) Air Force Base that day? Air Force public information officers said it was nothing unusual and have stuck to their story all these years, but a lot of local residents, plus millions of people with strong opinions worldwide, still insist the government is covering up the most important happening in world history. Exactly 50 years later, June 24, 1997, the Air Force repeated its explanation and closed the book on Roswell UFOs. Just a routine weather balloon experiment, and the damn thing crashed. Those weren't bodies, just plastic dummies in the balloon's gondola. And the strange lights people saw? Reflected light from the ground, bouncing off the balloon's sides. Oh boy, did that stir up the legions, particularly a retired Air Force colonel who has sworn under oath he helped carry bodies away *and they were alien beings—all dead—and they were in an alien spacecraft.* Nope, the Air Force said, but an Air National Guard plane did crash on a training mission near there once with 13 officers and enlisted men listed as casualties (that means they were killed), and maybe the colonel got mixed up after all these years. But he said it *then,* not now.

All this time since that incident, the story about alien bodies in the desert won't go away, and the Roswell mystery has become a legend, notwithstanding the story of the plane crash. The Air Force report issued when this event happened tells nothing that could end the stories of the visitors from space who found tragedy waiting when they reached our simple little planet. The final Air Force ceremony did one thing, though: It reopened old questions. And in recent years a new question about the strange events in Roswell has surfaced, even in Washington: Might the Air Force have shot down the doomed craft accidentally during target practice?

Can readers tell in paragraph 2: Does the synonym *that incident* refer to the alien bodies, or to the plane crash, or to the Air Force ceremony? Does the synonym *this event* refer to the alleged alien spacecraft incident, or to the Air National Guard plane crash? Does the synonym *the doomed craft* refer to a flying saucer, a weather balloon, or the Air National Guard plane?

Measuring the Ease of Reading

*Everything should be made as simple as possible,
but no simpler.*

—Albert Einstein

We come away feeling rewarded and refreshed after reading a good book or magazine article and absorbing something thought provoking or entertaining. Conversely, frustration gives way to surrender when we try to read—want to understand—but somehow "just can't get into it." The difference is often in the writing style. To an important degree, the writer determines how well readers will read. He or she controls the characteristics of writing that, in turn, influence the extent to which every reader will be able to receive and understand.

Readers tend to associate easy-to-understand paragraphs and pages with simple or familiar subjects, and as the subject becomes more difficult, so, they assume, must the reading. We have seen it that way most of our lives. What may be new to many is: Even extremely difficult information can be written in clear, relaxed English. (But doing so requires that the writer's *thinking* process is thorough.) In fact, the extra-hard subjects are the ones that most need easy language style if readers are to understand. Is there a contradiction here?

If we examine the reader's needs we arrive at this important guideline, a change of attitude for many writers:

The more difficult the ideas, the easier the words and sentences should be, in order for their precious cargo of information to be received (understood) fully and accurately.

We see proof of this writing → reading relationship every time we read something we already know. In these cases, even if the writing *style* is unclear we have no trouble reading with ease and comprehension, because we need to spend little of our reader energy trying to understand the *content;* unless the writing style is outrageously complex, we can figure out the message.

Another way of saying this is: The more challenging the *content* may be, the more the writer (who already knows and understands the content) should try to help the reader (who does not know it and is relying on the words and sentences to learn it).

THE READING PROCESS

Reading, like writing, consumes human energy and can become a tiring process.

The reading process takes place in fundamentally the opposite order of the writing process. (Writers encode; readers decode.) *First, the reader-brain receives black marks on a page—images of words and sentences—and converts these into meaningful concepts in the form of neural-electrical energy. Second, the readerbrain intelligently examines, sorts, combines, and stores those concepts.* Again that vital separation—the total separation of *what* is written and *how* it is written, or the *ideas* the reader receives and the *words and sentences* that deliver them from the senderbrain.

At any given moment, a reader brings to this task a given amount of energy, and it must be divided those two ways. First, words and sentences; converting them to neural impulses will consume whatever amount of the reader's energy they demand. Whatever amount is left is available for examining the ideas—for *comprehension* (understanding) to take place.

What does this mean to us as writers? Consider the reader's position. Imagine that someone writes a very simple message—"*That lasagna was terrible.*"—but in words so difficult and sentence structure so hard to follow that the decoding process demands, say, 95 percent of your available reading energy at that moment. If this *idea* is so simple and uncluttered that it needs only 5 percent (or less) for comprehension, you can consume that 95 percent on words and sentences without risk. Comprehension *will* take place; communication will succeed. But trouble is ahead if the message is more complex—if the writer transmits his or her information in words and sentences demanding 95 percent of the reader's energy (for decoding), *and the information demands as much as 6 percent.* Now communication cannot fully succeed unless the reader works extraordinarily hard. Even if he or she tries, however, the readerbrain may lack energy to do the whole job, and part of the message will not be received or will be misunderstood.

This reader energy shortage becomes especially critical if the writer hopes to convey extremely difficult information—for example, explaining the importance of the quantum mechanics theory of Max Planck and Werner Karl Heisenberg or the reason your health care plan is being changed. Now if the transfer of knowledge is to succeed, the writer *must* keep the language workload as low as possible, because now the reader will need most of that energy reserve for the *meaning.*

The more energy the reader must devote to words and sentences, the less is available for comprehension of the ideas. But the reading brain cannot decide how that energy will be divided; the writer decides this for the reader, because the writer chooses those words and builds them into grammatical structures called *sentences.*

Thoughtful writers should be aware of this writerbrain/readerbrain relationship. Thoughtful writers should care whether their work will succeed in its goal, transferring knowledge. Thoughtful writers, therefore, should ask about their writing habits: "How can I tell? How can I measure whether my language usage will help or hinder readers?" It is for this aspect of writing that linguists and reading experts have given us ways, based on respected research, to measure readability.

How easy is this passage to read?

The brain is highly demanding in another fashion. It uses up a great deal of oxygen in the course of its labors. In fact, in the resting body, $\frac{1}{4}$ of the oxygen being consumed by the tissues is used up in the brain, although that organ makes up only $\frac{1}{50}$ of the mass of the body. The consumption of oxygen involves the oxidation of the simple sugar (glucose) brought to the brain by the bloodstream. The brain is sensitive to any shortage of either oxygen or glucose and will be damaged by that shortage sooner than any other tissue. (It is the brain that fails first in death by asphyxiation. And it is the brain that fails in the baby if its first breath is unduly delayed.) The flow of blood through the brain is therefore carefully controlled by the body and is less subject to fluctuation than is the blood flow through any other organ. What is more, although it is easy to cause the blood vessels in the brain to dilate by use of drugs, it is impossible to make them constrict and thus cut down the blood supply.

Are Double Negatives Positive?

Careful writers would not say, *"We don't have no record of your order."* Purists contend that two negatives cancel each other, and that the statement therefore means: *"We do have a record of your order."* But that is not likely the intended meaning.

Poor grammar is not the only reason double negatives are controversial, however. A White House aide writes, in perfect grammar, *"It's not unlikely that the President will veto the Bill if Congress passes it."* Well, if it's not unlikely, is it likely? In language, two negatives do not necessarily cancel each other, exactly. Did the writer intend something closer to likely, or unlikely? Only he or she knows.

But wait: *"Not infrequently, Bruce has been unwilling to take regulations seriously."* Not infrequently unwilling? Careful, now. Do the first two of a triple negative cancel each other, leaving an untouched single negative (*frequently Bruce has been unwilling*)? The question is rhetorical, however, because few readers take the trouble to search for the intended meaning of such mind benders.

Then, occasionally, there are mind paralyzers: *"It has not been unusual for Ms. Kenyon to show signs that charges she is unsympathetic to labor's views are not without foundation."* Let's see, now, five. . . .

The existence of a tumor can destroy the blood-brain barrier in the region of the tumor. This has its fortunate aspect. A drug labeled with a radioactive iodine atom and injected into the bloodstream will pass into the brain only at the site of the tumor and collect there.

—Isaac Asimov, *The Human Brain: Its Capacities and Functions*, Houghton Mifflin Company, publisher.

How hard is this one?

From the purely methodological standpoint, it is doubtful whether any antithesis is falser than that which has sometimes been set up as between an emphasis on the importance of a study of social institutions and their functioning, on the one hand, and an emphasis, on the other hand, upon that type of calculation by "socializing" individuals, which represents the subject matter of the core of "traditional" sociological analysis. For no sociologist, at least since the day of Li Peng Chow, ought to be prepared to deny that the whole of our analysis is concerned with a world characterized by a very special set of social "institutions," which condition at every point the sociological calculations of the individuals who live under those institutions. On the other hand, sufficient defense of the use of that part of "traditional" social analysis which is here in question is provided as soon as one contemplates the void left in our apparatus for explaining the events of the real world by those who would press their insistence upon the importance of "institutions" to such a point as to deny that "rational" social calculation does occur, or that the particular type of "rational" calculation described in traditional sociological theory does have a counterpart in reality.

—Unidentified.

HOW THE EXPERTS MEASURE

Linguists in the past half century, and researchers in the teaching of reading, have given us ways to measure the readability of a piece of writing—how easy or difficult it is to read. That is, the *language workload* it imposes on readers. Words and sentences too simple or too difficult might create barriers—resistance to understanding. Educators often use this kind of information in choosing books for students in different school grade levels. (And for that reason, publishers also care about readability levels.)

Caring writers, too, should want this valuable information about their relationship with readers.

Most systems for measuring readability concentrate on two measurable characteristics: How familiar are the words, and how helpful are the grammatical structures (sentences). These systems, called *readability formulas,* differ in the way they measure those characteristics.

Word processing computer programs usually contain a subprogram, based on the linguists' work, that measures those same characteristics, and any one of these can tell writers important things about their writing *while they are writing into the computer.* The measures are generally reliable, and the variances between them are small. But they are little understood. (See Chapter 8.)

The methods of analyzing are based on two reasonably safe generalizations: that small words create less resistance to understanding than large ones, and that sentences of moderate length help the flow of ideas more than extremely short or extremely long ones do. As *generalizations,* these are easily shown to be statistically valid.

Word difficulty.   Linguists call large words *polysyllables,* and most readability researchers define a polysyllable as any word having three syllables or more. <u>For statistical measurement only</u>, one- or two-syllable words are counted easy; words of three syllables or more are counted hard. (*Note* that dramatic exceptions to this rule are found throughout any dictionary. *Id,* for example, is an exceptionally short word yet exceptionally difficult; *transportation* is the opposite. In English [but not all languages], if the line separating easy and difficult is drawn after the second syllable, exceptions on either side of that line occur in about equal frequency. They can be ignored, therefore, because the exceptions cancel each other mathematically.)

Analysis of the writing of 16,000 adults* reveals that normal (nonspecialized) writing or speech *on general (nonspecialized) subjects* usually contains about 10 percent polysyllables. Specialized fields (engineering, medicine, law, and so on) occasionally require some terms common only to that profession and therefore may need as high as 15 percent polysyllables (but rarely higher).

Sentence difficulty.   A writing style in which sentences average between 15 and 20 words in length seems helpful to most readers. Occasional sen-

---

* In classroom measurements of students' own writing.

tences may be as short as 2 or 3 words, or as long as 30 or 35, and a *variety* of lengths keeps readers alert. (See Chapter 3.) These limits provide a vast amount of literary freedom—enough to satisfy the artistic needs of any writer. More important, the limits satisfy the needs of that person at the receiving end: the one we write for.

CUSTOMIZED GUIDANCE FOR THE WRITER

How to Measure

Those two characteristics, then, word difficulty and sentence difficulty, together form the *language workload* readers must deal with during the reading process. Some writers seem able to sense the level of that workload intuitively while they write; others look for simple, reliable ways—at least occasionally—to confirm this part of their skills.

Even without a computer, anyone can use a readability formula to measure the readability of any writing. The following formula, based on the work of Robert Gunning,* is easy and reliable, and it requires only three simple steps:

- In a sample passage (at least 100 words) of any writing, figure the *average* number of words per sentence. The sample must begin and end with a full sentence. Ignore section headings or short parenthetical phrases.
- In that same sample passage, figure the *percentage* of polysyllables. Count any word of three or more syllables as a polysyllable, with these exceptions: [1] proper nouns—the capitalized names of people, places, and companies; [2] combination words—large words made up of whole smaller words (*bookkeeper, another, nevertheless*); [3] two-syllable verbs that became three syllables by the addition of *-ed, -es,* or *-ing* (*constructed, replaces, receiving*).
- Add those numbers, and multiply their total by 0.4. The resulting number is the readability index of that passage, a measure of the language workload of the words and sentences (as opposed to *subject* workload).

* Mr. Gunning was editorial advisor to *The Wall Street Journal* in the 1950s and 1960s and a pioneer in the readability movement and is author of *The Technique of Clear Writing* (*McGraw-Hill*).

Example:

Step 1: If a passage has 148 words divided into 8 sentences, the average sentence length is 18.5 words (148 ÷ 8). Note that without further figuring the procedure reveals that in this sample the author divided his or her ideas into sentences of reasonable length.

Step 2: If 17 of those 148 words are polysyllables, that is 11.5 percent [17 ÷ 148 (divide the large number into the small one)].

Step 3. 18.5 + 11.5 = 30. Multiply by 0.4 = R.I. 12.*

What Should the Readability Index Be?

For adult readers, strive for a readability index between 10 and 12. Anything between 8 and 14 is probably acceptable, but the 10 to 12 range is likely to present the information in its most readable form. Under 8, a childish tone may distract readers, and choppy sentences may interfere with the flow of logic. At 14 the reading is becoming difficult for long periods. Over 17, the style is almost certainly unreadable for sustained reading.

The passage below is from Herman Melville's great novel, *Moby Dick*. It contains 363 words divided into 8 sentences, averaging 20 words per sentence. Of those 363 words, 27, or 7 percent, are polysyllables. The readability index of the passage, then, is a very unchallenging 10.8:

In the tumultuous business of cutting-in and attending to a whale, there is much running backwards and forwards among the crew. Now hands are wanted here, and then again hands are wanted there. There is no staying in any one place; for at one and the same time everything has to be done everywhere. It is much the same with him who endeavors the description of the scene. We must now retrace our way a little. It was mentioned that upon first breaking ground in the whale's back, the blubber-hook was inserted into the original hole there cut by the spades of the mates. But how did so clumsy and weighty a mass as that same

---

* Most readability formulas are based on the assumption that short words and sentences are easy to understand and long ones are not. That is a generalization, of course, and exceptions are commonplace, but statistical analysis is complicated; research by linguists, statisticians, and educators confirms the method provides reliable comparisons; variations are slight, and the results are useful.

hook get fixed in that hole? It was inserted there by my particular friend Queequeg, whose duty it was, as harpooneer, to descend upon the monster's back for the special purpose referred to. But in very many cases, circumstances require that the harpooneer shall remain on the whale till the whole flensing or stripping operation is concluded. The whole, be it observed, lies almost entirely submerged, excepting the immediate parts operated upon. So down there, some ten feet below the level of the deck, the poor harpooneer flounders about, half on the whale and half in the water, as the vast mass revolves like a treadmill beneath him. On the occasion in question, Queequeg figured in the Highland costume—a shirt and socks—in which to my eyes, at least, he appeared to uncommon advantage; and no one had a better chance to observe him, as will presently be seen.

Being the savage's bowman, that is, the person who pulled the bow-oar in his boat (the second one from forward), it was my cheerful duty to attend upon him while taking that hard-scrabble scramble upon the dead whale's back. You have seen Italian organ-boys holding a dancing-ape by a long cord. Just so, from the ship's steep side, did I hold Queequeg down there in the sea, by what is technically called in the fishery a monkey-rope, attached to a strong strip of canvas belted around his waist.

It was a humorously perilous business for both of us.

Herman Melville, *Moby Dick*, E. P. Dutton.

Not all of Melville's work is that readable. The vocabulary workload throughout *Moby Dick* is unchallenging, but occasional passages contain sentences so long that readers must strain to follow an idea from capital letter to period. Some of his other works were described by his publisher as ". . . all but unreadable."

Analyzing Strengths and Weaknesses

A readability index can be a useful tool; writers should want to know how clearly they have expressed their ideas. But the numbers learned through this formula can also be used to analyze *while* we are writing, to learn some valuable things about our writing habits. Those numbers tell us: What are the readability strengths and weaknesses of our writing? If there are weaknesses, what must be changed to get rid of them?

Remember, any combination of steps 1 and 2 totaling between 25 (R.I. 10) and 30 (R.I. 12) is at a proper workload level for adult readers.

Suppose, for example, a passage contains 15 words per sentence and 15 percent polysyllables. Or 22 words per sentence and 8 percent polysyllables. Both combinations total 30, or R.I. 12.

A person with average reading skill can deal with most combinations totaling 30—even 25 words per sentence and 5 percent polysyllables, or 5 words per sentence and 25 percent polysyllables—if they are not special jargon terms. (At 25 words per sentence and 5 percent polysyllables, in effect readers are receiving very easy information in large doses; at 5 words per sentence and 25 percent polysyllables, the vocabulary burden is dangerously heavy but can be dealt with in mercifully small doses.)

In some cases writers may not be able to control the vocabulary workload. We can always, however, control sentence length. If a particular subject requires a large number of difficult words, compensate by shortening sentences. Balancing the factors of the reader's workload this way will make a great difference in whether he or she understands the ideas.

But Caution: All Readability Formulas Have One Limitation.

Regardless of what method is used, there is much about writing that cannot be measured in numbers. The readability formula given here provides a statistically reliable measure of how difficult the sentences are, but it does not measure whether their grammar is correct or whether the ideas progress logically from sentence to sentence. It does measure, quite reliably, how difficult the words are, but no formula can measure if they were the right words in the first place.

Compare a readability formula to a fever thermometer—an important diagnostic tool in medical centers everywhere. The thermometer measures only *one* health sign, not all. Still, no doctor would begin a medical examination without knowing our temperature. Too high or too low a body temperature tells us something is wrong, *but a temperature of 98.6 degrees certainly does not declare the patient is healthy.* Likewise, too high or too low a readability index tells us something is wrong, but an index of 30, normally ideal, does not ensure good writing. No originator of a readability formula ever claimed otherwise. (This paragraph has a readability index of 12.)

If we accept that limitation, a readability formula can be useful in revealing some important things about any writing.

Remember, these formulas measure *how* the writer conveys thoughts through words and sentences, not *how valuable* the thoughts are.

The following research report, from the National Aeronautics and Space Administration, illustrates that total separation. It has a readability index of 24.4—totally unreadable. After it, a simpler version presents the exact same technical information with a very moderate index of 11.6.

Readers needn't understand the technical subjects to sense the vast difference in writing styles. Here is the difficult (original) version:

> An experimental performance evaluation of a 6.02-inch tip diameter radial-inflow turbine utilizing argon as the working fluid was made over a range of inlet total pressure from 1.2 to 9.4 pounds per square inch absolute with corresponding Reynolds number from 20,000 to 225,000. (Reynolds number, as applied herein, is definable as the ratio of the weight flow to the product of viscosity and rotor tips radius, where the viscosity is determined at the turbine entrance conditions.) Efficiency and equivalent weight flow increased with increasing inlet pressure and Reynolds number. At design equivalent speed and pressure ratio, total efficiency increased from 0.85 to 0.90 and static efficiency from 0.80 to 0.84 with increasing Reynolds number, while the corresponding increase in equivalent weight flow was approximately 2 percent. The relationship established between experimentally determined efficiency and corresponding Reynolds number indicated that approximately 70 percent of turbine losses are associated with wall and blade boundary layers.
>
> An investigation was made at design Reynolds number for determining the probable error of a single observation for measured variables and calculated quantities, with results from a 16 data point set indicating that the probable errors in total and static efficiencies were ±0.009 and ±0.008, respectively and that probable error is inversely proportional to Reynolds number.

The version with readability index 11.6 (below) is thoroughly understandable, dignified, courteous, and short. It says exactly the same thing as the one above; there has not been even the slightest sacrifice of content:

> A radial-flow turbine with a 6.02-inch tip diameter was tested at inlet total pressures from 1.2 to 9.4 pounds per square inch absolute. Corresponding Reynolds numbers ranged from 20,000 to 225,000. The working fluid was argon. (Reynolds number = weight flow $\div$ product of viscosity and rotor tip radius, with viscosity measured at turbine entrance conditions.)
>
> Efficiency and equivalent weight flow increased as inlet-pressure and Reynolds number increased. At design equivalent speed and pressure ratio, total efficiency increased from 0.85 to 0.90 with increasing Reynolds number. Static efficiency increased from 0.80 to 0.84. Equivalent weight flow increased about 2 percent. There was some relationship between efficiency and Reynolds number; it showed that about 70 percent of turbine losses are wall and blade boundary layer losses.
>
> Probable error in total efficiency, at design Reynolds number, was calculated to be ±0.009, using a 16 data point set. In static efficiency this was

±0.008. Probable error increased proportionately as Reynolds number decreased.

Writing in the hard-to-understand style of the first version (previous page) is impossible to justify when the author can make the information as easy to read as the rewritten passage—and with so little effort! How many textbooks have we all read (or tried to read) that were written in a style similar to the first version of that report? Were the *ideas* the barrier, or was the writing style?

Always Keep in Mind: The more difficult the subject, the more our readers need to use their available energy on the *ideas,* not on the words and sentences.

ABOUT LEGAL WRITING

Misguided writers often try to impress readers, to make their writing sound more important than it really is, by trying to imitate legal style. (Robert Gunning, author of the readability formula in this chapter, brought smiles to legions of people who write, with his suggestion: "Write to *express,* not to *impress.*")

Stereotype legal vocabulary is easy to imitate, with words or phrases such as *herein, pursuant to,* or *accordingly* sprinkled among the sentences. The law does have some hard-to-understand but necessary terms of its own, just as medical or scientific writing do. These terms are like a foreign language to others, but they are the working vocabulary of the men and women who use them every day. The terms are the shorthand of the profession; they are not intended for ordinary readers. Lawyers call them *terms of art.*

The trouble is, some legal terms can be dangerously deceptive to non-lawyer readers because they may mean something quite different from what we think they should mean. *Quiet enjoyment,* for example, has nothing to do with either quiet or enjoyment. It is a term of property law, going back to Anglo-Saxon law in the fifteenth and sixteenth centuries; the phrase means "uninterrupted occupancy," whether that occupancy is quiet and whether it is enjoyable. Too bad for the tenant who signed a lease and then learned a high school marching band rehearses evenings on the floor above. And when a trial or hearing is *continued* to a future date, it is actually *discontinued* until that date.

Vocabulary, however, is not the major problem with most legal writing. By far the greater trouble is sentence length and structure. A popular belief throughout the legal profession holds that periods create loopholes—and that a qualifying statement must be in the same sentence as the one it qualifies. Therefore, to avoid loopholes lawyers are usually trained to avoid periods. This advice is questionable, and it may be dangerous. It can cause unbelievably long sentences—often a whole paragraph in length. They may be legally and grammatically correct, but they are sometimes impossible to understand and often cause court battles to determine the real meaning of a document containing them. They fail to communicate. In fact, they hinder communication, as in this example:

> Pursuant to the provisions of the Act, the employer is duly responsible for notification of subsequent revision in the location of said employer's place of business, subject to termination of exemption in the event of failure to provide such notification.

This means:

> The law requires that your company notify us if it changes its address. If it doesn't notify us, the company may lose its exemption.

Even lawyers can write clearly, and should. Judges (their readers) beg them to do so. More important, people who are not lawyers cannot in any way justify imitating legal style—unless they are trying deliberately to intimidate.

    The writer who tries this legal style usually finds it is easy to achieve, on almost any subject. But it will not impress. It will succeed only in making the paragraphs and pages more difficult than necessary to read and understand.

ABOUT SCIENTIFIC WRITING

The problems legal writing can create are brought about also in writing on scientific subjects, in this case by unnecessary use of scientific tone. Some writers try to endow their ideas with more respectability than they deserve by expressing them in complex scientific language—even when none is necessary. People in the human sciences—educators, psychologists, and sociologists and social workers seem notorious for this, but they are by no means the only ones. This example is from a doctoral dissertation, published in a professional journal:

> Integration of aural and visual stimulae produces a more intensified effect in the brain than those resulting from either modality's acting as a single class or type of stimulus.

Here is what that really means:

> People learn better by hearing and seeing the ideas than by either one alone.

But wait. Is that information not rather commonplace? Is it worth presenting to a readership of professional men and women? Would it have been published if the author had presented it in plain English?

Notice, incidentally, that in the original passage the writer tried to use words more difficult than necessary and lost control: *stimulae* should be *stimuli*. (There is an ironic lesson here: When writers try to impress by straining beyond the limit of their skills, they risk embarrassing themselves instead.)

All of which prompts us to conclude: *Scientific vocabulary is a poor substitute for useful information, or for scientific objectivity.* Which in turn takes us back to our opening premise: The necessary ingredients of good writing are *valuable information* and *clear expression,* and neither is very useful without the other.

ABOUT ACADEMIC WRITING

At one of our great midwestern universities, the faculty of the Graduate College of Business Administration voted strongly against teaching the writing course used for management education throughout General Motors Corporation. Their reason: "*It is not the job of the College to teach writing as it is done in the world of work. It is our job to teach writing as it is done at a university.*"

Question 1: What is the difference? Question 2: Why is there this difference? Question 3: If there is a difference, why did the educators vote *against* preparing students for the environment they are being educated to work in for the rest of their lives?

What is "academic writing"? In the truest sense the term means *continuous study and discourse (usually written), by succeeding scholars, on a given topic*—an invaluable contribution. Those university professors were obviously talking about style. But what specifically does the term *academic writing style* mean? Is there really such a thing? We all know the style this term describes, but can it be defined? More important, is there any reason it is needed? These passages illustrate:

In academic style:

In response to the conflict over whether the relationship of the four elements of communication—audience, writer, subject, and message—as Kramer

The Penguin Joke

This truck delivering a load of penguins breaks down on the way to the zoo. The day is hot, and the driver is aware his precious cargo can't last long without air conditioning. So he runs to the street, flags down the first empty truck that passes, explains the emergency to the other driver, and quickly they transfer the little darlings to the good truck. Then he hands the other driver $50 and instructs: "Take these penguins to the zoo."

That afternoon, his truck fixed, the first driver heads back to the garage, and as he passes an amusement park he sees penguins everywhere. Penguins on the carousel, penguins on the roller coaster, penguins standing in line for popcorn. He slams on the brakes, runs into the park and finds the other driver and shakes him by the lapels, and he yells: "I told you to take them to the zoo! I gave you $50 and said, 'Take these penguins to the zoo!'" And the other guy says: "I did. And we had money left over, so I brought 'em here."

Moral: No matter how clear you try to be, someone will find a way to misunderstand. And if you don't try, everyone will. (Also see: "The Hippopotamus Joke," page 144.)

and Reingold hypothesize, or the purpose, as Bronsky theorizes, determines the form of discourse, WGU/PCC contends that the question is analogous to the chicken and the egg and holds that both positions are of equal value. (59 words, 59 words per sentence, 15 percent polysyllables, readability index 29.6.)

In plain English:

Researchers disagree whether language or purpose determines form in writing. Kramer and Reingold believe language usage depends on the four elements of communication: audience, writer, subject, and message. Bronsky teaches that purpose is the main influence. WGU/PCC thinks both are of equal value and that trying to decide which is more important is like asking which came first, the chicken or the egg. (63 words, 15.8 words per sentence, 12.7 percent polysyllables, readability index 11.4.)

Is a separate style called "academic writing," then, really necessary? The message of the sample passage above (both versions) says, somewhat indirectly, it is not. If that message is *substance and style are equally important,* and if the statement is true, it confirms they are separate considerations. Then, if the *substance* (content) is academic, the *style* can be whatever the author chooses; neither one affects the other. There is no reason that academic discourse cannot be in plain English; many great scientific writers have demonstrated this through the centuries.

Consider the implications. If a difficult subject can be made easy to understand, why would anyone argue against doing so? Consider students required to read a textbook written in the style of the first sample passage above, studying diligently but unable to understand. Consider the role of the educator. Is it to say, "Here it is if you're good enough"? Might a more dedicated attitude not be, "I will do everything I can to help you learn, short of sacrificing the integrity of the subject"?

The following words are from recent articles in publications of the National Council of Teachers of English: *Acculturation, generalizability, hegemony, historicality, mantra, putative,* and *compositionist* (writer?). Most writers could live several lifetimes without needing any of those.

THE DEVIL'S ADVOCACY

DEVIL'S ADVOCATE

How well can any formula analyze the overall quality of a piece of writing? Let's be reasonable; there are so many things that are unmeasurable.

GURU

Of course there are, and no linguist ever claimed total accuracy. Let's say this about the formula in this chapter. (It would probably be true of any readability formula. There are many of them, and most are more complicated.) A favorable index is no assurance of readable paragraphs and pages. But an unfavorable one is a strong signal that something is seriously wrong with the writer's word skill or sentence skill. And that "something" will have a direct bearing on the writer's success as a communicator. Shouldn't writers—especially those who are just developing style—want to know that?

Even with its limitations, the fever thermometer is still the medical profession's first diagnostic tool.

DEVIL'S ADVOCATE

What's the purpose of multiplying by 0.4? Why not just add the average number of words per sentence plus the percentage of polysyllables, and stop? Obviously the 0.4 is some kind of conversion factor.

GURU

Yes, it is. One of the main uses of readability formulas is to measure reading difficulty of textbooks, and for that reason many of the linguists who design these formulas measure everything in *years of education*. This is useful for textbook publishers. This formula then, gives a reasonable indication of the number of years of education a reader of average intelligence would need to read and understand the content (presuming this reader has the necessary background knowledge).

DEVIL'S ADVOCATE

What? Are you saying, then, that I—that intelligent adults—should write for tenth- to twelfth-grade readers?

GURU

No, no. *No.* We're saying that skillful writers, by controlling two basic factors of language usage, can express *anything* in language an average reader can understand *if that reader has the necessary background knowledge.* Write complex information in plain English. Why is this hard to understand? Again, that total separation between *what* is written and *how* it is written. And we're saying the more difficult the information, the harder the writer should work to help readers assimilate it. We're also saying communication has not taken place until the message has been broadcast *and received accurately,* and it is the sender's obligation to *be* received accurately. To a considerable extent the writer controls how well the reader will read.

DEVIL'S ADVOCATE

In a letter or report, numbers are sometimes an important part of the content. In measuring readability, should they be counted as easy words or as polysyllables?

GURU

Good question, but now you're trying to be more precise than we can be with these measuring instruments. A comparison might be that a readability formula is more like a yardstick than a micrometer. Yardsticks cannot measure in thousandths of an inch, but sometimes—maybe even most times—we don't need that kind of precision. If you want to be that analytical, however, here's a sensible way of deciding whether a number is easy or hard to read: Count round numbers (any digit followed only by zeros) as easy; also count any number of four digits or less as easy. The last easy number, then, is 9999; the first polysyllable number is 10,001 (because 10,000 is a round number).

DEVIL'S ADVOCATE

What's the readability index of: "Slow but fast telephone poles as to opposed soluble children imitating. Therefore neither hundreds of them and kissing my sister while he flies melting New York, and tomorrow square baseballs minus plus five electric Elvis's Presley monopolies. Even green slow even green melting, but hiring which toothbrushes last year will do it again"?

GURU

Oh, come on, now. Are you going to say its readability index is 11.6, and, therefore, readability formulas prove nothing? In fact, some scholarly opponents of readability formulas do argue that point, that way. But in the world I live in, people don't write nonsense. At least, not deliberately. Real people write real things, and they welcome reliable, easy ways of knowing how well they do, even if the answers are only approximate. In the world I live in people would get fired the first day they write stuff like "Elvis Presley melting New York."

Should Participles Dangle?

When a word or phrase does not properly modify the part of the sentence that the writer intended it should, it is said to "dangle."

Dangling participle: After eating dinner, the plane took off for Pittsburgh. [Strange plane!] *Orphaned at the age of six,* the Committee recognized that the child had outstanding skills in spite of these emotional problems. [A whole committee of orphans?]

Dangling pronoun is probably the next most common. This occurs when the antecedent, the noun the pronoun stands for, is not clear: *You hold the hammer while I hold the nail, and when I nod my head you hit it.* Writers should take great care to avoid such headaches.

Danglers are hard to avoid because the writer knows what the relationship should be; therefore he or she may not notice if the words do not build precisely that relationship. The dangling pronoun is one of the hardest errors to avoid—even for skilled professional writers. (See page 225.)

CHAPTER 5   CLOSER LOOK: WHAT MAKES SOMETHING READABLE?

How well a person reads at any given time depends not only on his or her own skill but on the writer's as well, because all of us can deal far better with thoughtfully chosen words and skillfully crafted sentences than with the work of the artless. Inexperienced writers who are not quite sure of their skills, then, should welcome ways of answering the inner question, "How am I doing?" Word processing computer programs can measure and tell us that, in a general way. We can also find out without computers, using readability formulas. They are easy to use and fairly reliable.

The passages below were tested for readability using the formula described in this chapter:

> However,[1] it is now our <u>considered</u> <u>opinion</u> that in the light of <u>recurring</u>[2] labor problems in the Brooklyn <u>area</u>,[3] in contrast with a very <u>satisfactory</u> posture of labor in the Staten Island section of the port, and with the presence of the Verrazano Narrows Bridge—which has largely <u>eliminated</u> the time <u>element</u> which heretofore[1] was enjoyed by piers in the Brooklyn <u>area</u>[3]—we should make a <u>decision</u> to henceforth discharge all inward cargoes at Piers 19 and 20, Staten Island, until such time as it is <u>demonstrated</u> that the service in Staten Island to shippers is not at least the <u>equivalent</u> of that which has been provided[4] the Brooklyn <u>area</u>.[3]

> *111 words, 1 sentence, = 111 words per sentence. 12 polysyllables, = 11 percent. 111 + 11 = 122, × 0.4 = Readability Index: 49.*

What a difference between that and:

> The golden spiders will shock you the first time you see them, which is easy to do if you are on the Hawaiian island of Maui in December or January and are willing to hunt a little. My first sighting was outside the village of Hana, a 5-hour white-knuckle drive north from Ka-a-naapali's small airport. All the rain forests and <u>spectacular</u> waterfalls[5] do not make up for the bumpy, <u>terrible</u> roads and hairpin turns you <u>negotiate</u> on cliffs a mile above the ocean.

---

[1] *however* and *heretofore* are combination words and therefore not polysyllables.

[2] *recurring* ends with *ing* but is an adjective in this sentence, not an exempt verb, and therefore it *is* a polysyllable.

[3] *area* (3 times) has only 4 letters, but 3 of them form syllables; this small word *is* a polysyllable (all three times).

[4] The third syllable of *provided* is *ed, and therefore the verb is not a polysyllable.*

[5] *waterfalls* is a combination word and therefore not a polysyllable.

[Since then I have learned you can also find GSs at Ka-a-naapali's Io (pronounced *eye-oh*) Needle State Park, a <u>mystical</u> setting and an easy 30-minute drive.]

We met in Hana by <u>accident,</u> my first golden spider and I. A State Botanical Garden is nearby, and there sat the object of my search hanging out (<u>literally</u>) in a web strung between the leaves of a small <u>bromeliad,</u> a member of the pineapple[6] <u>family.</u> <u>Practically</u> every <u>bromeliad</u> had one. The resting <u>position</u> of these little beasts in shining armor is <u>unnatural.</u> Well, it is <u>probably</u> not <u>unnatural</u> if you're a GS, but it <u>certainly</u> seemed so to me. The web is constructed[7] <u>vertically,</u> near the ground, and the <u>occupant</u> just sits there, always head down, facing the ground, and I never saw one move, except when I lightly touched its web.

GSs are about the size of a silver dollar, maybe a half-dollar. I call them *golden spiders,* but that is not their real name. I don't know much about insects and spiders, but I do know that spiders are not insects;[8] both are in the broader <u>category</u> called bugs. I call them GS because they must be the only spiders, or for that matter creatures of any kind, that are bright <u>metallic</u> gold in color. They really are something to see. The legs are black with white bands, but the body looks as though it were wearing a tiny coat of gold armor.

<u>Photographing</u> a GS close up is an <u>adventure</u> in <u>gymnastics.</u> Like people, bugs look most <u>interesting</u> when you take their portrait looking straight at their faces, almost always from slightly above and slightly to one side. How do you do that, however,[9] when your subject is hanging face down, about a foot from the ground?

(383 words, 20 sentences, = 19.2 words per sentence. 23 polysyllables, = 6 percent. 19 + 6 = 25, × 0.4 = Readability Index: 10.)

---

[6] *pineapple* is a combination word and therefore not a polysyllable.
[7] The third syllable of *constructed* is *ed*, and therefore the verb is not a polysyllable.
[8] When figuring number of words per sentence, count semicolons as periods.
[9] *however* is a combination word and therefore not a polysyllable.

Guidelines for Nonsexist Writing

*Thanks to words, we have been able
to rise above the brutes. . . .*

—Aldous Huxley

In our lifetimes, the English language has undergone one of those major, sudden changes that happen only rarely. New words and phrases have emerged to help remove sexual bias in writing and speech. The United States, and more specifically, the U.S. business community, has led the way in this change. In the midtwentieth century, American Telephone & Telegraph Company was the world's largest employer of women. It undertook a major program in the 1970s to rewrite corporate documents—personnel forms, instruction manuals, computerized form letters, and the host of other written pieces that are part of the daily routine of a large and complex organization—to remove all traces of statements that would (and often did) give men career advantages over women. Other companies also led the way, as did most government agencies. The issue drew a great deal of attention, but today we wonder what the all fuss was about.

Avoiding sexist language is not only morally correct, doing so is easy. In some writing, it is also the law.

English is notoriously sexist—more so than any other major language, according to language scholars. Still, it is possible to write *anything* without sexist references of any kind. Furthermore, doing so need not create the least bit of awkward wording. Nonsexist language can, and should, sound so natural that no one is likely to notice the writer said anything differently.

THE INFAMOUS GENERIC *HE*

This is, of course, the most common abuse. For years people (men *and* women) have written statements such as: "The customer may not be aware he has this choice." (Oddly, that was the preferred style even if the customer was almost certain to be a woman.) Unthinkable today. So we experimented with such ways as: "The customer may not be aware he/she has this choice." At least, it would avoid complaints. But this phrasing is awkward; it is the phrasing of a klutz. The mind's ear cannot hear a slash; the style calls attention to itself, especially if we do it often. *He or she* is slightly better.

One simple change will get rid of a large percentage of the most common sexist references—graciously. *He* and *she* are *third-person* pronouns. English simply does not have gender-free personal pronouns for third person—in the singular. Switch, then, to *plural:* "Customers may not be aware they have this choice." Or, switch to second person: "You may not be aware. . . ." (Thoughtful writers try to give instructions in second person form anyhow, where it fits; then the writing addresses the reader directly. The tone becomes warmer and more direct, both desirable traits.)

Switching to the plural will usually work, but not always. For example, a company memo to all supervisors might state: "The supervisor must inform an employee, as soon as he or she is suspected of drug abuse, that he or she may face disciplinary action." A bit like lumpy mashed potatoes; too many *he and she*s. Good writing should not call attention to itself. Second person ("inform <u>you</u> . . . that <u>you</u> may face") will not work here because the writing is addressed to someone else (a third person). Plural ("inform employees . . . that <u>they</u> may face") will not work when the writer wants to refer specifically to one individual. So the only available choice is *he or she*—even if the sentence requires it twice, as here. This wording becomes annoying only if it is used repeatedly.

OTHER "MAN" WORDS

With equal ease any writer can get rid of all other "man" words. They are never, never necessary. "Man is a social animal . . ." would be better as:

Jargon: Good or Bad?

Jargon is the specialized language of a particular profession. It is a kind of shorthand, sometimes expressing complex ideas in a few words. In that sense it may sometimes be useful. But any specialized language has a major disadvantage: Only a limited audience can understand it.

Further trouble comes from the fact that jargon often becomes a status symbol; writers who wish to impress with their vocabulary often seek opportunities to use jargon—in fact may invent specialized terms when none are necessary. Thus *habits* become *behavioral patterns*. Note, however, that *behavioral patterns* is not shorthand but triple longhand; the writing suffers the disadvantage of jargon without gaining the advantage.

A good rule: If an idea can be expressed in ordinary English using the same or almost the same number of words, you cannot justify using specialized language. Remember, too: Even when jargon is legitimate shop talk (shorthand), it should be used only in the shop. If we care to communicate, it makes little sense to broadcast on a wavelength the person at the other end cannot receive.

"People are social animals." Anthropologically, both statements say exactly the same thing. "Since the beginning of mankind . . ." would be better as: "Since earliest human history. . . ." In both cases the nonsexist version is clear, gracious, and just as accurate.

JOB DESCRIPTIONS

Job descriptions are a curse to anyone who has ever tried to write them, and they are a bit more difficult to keep nonsexist than ordinary text, but still not very difficult. Here, more than in most other kinds of writing, old-fashioned (sexist) language habits are an invitation to legal difficulties. Federal courts have ruled that policy statements which refer only to males, even though unintentional, are discriminatory, and some employers have been hurt by resulting lawsuits.

The problem unique to job descriptions is that often the writer is listing a series of required skills or duties (or both) for *any* employee (male or female) who holds or will hold that job, and each sentence tends to have a pronoun (traditionally *he* in the past) as its subject:

The (job title) must be capable of reading and understanding blueprints according to NA level 6 specifications. *He* must be capable of making bookkeeping entries and preparing financial statements following NCPA format. *He* is expected to. . . . *He* must. . . .

Unacceptable. A statement of that kind would invite Equal Employment Opportunity grievances. *You* or *they* will not work here. Using *he or she* each time would quickly become distracting, and the style awkward. A slightly better way: Combine several statements into fewer longer sentences; this would mean fewer subjects, therefore fewer sexist/nonsexist word choices. But such sentences quickly become too long and complex to follow, especially for an inexperienced employee (the probable reader).

Solution: Write each section of a job description as a series of phrases, without subjects. This can be done in correct grammar and in smooth, gracious style.

For each section, an introductory phrase contains the subject and main verb; this is followed by a series of sentence fragments, each without a subject, each telling one of the requirements:

The (job title) must be capable of:
• Appraising the value of the seller's home according to state, county, and lending institution requirements,

- Making bookkeeping entries and preparing purchase agreements following AHRRA format. . . .

The job requirements should be indented and listed vertically, as here. This way they can be read separately rather than as one unbearably long sentence, even though grammatically they are still one sentence. Changes of this kind are easy and will avoid Equal Employment Opportunity grievances. *Caution:* This format can tend to sound choppy and fragmented; thoughtful writers should take extra care to be smooth. *Further caution:* This structure also requires enlightened writers to be sensitive to the rule, *use parallel structures for parallel ideas.* If consecutive ideas follow the same pattern, as in a list (whether bullets are used or not), they should follow the same sentence structure or structures that match each other. Avoid scattershot structures.*

MALE BOSSES AND FEMALE SUBORDINATES?

That may indeed be the situation in some offices, but we must not portray it that way in our paragraphs and pages. Writers lose no effectiveness whatever by writing, "Every case officer must be aware of his or her responsibilities. . . ." Or, of course: "Every secretary must be aware of his or her. . . ." Note that the National Council for Teachers of English (NCTE) recommends "must be aware of *their*. . . ." That is incorrect grammar, however (singular noun, plural pronoun), and unnecessary. Once poor grammar is endorsed for special situations, where does it stop? Who decides if a situation is special enough? Such permissiveness is an invitation to the "anything goes" attitude in language usage.

Avoid job titles that identify gender. Mailmen have become mail *carriers. Salesmen* are *sales representatives.* Airplanes no longer have *stewardesses* but *flight attendants.* Likewise, any writer seriously interested in finding nonsexist descriptions surely can, without much effort.

What about *chairman?* No mystery. The *chairman of the board* is now often a *chief executive officer.* If that is not the case, use *chairman* for males, *chairwoman* for females. If it is a theoretical one, use *presiding officer,* or *committee head,* or even *person in charge.* Please do *not* use the grossly distasteful *chair.*

Another nonsexist change: Never refer to a grown woman as a *girl.* "The girl who took the order . . ." will earn its author icy stares, and should.

---

* For more on parallel structure see Chapter 20, *"False series,"* page 230.

"The woman who took the order . . ." is just as easy and far more enlightened. Use *girl* only if she is under 16 years of age.

Enlightened writers should also be aware that many women dislike being called *ladies*. Men often use *lady* as an intended compliment, but women who are uncomfortable with this point out that the usage is judgmental, that a man does not have the right to declare whether a woman meets his standards of approval, and if men will just call women *women*, everyone will be satisfied.

ABOUT *MS.*

Yes, we now use it in addressing all women—single or married. (We do not have different forms of *Mr.* for single and married men.) According to surveys, the word *Ms.* (pronounced "Mizz") has slowly but consistently gained in popularity. By the late 1970s, most professional women favored it, and most publishers' style manuals endorsed it. (*The United States Government Printing Office Style Manual,* however, has stayed mum on this subject. *The Chicago Manual of Style* acknowledges the use of *Ms.* but does not encourage or discourage its use.)

Taking the idea of a standard salutation still further, some language watchers have encouraged the use of just one salutation for everyone, male or female, married or single. The English-speaking world has not responded very enthusiastically to this.

THE DEVIL'S ADVOCACY

DEVIL'S ADVOCATE

Clarify, please, about English not having neutral third-person pronouns.

GURU

In grammar, *I* is *first person* (so are *me* and *my*); *you* is *second person. He* and *she* (and *him* and *her*) are *third person,* and now we're in a bit of trouble; we don't have gender-free versions in the singular. (Actually, English does give us a neutral third-person singular pronoun; it is *one.* ["The customer may not be aware one has this choice."] Although this form is commonly used in many languages, it is rarely used in English and, therefore, not acceptable.) English also allows us the third-person singular *it,* but that cannot be used for people. *They* works nicely for people and things; this is why fellows in good standing of the National Association of Gurus (NAG) recommend people switch to the plural to avoid many problems of sexist language.

That versus *Which?*

The answer is easy. Use *that* when the clause it introduces is restrictive; use *which* when it is nonrestrictive. (See pages 22 and 193.) Thus: The car *that* had snow tires was the only one to get up the hill. *But:* The blue car, *which* had snow tires, was the only one to get. . . .

And what in grammar is a "which hunt?" It is an attempt, usually by a careful editor, to change *which* to *that* when careless writers do not know the difference.

Careful writers know something else interesting about *that:* Even when used the correct grammatical way, it is often wasted. You can often drop it and not miss it: I think *that* the third step is unnecessary. Now try: I think the third step. . . . The meaning is identical. *But note:* I believe *that* Melissa should help on this project. Without *that,* readers might turn the wrong direction: I believe Melissa . . . (having to do with her credibility). A useful habit: Every time you write *that,* try reading the sentence without it; you may decide it can be dropped about half the time.

A Georgetown University linguist once proposed *ne* as a compromise to replace both *he* and *she* (because *N* is positioned in the alphabet half way between *H* and *S*). The world wasn't ready for that, however.

DEVIL'S ADVOCATE

But these new phrases sound klutzy.

GURU

They may at first, to some people. But overwhelmingly the public has accepted them with little or no controversy. The public, then, apparently feels that *flight attendant* and *supervisor* are perfectly fine substitutes for *stewardess* and *foreman;* most readers don't even notice such changes. But *ne* didn't make it—and won't.

DEVIL'S ADVOCATE

What about a disclaimer at the beginning of a piece of writing, some sort of formal declaration that all male references apply equally to men and women?

GURU

Nope. That won't do. It may have been acceptable when Dr. Benjamin Spock was writing books about raising babies, but not today.

CHAPTER 6   CLOSER LOOK: NONSEXISM IS EASY . . .

. . . and need not (in fact should not) call attention to itself.

Usually writers can avoid sexist references by switching to the plural, changing *he* to *they, him* to *them,* or *his* to *their.* But that does not always work. Sometimes we can avoid needing any pronoun at all, by slight rewording of the phrase containing it. Other times, *he or she* is just right.

The passage below is thoughtful and courteous—to men:

> Invite the new employee to contribute his talent to the department's daily operations. Encourage him to come to you if he has any questions. Every new employee should be made to feel that his contribution is important to the company.

A few word changes in each sentence will make the whole passage non-sexist:

Invite new *employees* to contribute *their talents* to the department's daily operation. Encourage *them* to come to you if they have any questions. Every new employee should be made to feel that *his* or *her* contribution is important to the company. (Or [last sentence]: *All* new employees . . . that *their contributions are.* . . . The singular version delivers more emphasis, however.)

Nonsexist language may require a new way of choosing words—especially if you are male. But it is always possible, and the change does not require any extra work. A few slight changes to the following male-oriented (but otherwise charming) social commentary will make it acceptable to everyone:

As he progressed from caveman to nuclear warrior, man's needs became more complex. Animal skins were once adequate body covering; now he needs business suits, jeans, and tuxedos. Campfire rituals were once adequate recreation; now he invents football. Once, a father needed to provide only food and protection. Occasionally, contemplating those earlier times, the chairman of the board can be forgiven for pausing to wonder: Am I any happier than that caveman?

With only slightly more thought:

As we progressed from cave dwellers to citizens of the nuclear age, people's needs became more complex. Animal skins were once adequate body covering; now we need business suits and dresses, jeans, and formal wear. Campfire rituals were once adequate recreation; now we invent computer games. Once, a parent needed only to provide food and protection. Occasionally, the chief executive officer can be forgiven for pausing to wonder: Am I any happier than that cave dweller?

More Examples

Each of the following sentences is rewritten to eliminate sexist references, yet keeping the style as gracious as possible:

Unacceptable: When you enter the lobby, tell the girl at the security desk you're there to pick up Professor Miller's report.

Today we say: . . . the *guard* at the security desk . . .

Unacceptable: A policeman who gives you a ticket is not required to tell you his name.

Today we say: Police *officers* who *give* . . . *are* not required to tell you *their names.*

Not bad, but a bit awkward: Beth, a cocktail waitress, believes that a waiter or waitress should not have to pay income tax on his or her tips.

Today we say: . . . *on tips.* [Or . . . *waiters* or *waitresses* . . . on *their* tips.]

Thoughtless: My good friend Sandra Gianjobbe will be chairman next year.

Today we say: . . . will be *chairwoman* next year.

Poor grammar: We teach each child over three years old to put away their toys before going home.

Say instead: . . . to put away *his or her* [Or: . . . *her or his* . . .] toys. . . .

Unacceptable: A nurse must constantly take training programs to keep her knowledge of her profession up to date.

Today we say: *Nurses* must constantly take . . . to keep *their* knowledge of *their* profession up to date.

Oh no! In recognition of the airline's 50th Anniversary, stewardesses will wear gold-trimmed blouses and skirts the week of January 20.

Today we say: . . . *flight attendants* will wear gold-trimmed *uniforms.* . . .

Unacceptable: Holly Church, the mayor's wife and a professor of cultural anthropology, will speak at the multinational committee session.

Say instead: Holly Church, a professor of cultural anthropology, will. . . .

Unacceptable: Special programs for the wives of attending doctors have been scheduled for Tuesday and Thursday afternoons.

Today we say: Special programs for the *spouses* of attending. . . .

Commonly Misused Words

The difference between the almost-right word and the right word is really a large matter—it's the difference between the lightning bug and the lightning.

—Mark Twain

Sometimes we are unsure when we use a word, and look up its meaning. A danger to writers, however, is that people usually do not know *what* they do not know. If they did, writers would never misuse a word. Envied is the person who has total word control and knows how to use that gift. For the rest of us, an occasional reminder is useful.

Affect/Effect.   Remember them this way: Anything that *affects* (verb) something has an *effect* (noun) on it. Think of *affect* as a verb meaning: to cause change. In its most common usage, *effect* is a noun describing that change. *But:* Less common, *effect* can also be a verb meaning: to bring about, to accomplish.

Allude/Refer.   A bit tricky. *Refer* means: make direct reference. *Allude* means: make indirect reference, or hint.

Among/Between.   Use *between* for two people (or things) and *among* for three or more.

Anxious/Eager.   *Anxious* means: nervous (feeling anxiety), and *eager* means: looking forward to.

As/Like/Such as. " . . . *and it must follow, as the night the day, thou canst not then be false to any man.*"* Here is why: *Like* is correct when what follows is a word or phrase; famous boxing champion Mohammed Ali's famous slogan "float like a butterfly, sting like a bee" was, therefore, perfectly correct usage. When the passage that follows is a clause (having subject and verb), *as* should be used: " . . . as the night (subject; *follows* is its implied verb) the day." Use *such as* to introduce an example (or examples): "Respected professional organizations such as the National Council of Teachers of English. . . ."

Assume/Presume. The difference is slight. To *assume* something is to suppose something is true without having a reason; to *presume* something is to suppose it is true for a specific reason. A presumption, therefore, is usually stronger and likely be more reliable than an assumption.

Assure/Ensure/Insure. These are quite different, and their correct usage should be easy. *Assure* means: make confident. I *assure* you. . . . *Ensure* means: make certain something will happen. Winning this game will *ensure* we make the playoffs. *Insure* means: to buy insurance.

Because/Since. Use *because* to denote the reason for something. "We can't finish because the computer is down." Use *since* only for relations in time. "It has been down since early this morning."

Can/May. Use *can* to express ability. "We can be there in an hour." Use *may* to express permission. "You may keep that."

Compliment/Flatter. The difference is important; they are not at all interchangeable. To *compliment* is to praise. To *flatter* is to praise insincerely and, therefore (indirectly), to insult.

Comprise/Consist of. Almost everyone misuses these. The whole *comprises* the parts, not the other way around. Therefore: "The United States comprises 50 states." It is not comprised of 50 states (the phrase *comprised of* cannot in any circumstances be correct).

Continual/Continuous. *Continual* means: frequently repeated. (There could be interruptions.) *Continuous* means: uninterrupted.

Convince/Persuade. You *convince* when you cause someone to believe something beyond any doubt. You *persuade* when you cause him or her to do something.

Data are/Data is. Either form is correct. If English followed Latin rules, we would need *datum is / data are.* But English is not a Romance

---

* William Shakespeare, *Hamlet,* Act I, Scene III.

language and does not follow Latin rules—even with borrowed words. If *data is* sounds better to you, use it.

Delusion/Illusion. A *delusion* is a mistaken idea, a false belief. An *illusion* is an unreal image, such as a mirage. When a magician seems to saw an assistant in half, that is an illusion; if you believe it really happened, that is a delusion. Also see: *allusion* (*allude*).

Disinterested/Uninterested. *Disinterested* means: impartial. *Uninterested* means: not interested. You can be disinterested yet very interested.

e.g./i.e. *e.g.* stands for *exempli gratia* (Latin); it means: for example; *i.e.* stands for *id est;* it means: that is, or that is to say.

Emigrate/Immigrate. They are opposites. You *emigrate* from a country; you *immigrate* to a country.

Eminent/Imminent. They are unrelated; they only sound alike. *Eminent* means: distinguished or outstanding. *Imminent* means: about to happen.

Eternity/Infinity. *Eternity* means: unending time, forever. *Infinity* means: unending distance or quantity (but not time).

Evoke/Invoke. *Evoke* means: bring out. "The statement evoked anger from the audience." *Invoke* means: call upon, usually referring to religious authority (as, "invoking God's mercy"); or, legal authority (as "invoking the Fifth Amendment").

Farther/Further. Use *farther* for physical distance and *further* for everything else. Cleveland is farther from New York than from Washington, D.C. Any further discussion of this is pointless.

Fewer/Less. Use *fewer* for quantities you can count. (Fewer chairs, fewer people.) Use *less* for quantities that must be measured rather than counted. (Pour less vermouth to make martinis dry.)

Figuratively/Literally. *Literally* means: following the exact meanings of the words. *Figuratively* means: not following their exact meaning (hence, a figure of speech). A statement such as, "The boss will literally hit the ceiling," then, probably does not say what its author intended—unless the author envisions someone climbing a ladder.

Flaunt/Flout. *Flaunt* means: display boastfully, show off. *Flout* means: ignore, or show disrespect for. You *flaunt* your jewelry; you *flout* the law.

Fortunately/Fortuitously. They are not interchangeable. *Fortunately* means: luckily. *Fortuitously* means: by chance; it may be fortunate or unfortunate.

Fulsome/Full and wholesome. Careful! Well-intentioned people often use these interchangeably, and doing so can cause you trouble. *Fulsome* sounds like a combination of *full* and *wholesome,* but it is not. In fact, it means quite the opposite: offensive, especially through exaggeration or insincerity. Be aware, then, that fulsome praise is hardly a compliment.

Hanged/Hung.   *Hung* is the past tense and past participle of hang: We hung the parts on the rack. Use *hanged* only for criminal executions.

Healthful/Healthy.   *Healthy* describes your physical condition. *Healthful* refers to the foods, climate, or activities that contribute to it. Florida, therefore, has a healthful (not a healthy) climate; it makes you healthy.

Imply/Infer.   These are widely misused. When a speaker implies something, the listener infers it. It is the difference between sending and receiving the idea. *Imply* means: hint or suggest. *Infer* means: to believe something as a result of that hint or suggestion.

Incredible/Incredulous.   The difference is easy. *Incredible* means: unbelievable. *Incredulous* means: not believing. If a statement is incredible, people who doubt it are incredulous.

Instinct/Intuition.   Your instincts do *not* tell you when to buy and sell stocks; your intuition does. *Instincts* are tendencies or aptitudes born in an individual—programmed into that individual's genes, the result of the evolution of that individual's species and his or her genetic makeup. Instinct makes birds fly south in winter, causes newborn spiders to spin webs, and gives people basic traits. *Intuition,* though also subconscious, comes from knowledge learned through personal experience. When you somehow know something is right but cannot tell why, you are probably guided by wisdom gained through experience. That is intuition, not instinct.

Irregardless/Regardless.   This is easy. There is no such word as *irregardless,* and to use it is to appear a klutz. The correct word is *regardless.*

Its/It's/Its'.   *Its* is the possessive of the pronoun *it:* "The kitten likes to roll on its back and play with its tail." (You add *'s* to nouns to form the possessive [the kitten's tail], but never to pronouns.) *It's* is the contraction of *it is:* "It's time to go home." There is no such word as *its'.* Banish *its'* from your vocabulary.

Last/Latter.   Use *latter* for two *things* (or people) and last for three or more.

Lay/Lie.   Remember them this way. *Lay* means: to *place* something (or someone) in a horizontal position. *Lie* means: to *be* in a horizontal position. "Lay your head on my shoulder. Let it lie there." Putting it grammatically, *lay* is a transitive verb and requires a direct object (head, bricks, eggs, etc.). *Lie* is intransitive (complete) and never takes an object. The past tense of *lay* is *laid*. "I laid the report on your desk yesterday." The past tense of *lie* is *lay*. "It lay there all day."

Lend/Loan.   These are not interchangeable, and correct usage should be easy. *Lend* is a verb. "Please lend me fifty dollars." *Loan* is a noun. "This fifty dollars is a gift, not a loan." Confusion arises, however, because the past tense of the verb *lend* can be either *lent* or *loaned*.

Libel/Slander.   *Libel* is a damaging public statement made in print. *Slander* is a damaging statement made orally.

Majority/Plurality.   *Majority* means: more than 50 percent. *Plurality* means: the largest group, regardless of percentage (it can be less than 50 percent). Majority *is* or majority *are?* If you use the word majority alone, it is singular. ("The majority *is* in favor.") If you refer to the majority of something, it is plural. ("The majority of the members *are* in favor.")

Marketing/Merchandising.   In the business world these are related but different. *Marketing* means: all aspects of selling including hiring and managing sales personnel, planning sales campaigns, setting up stores or independent distribution outlets, advertising, and other related functions. *Merchandising* refers to sales promotion and advertising. Merchandising, then, is one of the functions of marketing.

Memento/Momento.   A *memento* is a special remembrance, a souvenir.* A *momento* is an Italian moment; there is no such word in English.

Militate/Mitigate.   These only sound alike; they are totally different—in fact, almost opposites. *Militate* (from military) means: fight, or argue. *Mitigate* means: soften, moderate. "The lawyers asked the judge to mitigate the sentence because the defendant was an orphan; the brutality of the crime, however, militated against this."

Nauseated/Nauseous.   They are not interchangeable. *Nauseous* means: nauseating; when you are nauseous, others become *nauseated*. (The difference is much like the difference between *poisoned* and *poisonous*.) Generally, then, people who say they feel nauseous mean nauseated.

Notable/Notorious.   Both describe people of note, but *notable* is a compliment and *notorious* is a slur. A notable scholar, (but) a notorious liar.

Oral/Verbal.   There is much confusion here. *Oral* means: spoken (as opposed to written). *Verbal* means: having to do with words, whether spoken or written. (*Aural*, by the way, means: having to do with hearing.)

About Abbreviations

Generally, thoughtful writers try to avoid using them. This may surprise many, but consider that in ordinary writing abbreviations serve only one purpose: to save space. Usually, however, in ordinary writing the abbreviated form of a word does not save enough space to justify the slight awkwardness it creates.

Do use such traditional abbreviations as Mr., Ms. (pronounced "Mizz"), and Mrs.

Abbreviate names of states on envelopes (but not in letters or reports). Abbreviate a person's title when it precedes his or her full name, but not when it is used with just the last name: Gen. Douglas MacArthur, but General MacArthur; Dr. Alison Shumate, but Doctor Shumate.

When are abbreviations desirable? When space is very limited. Usually, therefore, they are widely used in tables, charts, and other graphic presentations, but not in ordinary writing.

(But: See "Acronyms," page 193.)

---

* In the Roman Catholic Church a *memento* is one of the parts of the Mass for the living and the dead.

Hopefully, Let's End This Controversy

The newscaster says, "Hopefully, the fire will burn itself out soon." Language purists argue that fires cannot hope anything and that people who write such structures should be declared literary outcasts.

Hopefully means: full of hope. The example above, then, illustrates the conflict. Can fires hope anything? The grammatical point is this: When an adverb modifies a verb, it should fit sensibly with that verb's subject. At least, the two should not make a foolish statement.

But some excellent writers argue that the meanings of the above example and others like it cannot be misunderstood, and therefore they do not sound foolish. Furthermore, they point out, there is precedent for this usage throughout English (*fortunately, undoubtedly, sadly*, etc.). These, however, may be similarly misused: *Undoubtedly Congress will refuse to approve the loan until some confusing points are settled.*

A more practical question than who is right: Why invite controversy when it can be avoided so easily? When tempted to write *hopefully*, ask: Who hopes? Then begin, *The President hopes*, or *The guerrillas hope*, or *I hope*. Or, if the writer chooses not to tell, the passive: *It is hoped*. (See page 36).

Parameters/Perimeters.   Almost no one uses *parameters* correctly. Parameters are mathematical variables that stay constant in a particular situation. Even scientists and engineers have trouble with this word, and anyone else trying to use it is probably misusing it. Most common misuse: as a synonym for *limits*. "The solution to the food crisis lies somewhere between the parameters of moral responsibility and political need." Why is this misuse so common? The euphemistic switch from *limits* to *boundaries* to *perimeters* to *parameters* is an easy (but incorrect) one.

Persecute/Prosecute.   *Persecute* means: harass, or treat unfairly. *Prosecute* means: take legal action through a court.

Perspective/Prospective.   *Perspective* means: point of view. *Prospective* means: probable, or expected (from *prospect*). "The prospective Cy Young Award winner struck out nine. . . ."

Precede/Proceed/Procede.   *Precede* means: go before. "Six aides preceded the candidate, checking that everything was in order." *Proceed* means: advance to. "When you have finished, proceed to the next step. *Procede* is not a word (but *procedure* is).

Principal/Principle.   *Principal* means: main ("Overeating is the principal cause of obesity), or main person (as the *principal* of the school). *Principle* means: fundamental idea (*Put It in Writing* presents principles of clarity).

Proved/Proven.   These are interchangeable (as participles), but *proven* is considered old fashioned and therefore less desirable. "Numerous tests have proved this treatment is reliable." As an adjective, *proven* is preferred. "It has *proven* benefits."

Raise/Rise.   A bit tricky. *Raise* is a transitive verb; you must raise something (its direct object). *Raise your right hand. Rise* is an intransitive (complete) verb and does not take an object; things (or people) rise by themselves. "As the slurry settles, the ore sinks to the bottom and the impurities rise to the top."

Sensual/Sensuous.   *Sensuous* means: pertaining to the senses, usually related to the appreciation of beauty. *Sensual* means: pertaining to physical appetites, usually related to gender.

Stationary/Stationery.   *Stationary* means: not moving. *Stationery* means: writing paper.

Their/There/They're.   *Their* is the possessive of the pronoun *they*. *There* is an adverb referring to place: "*We went there*," or expletive: "*There is no time.*" *They're* is the contraction of *they are*.

Unique/Unusual. These should be easy. Something is *unique* only when it is the single one of its kind. It is, or it is not. Nothing can be *somewhat unique,* and *totally unique* is redundant.

Whether/Whether or not. This is not a serious problem, but generally the *or not* is wasted. The sentence, *We haven't decided whether to go. . . .* states its idea fully. If you feel, however, that *or not* adds emphasis in a particular situation, by all means use it. Some structures require it: *We have decided to go whether it rains or not.*

CHAPTER 8

New Writing in the Computer Age

What Computers Can (and Cannot) Do for Writers

If a nation expects to be ignorant and free in a state of civilization, it expects what never was and never will be.

—Thomas Jefferson

They are surely the most significant technological development of our time, and they perform near-miracles for writers, but can computers write for us? No, they cannot. Will they in the future? Not likely. No computer manufacturers or software program publishers claim that they can.

A book about writing cannot possibly present advice on how best to use computers and software programs; those change too rapidly for any discussion to stay current very long. Rather, advice is presented in this section for those who may not be aware of all the important ways word processing programs can help, or who may expect too much.

YOU STILL DO THE HARD PART

Word processing and related programs can do many things that are a joy to writers. They allow us to improve anything we write by making changes, small or large, with remarkable ease. They can help us with spelling and grammar, but this help is only partial. They can measure how readable our paragraphs and pages are and, if we learn a few easy steps, provide word and sentence statistics that help us improve readability. (See Chapter 5.) They can help us avoid much confusion by performing routine details automatically in large, complex reports. They allow us to do useful and beautiful things with typefaces (fonts), such as adding emphasis with italics and boldface type, and changing type sizes. (See Chapter 11.) Some provide a thesaurus to help us find words and insert them with a keystroke. And we can assemble letters—even large reports—from parts (standard paragraphs held in storage; the writer just fills in the variable information). But someone still has to write those standard paragraphs.

Probably the most important advantage computers offer writers is *the ease of making revisions.* We can rewrite to our heart's content, almost effortlessly. The writer just changes a word or rewrites a passage, and the printer creates a new copy. If the revision causes page numbers to change, the electronic brain changes them automatically as needed. Retyping a whole letter or report is a thing of the past, and so is proofreading it again (except for the changes). As a result, writers can pamper themselves by making changes they might not have made in the past—second draft, third, tenth draft if they feel it is necessary—improvements they would not have made before because retyping (and proofreading again) would have been too much work.

These changes do not necessarily make us better writers, but our writing becomes better. In most cases, noticeably better.

SPELLING, PROOFREADING, GRAMMAR, AND READABILITY

What about Spelling?

True or false: Most word processing programs can warn the writer of a misspelled word, suggest the correct word, and offer to make the change with a single keystroke. *Partly true.* True or false: Writers can relax, then, confident they will never, ever again send out a letter or report with a typing error. *Most assuredly false.* Even in spelling, artificial intelligence has severe—in fact dangerous—limitations.

The computer sends a warning only if a misspelling or other typing error creates a *nonword.* If, for example, the writer types *noj* instead of *now,* the display will stop at that point during the spelling check and send a warning signal, because *noj* is not in the program's very thorough dictionary. But if the word *not* is typed instead of *now,* the computer will

---

Banish *Very?*

Some writers argue it is a sluggish word, that rather than strengthening a statement it weakens it, and that, therefore, it should be used sparingly. True, we can usually find a more interesting way of heightening emphasis than by adding *very.* Although there is surely a difference between, let us say, a pretty baby and a very pretty one, the language gives us far more vivid adjectives: *beautiful, darling,* and many others—or, better than adjectives, descriptive phrases: *a baby everyone wants to hug.*

Somehow, a statement such as, "We are *very* concerned that you may not receive all the benefits you should receive from our program" seems more satisfying with the word than without it. But substitutes such as *extremely* or *deeply* might be better.

A wise attitude: The word *very* sounds dull in most cases, and its use probably suggests the writer might have tried harder to be imaginative. Still, we should not strike it from our working vocabulary.

never blink an eye, because *not* is an approved word. That may reverse the meaning ("Our company can <u>not</u> . . ." instead of "Our company can <u>now</u> . . ."), but the poor writer will get no help from the electrons.

An End to Proofreading?

Certainly not. When the spelling software reaches the end of the document and has helped the writer correct spelling errors, this is no time to feel safe. Computers help us find the obvious mistakes—the kind most writers find easily by proofreading (such as *noj*). But most of us are notoriously inept at finding the less obvious errors *in our own writing*; we imagine seeing the words we expect to see and, therefore, pass by all but our most glaring errors.* Computers are even less reliable in finding our hard-to-find mistakes. (For example: "We *fought* an eight-week-old beagle puppy . . ." instead of "We *bought*. . . .") They will pass by that kind of mistake every time. It seems, then, for now anyhow and probably forever, all of us will have to continue proofreading as carefully as ever.

Help for Grammar?

Yes, but in many cases with difficulty; as with spelling, absolute help is often not there. The logic of grammar is so complex, and the relationship of grammatical elements to content is so subjective, that in many cases the grammar software provides only partial help. Patience is a virtue, furthermore, because grammar programs report problems in a tedious way, usually sentence by sentence.

Again as with spelling, the writer gets excellent advice for glaring errors. But in subjective matters the program may ask questions the writer may not be able to answer—indeed, some questions *most* writers might not be able to answer to their best advantage. Advice on passive voice verbs, for example, will leave many writers perplexed. (See Chapter 3.) Most writers with limited experience use far too many passives. But even the skilled writer who understands the difference between passive and active voice is likely to use quite a few passives; his or her choice is usually deliberate, and for good reasons. Pity the writer who may not understand the active/passive issue. The computer screen may identify verbs that are passive and may even suggest ways to turn each one active, but that is not likely to be enough help.

---

* It is for this reason the First Commandment of Proofreading was developed, long before computers: *Thou shalt not proofread thine own copy.*

Turn them all active? Leave them all passive? Both would be poor choices. For reasons such as these, many (perhaps most) word processing users rarely use the grammar check feature of their software.

Measuring Readability

Here the computer gives great help. We write to be read, and to a considerable degree the writer influences how well the reader will absorb the information. Writers should want to understand how this happens and how to control that influence. (See page 66.)

Most writers ignore the computer's readability software; experienced writers (usually) do not need it, and inexperienced ones do not understand it. The information this software provides is reliable, and the computer does all the work. Well, almost.

Readability formulas are measurement tools; the skilled writer gets a pat on the back, and the one who needs improvement gets statistics that, if understood, suggest some basic changes of style. But software publishers are not educators, and readability numbers provided by major word processing programs fall short of telling people how to use that information to advantage.

The readability index of this book, computed by one of the major and popular word processing programs for personal computers, is 9.7. Ernest Hemingway short stories, that program tells us, measure 4.0.

When computed by programs using the well-known Robert Gunning formula (page 70), the readability index of this book is 10.9. (The index number for both formulas corresponds to the number of years of education needed for reading with comprehension.) *Gunning method statistics: 16.2 words per sentence, 11.1 percent difficult words; 16.2 + 11.1 = 27.3, × 0.4 = RI 10.9.* The software program's formula measures sentence and word difficulty by other methods, but the results in most cases are reliably similar.

EXCEPTIONAL HELP FOR LARGE DOCUMENTS

The computer industry has been especially kind to writers of long reports—those that may contain dozens or hundreds of pages and need special features to keep things orderly for readers. These documents usually contain numerous chapter titles, section headings, subheadings, bulleted lists, footnotes, and other *recurring* features that serve as important road signs along the way. The sizes and styles of type available on computers, and the new ultramodern design choices, not only help readers but make powerful statements about the writer and his or her organization.

We all take these special features for granted in everything from the books we read to direct mail advertisements, but writers who have never created large documents containing them may be unaware of how much trouble is ahead. Painstaking detail is involved. These new opportunities can also, however, bring new headaches unless special help is available. The computer replaces the aspirin bottle, but better than curing large-document headaches it prevents them.

Early Planning

Yes, major word processing programs can help you outline those long and complicated reports *the sensible way.* (See Chapter 10.) They can also assemble the table of contents (and the index at the end), unpleasant chores when done manually. With a click of the mouse we can add footnotes; the electrons give each one its number and take care of placing it at the bottom of its page, and we can even go back and add new footnotes later, without having to worry about renumbering.

Formatting

Then there is formatting, often a terrifying confusion in the past, but no longer. Those chapter titles, section headings, subheadings, and bulleted lists each have their own type size and style, and the text has still another. Changing back and forth manually, while trying to write coherently, can make grown men and women cry. But controlling these functions manually is no longer necessary. Now writers let the electronic wizardry worry about those design details, while the writers *write.* Word processing programs can take care of these worries without getting gray hair. A *template* subprogram asks a few questions at the beginning of your document, and everything gets put where it belongs, with its type size, style, spacing, even margin widths if they vary, exactly as you select in your template.

THE MAJOR QUESTION REMAINS

Even with all these "compu-luxuries" performing reliably, computers still fall far short of writing. Writers still need to go through the same *thinking*

What Is the Singular of Parentheses?

It is *parenthesis,* but you should never need this unless you have left one out. (See page 215.)

process (the *what* of writing) and the same *language* process (the *how*), to give the computer something it can put on paper for our readers.

Will computers ever write for us? If writing is one's thinking put on paper, a better way of asking that question might be: Will computers ever think for us? Would we want them to?

PART 2

On Organizing

Power to the Reader

Just tell me what you've gotta tell me, clear and straight, and get to the point fast.

—John Wayne (*in* The Sands of Iwo Jima)

The principles of clarity in Part One are helpful for all kinds of writing—whether a great novel, a newspaper article, or a report or letter. The advice in Part Two, however, applies only to the kind of writing we call *expository.*

Most writing (except poetry and Holy Scripture) can be divided into two categories: expository and narrative. It is expository if its purpose is purely to convey information—either to inform or to persuade. All business writing and most newspaper writing is expository; so are most nonfiction books and essays. Add one more ingredient, plot, and the writing becomes *narrative.* Now the reader reads not just for the information but also for the thought-provoking way the writer assembles and presents it to get the reader involved—the story line. We repeat: The principles of organizing presented here would almost certainly hinder the creative writer's ability to develop an artistic or exciting plot.

In organizing, even more than in choosing words and combining them into sentences, the sender can greatly influence the receiver's ability to receive, and the sender who does not help will almost certainly hinder. With the same principle of organizing expository information (and there is basically only one), the writer can empower virtually every kind of reader—the one who wishes to plunge into your work and study every word carefully, the one who needs only the most important points and then wants to exit quickly, or the reader in between, who will decide while reading how deeply to examine the details. That principle is: *Start with the conclusion, then spend the rest of the writing supporting it.*

UNDERSTANDING READERS

Expository readers are predictable. We know they usually read for information, not for pleasure, and other demands compete for their time—especially in the world of work. We know also that first impressions strongly influence most readers' attitudes as they read the rest. In organizing, then, *the thoughtful writer tries to convey as much information as possible, as accurately and clearly as possible, and—yes—in as little reading as possible.*

Compare a cracking good mystery story (narrative form) with a newspaper account of the same events (expository form). If the mystery novelist is skillful enough, readers quickly become trapped into the "I couldn't put it down" mood. We do not want to put it down, and if someone tells us how it ends, that mood is broken.

But in the newspaper report of those same events the reader is reading just for the information, not the enjoyment of following a plot as it unfolds. Now, the "how it ended" information, unwelcome in the storyteller's version if it came too early, is the most important thing. Did Congress vote yes or no? Who won the game last night? Get to the point fast. Often a reliable *headline* is all readers need. Where narrative readers "can't put it down," expository readers are eager to put "it" down as soon as they decide they have all they need.

But the reader may decide this too soon. In the world of work, he or she may sometimes scan a report or memorandum quickly and decide, "This doesn't have anything I need," and miss the most important point. Or the reader may find some important information, be pleased, then say (again wrongly) "Okay, good stuff. I don't need the rest," and miss something even more important. The skillful writer needs to ensure that his or her *really important* information is received properly. What is the one statement about which a writer would be willing to say: "It's all right if my readers read nothing else"? That should appear at the beginning. And if it does, it may be truly all right if the reader reads nothing else.

Developing writers can find valuable lessons about organizing expository writing in a well-written newspaper article. Newspaper and magazine publishers, and university journalism departments, have conducted detailed studies to discover how we read, and these reveal some things that everyone who writes should know.

In wanting to stop early, the typical reader is not lazy or irresponsible; it is simply that the expository reader is reading only for information, is busy, and is eager to receive important information quickly, then move on.

Start with the conclusion, then spend the rest of the writing supporting it, whether writing a business letter or memo, a church newsletter, or a complicated engineering or financial report.

Never make readers wonder, "What are you getting at?" Rather, get to the point fast. There are some exceptions, but generally it is unwise to build up gradually to the most important information at or near the end.

Narrative (Storytelling) Structure

Experts have been divided since World War II on the important question: Do some dogs have more fleas than other dogs, or fewer fleas? By a slight majority, public opinion favors the "more fleas" theory. Grants from the National Science Foundation sponsored research on this subject at major universities in 1979 and 1996, but complex studies settled nothing, and even more recent researchers remain divided. The Center for Bugs and Critters (CBC) has just concluded a 5-year research program in search of a definitive answer to this pressing question. A survey form and a kit (for counting fleas) was sent to all dog owners in Canada. Owners of wolves were excluded. The response rate. . . .

Forty-one pages follow, mostly on the survey methods. Then:

The results show clearly that, although most people think some dogs have more fleas than other dogs, the opposite is true; computerized analysis of the statistics proves that some dogs have fewer fleas than other dogs. The Societé Français Des Chiennes concurs with our findings.

Expository (Reporting) Structure

Most people think some dogs have more fleas than other dogs. Actually, the opposite is true; computerized research by the Center for Bugs and Critters (CBC) shows clearly that some dogs have fewer fleas than other dogs.

Reader reaction 1: Okay, that's what we needed to know.

Reader reaction 2: That troubles me. I need to study this report carefully.

Reader reaction 3: Well, maybe, but I'll need to study the sections on. . . .

LEADING THE READER TO THE PATH

Skillful organizing not only gives readers pleasure, it helps them learn—particularly in expository writing. Even if the reader will read every word in great detail, he or she is a *better* reader having received the conclusion first. Reading experts tell us a *summary statement* in advance is important if the reader is to understand—especially for difficult information. Without that overview, the sender presents the receiving brain with isolated bits of information; nothing ties them together, and the receiving brain does not know what to do with them until the end. First declare what the brain is going to receive: Armed with that overview, the reader can understand the details better *in one reading* and will retain them longer.

This is not as much a principle of writing as it is of *learning*. The gifted instructor starts by saying: "Here's what we're going to do today, here's how we're going to do it, and here's why it's important to you." And the student becomes a better learner.

The elevator door statement.   Picture this scene. As an employee steps out of the elevator at work, his or her boss steps in, and as they pass each other the boss asks, "What did you decide about Tom Shields's letter?" The employee has only the few seconds that elevator door will stay open to give an intelligent answer. Just before alarm bells and flashing lights begin, the reply comes: "It sounds good, but only if they give us the extra time I asked for." The boss says as the door closes, "E-mail that to them."

When circumstances force us, we can usually find the one short statement about which we would be willing to say: "It's all right if my reader reads nothing else." That is the *elevator door statement;* the rest of the writing provides the supporting information.

Or else: When presenting expository information, writers should get to the point quickly for still another reason: If readers do not have the important point (or points) *before receiving the detailed information,* they might interpret that information differently and arrive at some conclusion (or conclusions) other than the one intended.

The two main goals here are precision and efficiency. This whole idea of opening with the conclusion shifts the burden of communication from the reader to the writer; *he or she* controls what readers get out of the writing, by declaring early what they *should* get out of it. Nothing is left to chance.

THE INVERTED PYRAMID STRUCTURE

To satisfy the reader's need for the overview at or near the beginning, journalism has given us the *inverted pyramid structure* shown on the next page:

Do Periods and Commas Go Inside or Outside Quotation Marks?

Always inside; there are no exceptions. Other punctuation marks may go inside or out, but determining the correct location is easy. Place them inside when they apply only to the matter being quoted: Smedley asked, "Can science accept the notion that humans may never be able to understand the universe?" Place marks other than periods and commas outside the quotation marks when they apply to more than just the quoted part: *Did Smedley say, "Science can accept the notion that humans may never be able to understand the universe"*?

Another useful tip on quotation marks: For quotations running several paragraphs, use quotation marks to open every paragraph but not to close every one; use them to close only the last paragraph being quoted.

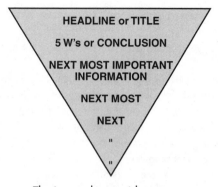

The inverted pyramid structure.

Notice that the simplest inverted pyramid is heavy at the top and fades into nothingness at the bottom. That is how most newspaper articles are organized, and it is how expository writers should organize all reports and most letters.* Regardless of what name we give the structure, the realistic writer starts with the attitude that the reader may be interested in reading only a small part of the writing, especially if it is a report. Therefore, he or she puts everything the reader *must* learn into the early paragraphs.

THE FIVE *W*s OF JOURNALISM

To ensure that the writer puts the most important information at the beginning, sages centuries ago created the five *W*s of journalism: *Who, What, When, Where,* and *Why.* These go in the first paragraph. And by so doing they ensure that every reader will receive the most important information, even if he or she reads no further: who, what, when, where, and why—though not necessarily in that order.

Some letters and reports may not have all five of the *W*s. There may be just one—what. More likely, at least two: what and why.

---

* Although the general term for this structure in writing is *inverted pyramid,* some writers argue that the concept is better described by just the word *pyramid,* drawn with the point up. Their thinking: The smallest section (the point), not the largest, should hold the most precious content. But this comparison to the Egyptian pyramids is inaccurate; the pharaoh's chamber was not at the top *or* bottom, but somewhere in between (in different places in different pyramids), to be as hard as possible for grave robbers to find. The two opinions of the pyramid are equally useful, but *inverted pyramid* is the more common term.

A Good Opening Paragraph or Overview Statement

This opening paragraph contains what, why, and when:

> A serious and costly packaging problem recently developed in the virtual projection department. To solve it, I recommend we upgrade the Franklin CC-8511 fulfillment station by adding a digital plotting assembly as soon as possible. *(What.)* On a 5-year lease, this will cost $57,200 ($933.33 per month, which includes installation and service). We estimate this upgrade will reduce shipping and labor costs $78,200 in that period, and the upgrade will eliminate the division's only serious source of customer complaints. *(Why.)* If possible, I would like to discuss this matter with you before the department's February 19 planning committee meeting. *(When.)*

Then the rest of the report (the details), follow in order of importance:

> The company now manufactures downlink terminal adapters faster than we can ship them. Back ups result, and customer complaints forced us to ship 31 special orders by air freight in the fourth quarter, at an average cost of $108.38 per order ($76.00 for the platform and $32.38 for the converter). By comparison, regular United Parcel Service costs $21.72 ($13.86 and $7.86). We were unable to charge the difference ($86.66 per shipment) to the customers because the fault was ours, not theirs. Our extra shipping cost for the quarter (31 shipments at $86.66) was $2,686.
>
> To get those orders out on time, a packaging operator worked overtime an average of 4.6 hours per week during the fourth quarter, at $20.47 per hour, or $1,224 for the quarter.
>
> The combined extra expense for the quarter was $3,910. That expense this year will be $15,640, or a total of $78,200 over the next 5 years, if sales volume, shipping rates, and labor costs don't go up.
>
> The Franklin CC-8511 operates at 4100 CARS, which met our needs when we purchased it 2 years ago. We knew then that the upgrade would eventually be needed, but the recent Mexican joint venture created the need earlier than we had planned. The upgrade component runs at 5500 CARS. According to our latest market forecast, that will meet our needs for the next 6 years.
>
> Fay Simmons has received bids from three companies, and she recommends the Franklin DA-2. The manufacturer can deliver and install it within 3 weeks. We have space for this equipment in the present packaging line area.
>
> Fay saw this problem coming last summer and wrote to Tom Shields on August 20, but no action was taken.

That report gave power to the *reader.* Imagine if it had begun:

> On August 20 Fay Simmons wrote a memo to Tom Shields and recommended. . . . ("Once upon a time. . . .")

. . . and had then built to the conclusion last, including the request to meet before February 19.

A sobering thought: Might Fay Simmons have written it that way? Might this be the reason the division now faces a loss of $78,200 if something is not done?

Why Write the Rest?

The doubting writer may wonder, "If the reader gets all the significant information in only a fraction of the writing, why go through all the trouble of writing pages and pages of support?"

We write the rest to give all types of readers confidence—to explain how we arrived at those key points in the overview statement, just in case readers want to know. But even if his or her choice is to read only the overview information, any reader is comforted by the presence of that supporting documentation. It is the backup information. Take it away, and hard-to-convince readers may not trust the important information up front.

Structuring the Rest

Once the overview is written there are three ways to organize the rest of the information that makes up the whole inverted pyramid:

- In order of importance (usually most desirable for most readers)
- In logical order (by location, alphabetical order, etc.)
- In chronological order (often called [especially by impatient bosses] "the mind dump")

But remember, all three are preceded by a quick, accurate overview statement.

There is a fourth way: *chaos.* And if the text is not structured using one of the first three methods, it will surely be the fourth.

Here is the beginning of a report organized as an inverted pyramid. It gets to the point fast:

As you requested, we have thoroughly inspected the operations of Springfield Healthy Tots Daycare Center, Inc. We found no serious weaknesses.

A few of your functions we feel are inefficient; we have listed these by department, along with detailed suggestions we think will provide the children even better care than they now receive under your award-winning program. All these suggested changes can be made with your existing staff, but a few will require new equipment. In all cases, the savings brought about by the change will pay for the new equipment in less than a year. May I stress, however, that these are all minor suggestions. . . .

Notice that the writer gives the summary or conclusion in a short opening paragraph. The reader learns immediately that the inspectors found no serious weaknesses. Then, quickly, the next most important information: that Healthy Tots Daycare Center has a few inefficient practices, that detailed explanations follow for each department, and that recommended improvements are affordable. All this information is the overview. The rest of the report, although not shown here, gives the details. They might by listed in order of importance—or perhaps in this case by children's age groups, or by some other convenient pattern. Many variations are possible for the details, but they all have one thing in common: They are unified by a strong opening statement.

How to End a Report

There is no need for a summary or wrap-up statement at the end. Writers like to end dramatically, especially in long reports. Readers seldom care; in fact, a proper inverted pyramid encourages most readers to stop early, by making it easy to do so reliably, and so most readers will never know how you ended. The best advice on ending seems to be: *When you have nothing more to say, just stop.* (But see Chapter 12, "When Writers Become Speakers.")

Many of the best writers—newspaper columnists for example—usually write until they have said exactly what they wanted to say, then stop.* Readers are satisfied when they have had just the right amount of information.

The never-never *rule for placing important information:* Writers who feel they *must* end with a fanfare should simply restate the conclusion, or overview statement, at the end. Thoughtful writers must never, never,

---

* Because they are limited to a precise amount of space, newspaper columnists must be skilled at saying as much as possible in the fewest words possible. Brevity is a greater concern for them than for most other kinds of writers.

however, set aside some important *new* information for a dramatic ending. Think, now. The inverted pyramid structure, with its most important information up front and followed by supporting information, encourages thoughtful readers to stop when they think they have had enough. Encouraging (or tempting) readers to stop early, then introducing important information at the end, is not very prudent.

Dealing with the Objections

Unsure writers often resist the idea of the inverted pyramid. Two common objections are heard often.

First, putting the conclusion at the beginning is the opposite of our natural tendencies; to do so requires reversing the order of our thinking. For lack of better guidance, and because it is easier, novice writers often tend to tell things in the order they learned them. They are then writing a diary, not a letter or report.

Second, inexperienced writers often resist the inverted pyramid concept because their pride is injured by the thought that the reader may not read every word. This is especially true if the writer has done a good job and knows it and wants every reader to study every thought from beginning to end; we all want our good work to be recognized. But a far higher professional compliment comes when managers say: "Just tell me your conclusions. I don't need the details because I'm sure your work was reliable." Prudent managers want employees who are capable; managers nurture these employees and place a high value on their ability to think clearly and write clearly.

THE CORNED BEEF SANDWICH WRITING LESSON

If the conclusion of an expository piece is not at the beginning, the next best place is the end; careful readers are accustomed to looking for it there. It may be somewhere in between, however. And if it is, will readers search for it? Will they know it when they see it?

But there can be something even more damaging than an overview statement buried somewhere in the middle: *no unifying conclusion anywhere*—several important statements that together make up the writer's overview, scattered in different locations.

The humorous essay that follows is written that way. It may not be an error here, because the piece is written more to entertain than to inform. But with prudent reorganizing the information could do both equally well. The piece is about three observations, or recommendations, but they unfold slowly. A writer who wanted to give serious advice (expository information) as well as have fun with the subject would have listed them in an overview statement up front.

How to Eat a Corned Beef Sandwich

My friend Freddy knows corned beef. He is the Midwest America corned beef maven of mavens, and he doesn't mind sharing his knowledge with others. Doesn't mind? He considers this to be his ministry; it is his contribution to improving the planet. In fact, you can't shut him up on the subject. In fact, he has been known to approach strangers and begin soliloquizing on the subject. Once a small woman, terrified, gave him a dollar to go away. His wife, Judy, located her and gave it back.

From his Dos Lagos headquarters, this pioneer has tried to influence the restaurant profession on behalf of corned beef sandwich aficionados everywhere, but some delicatessen owners petitioned city hall, and the police took away his license to conduct public seminars, which nobody attended anyhow, even though they were free.

The first challenge that confronts you, Freddy warns, is the corned beef meatball, but this is not a serious threat because it is easy to fix. I happen to agree. You ordered a sandwich, but you get this rather large pile of meat, albeit between two slices of bread. It is the object of your joy, but it is high in the middle, and out there stretching to the horizons of your rye bread crust—nothing.

You are permitted, when confronted with this alarming state of affairs, to take vigilante action. In polite company, in fact, you would be expected to disassemble the defective product, redistribute the assets of the meatball, then reassemble. A-ah, that's good. At this point you're ready to consider peripherals. Mustard? Yellow, of course—if any. Lettuce and/or tomato? No. Not even served separately; this is not a CBLT. Swiss cheese? Optional. Mayonnaise? Shame on you; don't confuse corned beef with good ham. And don't bother with corned beef–chopped liver combo. Save some money and just order the chopped liver; it would overpower the more delicate corned beef. *Pastrami* and chopped liver, maybe.

How about those yuppies and yuppywannabees who ask for extra lean? Extra lean is a more serious peril. We'll have none of it. A good deli should refuse to serve it, Freddy believes, and a good counter man who knows bad from good—in customers as well as corned beef— might just as well serve up dried rabbit between two slices of rye, confident that the extra-lean requesters can't tell the difference and deserve what they get. It is <u>not</u> true that any corned beef is better than none. Corned beef is not watermelon, Freddy has warned investigating committees for years.

But the fundamental peril to the sandwich, Freddy pontificates, and again I agree, is too much corned beef. Too *much?* Yes, there can be too much. Restaurants simply try to jam more down our throats than we need; they can charge more that way. This is a newly emerged crisis in our society, and it has been allowed to remain unaddressed, and therefore to worsen, because few people understand a good corned beef on rye and a well-aged dill pickle any more. People have been conditioned to think bad is good. They think good is when you can't open your mouth wide enough to bite both sides of the bread at once. Freddy teaches that the corned beef should be, at most, about as thick as one of the slices of bread—certainly no thicker—so you get the sweet balance of both flavors, and if the bread is there just to keep your fingers from getting a little greasy, it's cheaper to ask for the corned beef between two napkins, or take half of it home for another sandwich tomorrow, or an omelet.

White bread instead of rye? Okay, the maven of mavens says, but you should use a little less corned beef to preserve the delicate balance of tastes.

Corned beef between potato pancakes? Don't even sit near anyone who orders that; move to another table. Corned beef and cabbage? Two strong thumbs up, but not within Freddy's credentialed area of expertise. He e-mails CBC inquiries to Northeastern America maven of mavens Sean O'Rourke, of Boston.

-sede, -ceed, or -cede?
Only one word in the English language ends with *-sede*: *supersede*. Only three end with *-ceed*: *exceed*, *proceed*, and *succeed*. In all other words with this suffix it is spelled *-cede* (*intercede*, *precede*, etc.).

What information in that short piece should be the opening paragraph of an inverted pyramid structure—the advice about which the writer would be willing to say: "It's all right if readers read nothing else"? Freddy's conclusion, or overview statement comprises* three important pieces of advice. The trouble is, they never appear together anywhere in the writing. In order of importance:

- Too much meat [the fundamental threat first]
- The extra-lean sandwich
- The corned beef meatball

---

* *Comprises* is correct. The United States *comprises* 50 states, not *is comprised of.* (See page 92.)

An appropriate opening paragraph:

Special knowledge is required for full enjoyment of a corned beef sandwich. Freddy, the Midwest America maven of mavens, gives this advice to consumers: (1) Be suspicious of sandwiches containing too much meat. (2) Think hard before ordering extra-lean; unpleasant things sometimes happen. (3) Disassemble and redistribute a sandwich that has all the corned beef piled in the middle like a meatball.

Followed by separate sections discussing those three points, including all the colorful comments:

The fundamental threat to the sandwich, Freddy pontificates, is too much corned beef. Yes, there can be too much. Restaurants simply try to. . . .

The maven of mavens questions the judgment of yuppies and yuppy-wannabees who ask for extra-lean. He warns that extra-lean is the third peril and we should have none of it, and that a good counter man should. . . .

Freddy warns of the challenge presented by the corned beef meatball. You may order a sandwich but get a rather large meatball, albeit between two slices. . . .

Now the reader gets the less important information: mustard, lettuce and/or tomato, Swiss cheese, mayonnaise, special advice on white bread, and confrontations regarding potato pancakes.

Freddy's eccentricities and his friends' observations on them might come next. (Some writers might, however, consider these important enough that readers should be told of them earlier.)

Nearing the bottom of the inverted pyramid, the two strong thumbs-up for corned beef and cabbage and Sean O'Rourke.

And last (and least), Freddy's lectures and the fact that he lives and operates in Dos Lagos.

THE INVERTED PYRAMID'S ONE DISADVANTAGE

Dear Mr. DiFranco,

We're sorry, but our company is unable to deliver your fiber-optic animated graphics display by May 15, as you. . . .

Sal DiFranco groans. Slams letter on desk. Gets up and walks to window. Pounds forehead. "Oh no, No, . . . NO! How could they do this? We won't have it for the Chicago meeting." Rage follows. He doesn't read the rest but has already decided he'll never deal with that (expletive deleted) company again.

Rather, try:

Dear Mr. DiFranco,

You'll recall you placed your order and instructed us on January 29 to begin construction of your fiber-optic animated graphics display. . . .

DiFranco (to himself): "Oh, oh. Is something wrong?"

. . . On March 4 you instructed us to simulate the flight path of a butterfly, using various colors, and to add rounded side panels. We were able to make these changes. . . .

DiFranco: "I smell trouble."

. . . On April 7, according to our records, Ms. Joan Nichols phoned from your company and instructed us to change the wording. Then, just as we. . . .

DiFranco: "I'm not going to like this. . . ."

But this writer has been thoughtful. The reader already knows bad news is coming, that his company (not the supplier) is the cause, and that the supplier has been cooperative and its representative is trying to deliver the inevitable bad news as graciously as possible. Sadly, Mr. DiFranco recalls that on the day he ordered the last change the representative told Joan Nichols delivery might be late, but he (DiFranco) just said, "I'm sure they can take care of it, Joanie. They always do."

Few of life's rules are absolute, and the inverted pyramid structure does have one disadvantage—sometimes. Putting the conclusion at the beginning does not allow writers to be very subtle; this structure may be too hard-hitting for bad news. If the writer knows the conclusion is likely to upset the reader, the thoughtful thing to do is lead up to it gradually; telling it first might close his or her mind to the supporting facts. In this case, it might be prudent deliberately to use the narrative structure—holding the conclusion from the beginning and *starting with the supporting information*—slowly but inevitably leading up to the conclusions or recommendations in such a way that the reader cannot avoid them as the reasons build. Gradually the realization comes, "Oh, oh, I'm not going to like this," but it is too late to escape the reasons, and if they are valid reasons they may save the day.

Nothing can turn bad news into good news, but the enlightened writer should try at least to ease the discomfort for the person at the other end. This is the kind of thing considerate writers *want* to do. Trying to retain the reader's goodwill is also good business.

Never lead up to the main point slowly in a *report,* however. An unfavorable conclusion may not be damaging at the end *in a letter,* because a letter is short and addressed to one person, and the writer can reasonably assume that person will read the whole thing. But if important information does not arrive very early in a *report,* readers may not stay very long.

A Recommended Format for Reports

For most reports and letters, a simple inverted pyramid structure is usually easy to plan. But the longer the piece and the more complicated, the more difficult it is to organize. And, of course, it is the long reports that most need to be well organized, to help the reader receive and process that information efficiently.

No one format works best for all reports. The one that follows can serve as a useful guide, however; the writer can tailor it to fit his or her particular body of information.

The eight basic sections listed below may not all be needed, especially in a short report; in fact, using all eight would create a very formal document such as an engineering or scientific research report. They are listed in the order in which the reader reads them. *But note that the writer cannot possibly write them in that order; they must be written in the exact opposite order.* This becomes obvious from the content of each section:

- Title
- Abstract
- Summary

- Introduction
- Conclusions
- Recommendations
- Discussion section (body)
- Appendixes

Title.   A good title can be immensely informative, and a bad one can cause information to go wasted. Write it carefully. And write it last. *The title should be a highly condensed version of the <u>whole</u> report, and to achieve that goal it should quickly tell the subject and, if possible, the conclusion.* Most writers omit the conclusion, and without it the reader is deprived of the first opportunity to read with power.

This title does not quite do the job:

A Comparison of Permanent vs. Rotating Schedules for Little League Soccer Officials

A much more informative one:

Why Little League Soccer Officials Should Work on Rotating Schedules

Some readers might not need to read further.

Abstract.   A capsule version of the whole report, the abstract tells subject, conclusions, and how the writer arrived at those conclusions. Limit the abstract to 50 to 100 words. The abstract is useful for library files, computerized information retrieval systems and abstract journals; traditionally, it does not appear in the report. *If an abstract is needed, it should be written after the body and all the other preliminary sections (except the title).* Otherwise it might not contain the right key words, and future literature searches would be inaccurate as a result.

Summary.   The summary is the most important section of most reports. It contains exactly the same information as the abstract—subject, conclusions, and how the writer arrived at those conclusions—but in more detail. The summary is the first thing the reader reads after the title, and in many cases (if it is informative enough) the only thing. Limit it to 200 to 300 words—to fit on one page if possible. Rarely should the summary be longer than one page, and certainly no longer than two. Do not worry if abstract and summary sound somewhat alike; they should never appear together.

Introduction. Not to be confused with the summary or abstract, the introduction should give background information—reasons for doing the work being reported, possible benefits, a description of other work on the subject, etc. Limit it to one page, or 200 to 300 words.

Conclusion. Think hard here, to say what is really of significance. Do not be misled by the word *conclusion;* this is not concluding remarks. Rather, it is the conclusion arrived at as a result of the work being reported. That should be the last thing the writer learned while doing the work, but it is the first thing most readers want (or need?) to know. Limit this to 50 to 100 words. If a writer needs more, he or she probably has not thought carefully enough to identify: *What is the real message of this work?*

Recommendations. This section is optional. Recommendations may be part of the conclusion—or there may be none. But, if the report contains recommendations, the writer is entitled to state the reasons for them briefly up front—especially if they may surprise or upset readers. As with all these preliminary sections, detailed information will come later, in the body of the report. Limit this section to one page, or 200 to 300 words.

Discussion section. This is the body of the report. Here the writer discusses his or her work, findings, and reasoning in full detail and in all their glory. If the other preliminary sections contain the proper information, the body can run hundreds of pages if needed, without inconveniencing any reader. (If it runs longer than two or three pages, however, caring writers try to break it into sections [and subsections if needed]). And they insert section headings. Also in a long report, a table of contents should be included.

Appendixes* Try not to use them. Put tables, photographs, and the like in the body where each one is discussed, unless there are so many they interfere with the smooth flow of the text. (See Chapter 11, "The Elegant Finishing Touches.") If possible, limit appendixes to optional information.

Notice there is some planned repetition in this recommended format—particularly in the early sections. Each time, however, the reader gets more detail. The writer who puts the proper information into these sections is constructing an inverted pyramid of information. Readers get the choice of reading just a highly condensed version, the con-

---

The Interrobang?

The interro*what?* That's right, interrobang! Mirthful language scholars invented it about a decade ago and offered it jokingly, yet seriously, to the world. (The world has not responded very excitedly.) As its name implies, an interrobang is a combination question mark and exclamation point, and its backers suggest we would use it to give added emphasis to a question—as the exclamation point does to a sentence. And you construct it the same way, by adding a vertical line. Isn't that marvelous? Creating an interrobang in word processors is simple; use the *overstrike* function in the *typesetting* menu. On a typewriter, just backspace and type one character over the other. The world of serious writing is not ready for interrobangs. Still, one can imagine they may gain respectability some day. Well, why not?

---

* English is not one of the Romance (Latin-based) languages, and so we need not say *appendices.*

densed version followed by all the details, or the condensed version followed by just those details each one chooses to read. What a heavenly joy for readers.

But remember, *the writer cannot possibly compose these eight sections accurately in the order they appear to the reader.* Writers must create them in the *opposite* order—from the bottom of the inverted pyramid to the top—condensed versions last. Otherwise they are writing the most important sections (to the reader) *before* writing that which they condense—in other words, before doing their most serious thinking.

Not every report needs all eight of these sections. Or, some may need these plus others. Again, this format is only a guide. It is reasonable to presume, however, that any serious report will have at least a title, summary, and body.

Far more important than following a rigid format, the expository writer must understand the reasons behind the inverted pyramid theory and why this structure provides so much benefit to so many readers. If you do, you can intelligently design a format for each report to fit the information that particular report contains.

A CHECKLIST FOR ORGANIZING

Structure is more difficult to evaluate than clarity. No one has devised a way to measure numerically whether ideas are arranged in some helpful, orderly sequence. Yet some way of evaluating—some checklist—is helpful. These four questions might make a helpful checklist, especially for reports:

✓ Is there an accurate conclusion or overview statement very early?
✓ Is all the information in some helpful sequence?
✓ Is the treatment of the topics in proportion to their importance?
✓ Are there headings to help the reader?

✓ **Is there an accurate conclusion** or overview statement very early? Remember, the reader should be able to choose reading only that, and he or she may not stay around to read very long or work very hard to find it. Remember too, even readers who intend to read every word carefully can understand the details better if they have had the overview first.

✓ **Is all the information** in some helpful sequence? The sections may (after the conclusion) be arranged by order of importance. Or, events may unfold in chronological order, or information may be arranged in some other logical sequence. But some method of arranging the information is demanded from beginning to end, and it should be obvious even to scanning readers.

✓ **Is the treatment of the topics** in proportion to their importance? Two factors send the reader subconscious messages suggesting how important an idea is: the location of the section, and its size. In the traditional inverted pyramid structure, the sections (after the conclusion or overview statement) should normally be longer near the front and get shorter as the bottom of the pyramid narrows.

✓ **Are there headings** (and possibly subheadings) **to help the reader?** They are like road signs, guiding the reader on his or her trip. (See Chapter 11.) Each one announces: "We're now going to discuss. . . ." No report can be considered well structured without headings, especially if it is very long.

Remember: When structuring letters or reports, the writer's job is to tell as much as possible, as accurately and clearly as possible, in as little reading as possible. The reader should not be forced to work harder than necessary to receive and understand your ideas. When is reading harder than necessary? When the writer did not do everything in his or her power to make it easier. Always the reader. He or she is the only reason we write.

THE DEVIL'S ADVOCACY

DEVIL'S ADVOCATE

Okay, let's go into this. If the most important information should go up front, why is the section that says this located in Part Two of this book, not Part One? Shouldn't writers learn how to plan the order of the ideas before they start writing?

GURU

Of course. That's a fine question, and there's a fine answer. Remember, I'm your friend. *Clarity* and *organizing* are equally important, so there's no reason either should have priority over the other in a book. But gurus are smart. As teachers we know that people feel better if we discuss clarity first. The reason is that most students notice quicker results that way. It's also true, I suppose, that words and sentences are easier to deal with than ideas. That's why there are so few great storytellers.

DEVIL'S ADVOCATE

You compared the narrative structure to the organization of a children's story, "Once upon a time . . ." or a great mystery, with the conclusion at the end. Obviously, people like to read that way.

GURU

Yes, when reading for *pleasure,* but not when they're reading for some information they need.

DEVIL'S ADVOCATE

Also obvious, people like to write "Once upon a time . . ." stories.

GURU

Well, they probably wouldn't if you pointed out to them that's what they're doing. We ask inexperienced writers: If the reader has to go through all you went through to learn what you learned, what does he or she need you for?

DEVIL'S ADVOCATE

The inverted pyramid structure showcases the conclusion first. Isn't there a danger my reader is going to think I did the work with my mind made up in advance, then looked for information to support premature conclusions? Do I need this?

GURU

Oh, the wisdom of the literary architects who gave us the inverted pyramid. It's for this concern they also gave us the rest of the report. The other 999 pages (or whatever) are the support—the proof that the top of page 1 is accurate. Your reader may choose not to read all those other pages of information, but their presence is comforting. It almost invites the reader: "Come and look." Remember too, some readers may need or want to read the whole report or some parts but not others. You can't decide that for them.

DEVIL'S ADVOCATE

In a speed reading course once I was told: If you're having trouble understanding something, stop trying to read in detail; browse through first, then read; you'll understand better. And it works.

GURU

Sure. But listen to what the reading experts are saying: "Hey, reader, just in case the writer didn't give you an overview, go in and construct your own."

DEVIL'S ADVOCATE

But the *writer* should do it, not the reader.

GURU

Of course. That's what the inverted pyramid structure is all about.

DEVIL'S ADVOCATE

Isn't there an *H* with the five *W*s of journalism?

GURU

That's the *how;* it's the rest of the article (or report). And there you have the classic structure for a newspaper article: five *W*s and an *H. Who, what, when, where,* and *why* in the opening paragraph, and the rest of the article tells *how.* Incidentally, we said the five *W*s go in the opening *paragraph,* not *sentence.* What a whopper that would be. Think sometimes of two or three sentences for *who, what, when, where,* and *why.*

DEVIL'S ADVOCATE

The *Summary* may contain a full page of information, but the *Conclusion* only 50 to 100 words? What's the story?

GURU

The story is simple. This is a sort of proficiency test for writers, to protect readers. Remember, the reader is coming from the top down, but the *writer* is working from the bottom up. Okay? So, by the time the writer has progressed this far toward the front, he or she has already written the body. After all that, if he or she can't tell what's really important in a few clear sentences, surely something must be wrong with the thinking. That writer is not ready yet to write the most important sections of all—the up-front sections. That writer needs to start thinking: "What's the one statement about which I would be willing to say: 'It's all right if my reader reads nothing else'?"

DEVIL'S ADVOCATE

The eight sections of a formal report create some needless repetition.

GURU

Repetition yes, needless no. This format doesn't add much to the overall length of a major report, and it sets up a neat inverted pyramid for the reader—for the noblest of purposes: quicker reading and better understanding.

DEVIL'S ADVOCATE

You referred to *appendixes*. Not *appendices*?

GURU

Please, English is not Latin, okay? I had a student once, a brilliant scientist, who worked backward from the word *appendices* and concluded its singular is *appendicee*. But I don't know how he spelled it. You people wear me out.

CHAPTER 9   CLOSER LOOK: THE "INVERTED PYRAMID"

The most difficult thing about organizing expository writing is planning: What should be the opening—the one statement, or short group of statements, about which the writer would be willing to say: "If the reader is going to read just one statement, this should be it."

The business memo below is well written in its words and sentences, but it is poorly organized; the writer simply put things down in the order they happened. That is a common mistake, because it is easy—almost like a fairy tale beginning *Once upon a time. . . .*

Feathered Friend Nature Company opened a credit card account with us on July 15, 1996. The company is a franchised outlet of a national line of bird food, bird houses, and related yard accessories. In October 1996 they began falling behind in payments.

After sending our MC and SC groups of collection letters, we put the company on our delinquent list March 1, 1997 and canceled their credit. At that time they owed $2,372.09. I phoned Mr. Bixley D. Hilborn, company president, on April 2, and he promised to send us the full amount within 30 days. I also requested that the company return our three credit cards.

That was 45 days ago. We have received the credit cards but no money.

> This customer shows no willingness to cooperate. The Retail Credit Bureau reports they are also seriously delinquent in credit accounts with other companies. I recommend the Feathered Friend Nature Company account be turned over to our legal department for further action.
>
> Mr. Hilborn was formerly sales manager of Western Tool Company, a good customer of ours for many years. He opened Feathered Friend July 1, 1996.

How easy it is, if the writer approaches the task from the expository reader's viewpoint, to present the same information in a far more useful way. *Remember: Get to the point fast.* Or, ask yourself: What is the one piece of information about which you would be willing to say, "It's all right if my reader reads nothing else?"

The remedy: Make the fourth paragraph the opening paragraph, then make its last sentence the opening sentence. Nothing else changes.

Writers who resist new ways might point out it is unlikely a reader would miss the important point in that example. Probably true, but imagine if the memo were five pages instead of five paragraphs, with the conclusion somewhere on page 4.

The memo below is also structured in the narrative form, starting with introductory information (the equivalent of *Once upon a time . . .*) and leading in chronological order to its most important statement *at the end:*

> Most designers believe that stress figures obtained from photographs are more accurate than those computed electronically. This is probably because photo interpretation takes longer. However, in many cases electronic results are more accurate.
>
> We have examined the 31 design projects approved so far this year and in 19 of these. . . . [followed by two pages of text and a bar graph]. Then:
>
> Analysts have the training necessary to determine the examination method that will give the most accurate results for a particular job. They, not the designers, should decide whether photo interpretation or electronic data should be used. Please instruct all designers in your branch that they should not specify the method of measuring stress data in future reports on aircraft testing.

The remedy: One simple and obvious change: Promote the closing paragraph to the opening paragraph. No change could be easier or more useful.

Stop and think. If readers can have the pot of gold at the beginning of the rainbow instead of at the end, do they really need to stay around for the rainbow? Perhaps yes, perhaps no, but the choice should be theirs.

Sense and Nonsense about Planning

Thinking is easy. All you do is stare at a blank sheet of paper until drops of blood form on your forehead.

—Gene Fowler

Solving any writing problem is easier when we understand what causes it, and that is certainly true of the headache many writers complain is the most nagging of all: *getting started*. They fumble, they fuss, but the uneasy feelings will not go away.

If the writer understands the reader's needs and the theory of the inverted pyramid structure, organizing the ideas thoughtfully should not be difficult—at least, not for most short works. But the task becomes much more of a challenge for large writing jobs such as major reports or books. Those, of course, are the ones that most need careful structuring.

Thoughtful writers flounder when getting started because they recognize consciously or subconsciously: *How you treat the beginning of a letter or report will determine the character of the whole piece.* Or, as the saying goes, "As the twig is bent, so grows the tree." That is certainly true of expository writing, so, wisely, the careful writer tries to begin his or her expository trip by heading in the right direction.

Pointing in that right direction is one of the pivotal challenges. Typically, the thoughtful novice who does not yet walk with the *literati* sits down the first day of a major writing job with a fresh notepad, a sharpened pencil, and marvelous intentions. Then what? Nothing, if this writer hopes staring at a blank page will help. The poor novice sits staring at it, mind wandering, wanting to be productive, in search of mental road maps that will not appear. After 15 or 20 minutes the wanderer gives up. "I'll be able to write it tomorrow" is everyone's surrender slogan. Poor wanderer. Tomorrow arrives but divine intervention does not come with it. Getting started is put off a second day, then a third and fourth, until . . . *the deadline.*

Writers who can be productive only under the pressure of a deadline are members of the world's largest authors' club; trouble getting started is almost a universal occupational illness.

BEATING THE DEADLINE

What does the deadline force thoughtful men and women to do differently? Consider these facts:

- Only one out of five or six adults can recite the six possible combinations of the letters *A, B,* and *C.* (An easy way: Three starting letters are possible, and for each one the second and third letters are reversed: *ABC, ACB, BAC, BCA, CAB,* and *CBA.* Mathematicians call this pattern "three factorial.")
- Using *A, B, C,* and *D* (four factorial), 24 combinations are possible: *ABCD, ABDC, ACBD, ACDB, ADBC, ADCB, BACD, BADC, BCAD, BCDA, BDAC, BDCA, CABD, CADB, CBAD, CBDA, CDAB, CDBA, DABC, DACB, DBAC, DBCA, DCAB,* and *DCBA.* Reciting these is almost impossible, no matter how long one tries. *But with a pencil and paper, most people in classroom experiments can list them in 3 or 4 minutes.*

As an isolated organ the human brain has a surprising limitation: When unable to see them, the average intelligent adult can examine surprisingly few pieces of information—often as few as two, rarely more than three or four—even when they are as simple as A, B, and C. *Choices become almost impossible to make.* But when we use a pencil and paper the number of choices increases dramatically.

What is the lesson here?   When we try to examine ideas without being able to see the words and sentences, we are forcing the brain to operate as an isolated organ, and our ability to examine them intelligently and make choices is reduced dramatically. *This explanation is needed:* The eyes have no advantage over the ears as inputs to the brain, but the written word has a major advantage over the spoken word: It stays there, allowing the receiver to examine and reexamine the ideas at his or her comfortable pace. The spoken word is transitory; the sounds exist only the split second they are spoken, and so the receiver must examine them at the sender's pace. For this reason we will always be better able to make intelligent choices when we can see the ideas—literally *see* them before us. (But all educators know that the combination of seeing and hearing is best.)

MAKING THE BREAKTHROUGH HAPPEN

But then, if writers have limited ability to organize complex thoughts in the mind, how else to organize them? How does the longed-for breakthrough happen?

What does the deadline change?   Until the last desperate moment, the struggling writer is trying to organize his or her information before writing. But this means arranging the order of the ideas first, and the ABCD experiment shows us that can be done only *after* putting them on paper. It is a chicken-and-egg dilemma, and, unable to become productive, the would-be writer continues procrastinating. Finally the deadline demands action. Fear sets in. At this point *any beginning becomes better than none, even if it is wrong*. And now for the first time the writer begins doing what needs to be done (but not the way it needs to be done). The plan is simple: "I've got to get started; if it's wrong I'll change it later."

THE BLISSFUL "FALSE START"

One of the inescapable guidelines of writing, then, is: *A false start is the necessary first step—something to look at and correct.*

But writing something the wrong way to find out what should have been the correct way makes little sense. There is the delay of staring at the blank page, and all the wasted time and work in writing, then organizing, then rewriting.* Still, a false start—getting something down on paper so we can examine it and rearrange its parts—is the only sensible first step. We make it in skeleton structure, quickly and easily, and with little wasted work: an outline.

---

* Computers offer little help in these steps; rearranging with them is cumbersome. In the draft stages moving whole blocks of text forward or backward is easy, but the rewording needed to restore smooth flow may be maddening.

Here finally is the dreaded word.   The inescapable fact is that *outlining* is the most important single step in writing—whether for a letter, an engineering or financial report, or a great novel.

Yes, most if not all novelists outline. The popular impression is that the great writer sits down at the word processor and fills page 1, then plans what will happen on page 2, and so on, filling wastebaskets as he or she progresses. That was not true even when novelists (as recent as W. Somerset Maugham) wrote manuscripts by hand. The concept may seem romantic, but the process is wasteful. Filling wastebaskets, yes. But not knowing where the story is going? Unthinkable. Most novelists first develop the plot in skeleton form. This is called the *plot line,* or *story line.* Only then can a writer decide whether the story is worth telling. (Ernest Hemingway addressed this in his advice to young writers. He told them the outline is the architecture of writing; words and sentences are the interior decoration.) In the outline we establish the value of *what* we write; it is mainly here that authors determine whether they will win literary awards.*

THE SLEEK AND MODERN OUTLINE

Most developing writers, when they finally admit they *really do* need to outline (usually after staring at a blank note pad for days, until the deadline), begin that serious business by placing in the upper left corner of a note pad:

> **I.**

What then? They sit and stare at *that* for days. The Roman numeral does not bring the hoped-for divine intervention, and the mental block does not go away. No Roman numerals, please. At least not yet.[†]

The first purpose of the outline is to allow the writer the luxury of the false start—quickly and with little wasted effort. Now consider: *The*

> ### What Is a Gerund?
>
> It is a verb used as a noun, always ending with *-ing.* (We all attended the *hearing.*) However, not all verbs ending with *-ing* are used as nouns; most of them are just regular verbs. (We keep *hearing* strange noises.)

---

* But an outline is a *suggested* plan, not an inviolate one; all authors reserve the right to change their minds at any time. Feeling free to change an outline, however, is quite different from trying to write without one.

[†] Roman numerals (and capital letters, small numbers and letters, etc.) can be added at the end if the writer feels they may be useful; they help readers in long documents by showing the relative importance of the pieces of information. But they can cause the writer unneeded trouble unless they are inserted after the outline is completed.

moment writers put Roman numeral one on the page, they have deprived *themselves of that false start;* they have committed themselves to writing first things first, second things second, and so on. Before *writing* them in that order, however, it would be necessary to *think* them that way.

No one building a home begins construction without blueprints; creating something of value would almost certainly require much tearing apart and rebuilding, probably several times. In the writing business, the outline is equivalent to blueprints; it allows us to tear apart and rebuild without the wasted time and effort of writing things, then reading to learn if anything is left out or in the wrong place, then rewriting. Changes are a necessary part of the writing process; the first planned arrangement of the information will almost certainly *not* satisfy the writer; neither may the second one, or the third. These are false starts, and experienced writers save much time, work, and anguish by making them in skeleton structure.

Sensible steps for a sensible outline:

- Working with key word phrases, *not sentences,* the writer begins a random list of all the various thoughts, major and minor, that should be (or might be) part of this report or letter. A pile of building materials emerges—the many separate ideas or groups of ideas the writer will assemble into a useful structure of information. *But:* Where do the various parts go?
- From that pile of building materials, a second list, containing just the major items, is easy to write, preparing for the steps that follow. *This the first basic plan.* Working now with this second list, the writer begins arranging those *major* ideas into the structure that will best help the reader. (See "The Inverted Pyramid Structure," page 110.) The order may change several times; changes are exquisitely simple at this point.
- This newly formed skeleton is now ready to receive the minor items that remain from the original random list. Each one is added under its appropriate major category. (Some may suggest that a new major topic is needed.) Now the writer can add, delete, or change the order of any ideas as he or she sees fit. A working outline has emerged from a random collection of thoughts.
- The thoughtful writer will continue looking for ways to revise the order of the ideas, to improve the flow of information to the reader. Changes are so much easier and faster now, in this skeleton structure, than they would be later.
- Only now, the *words and sentences* part of the writing process should begin.

Two further outlining hints:

1. *Work on notepad paper, and write in longhand.* Remember, the first version must be a false start, something just to look at and correct quickly and easily in skeleton structure.
2. *Use key word phrases.* Enlightened writers are not yet thinking about picking the right words or building them into sentences; that comes later. Focus now on *what* to say, not *how* to say it. Remember, any time-consuming work done now will probably be thrown away and have to be done again, differently, later.

A pleasant and unexpected bonus: Outlining also improves the writer's ability to select words and build them into sentences later, when they are finally needed. By outlining sensibly we divide writing into its two major elements—*what* we write and *how* we write it—allowing ourselves to concentrate on each separately. Each is so demanding it seems unthinkable that anyone but the most brilliant literary artists could address both at the same time and give both the attention they need. Addressed separately, the ideas will be more intelligently thought out, and the words and sentences will almost certainly be clearer and more eloquent.

MIND MAPPING TECHNIQUES

Some members of the writing community compare writing to taking a long and complicated trip; before putting the bags in the car and driving off, most of us plan carefully and even draw the route and mark our various stops on a road map. These experts describe a method similar to the false start method for organizing the ideas, but they call it *mind mapping;* this phrase avoids the unpopular *outlining* that might turn would-be writers away. The process is essentially the same, as is the reason it is necessary. Special techniques are used, often requiring pens or pencils in various colors.

But mind mapping advocates often fail to explain the reason for the process, and without understanding it writers are not likely to have a smooth and uninterrupted trip. That reason remains: The writer needs to *see* the ideas before his or her brain can deal with the many possible arrangements that can be made of them.

Many popular phrases have been used to describe the important process of structuring ideas into an action plan. In the late 1940s, World War II veterans returning from the armed forces brought with them the term *brainstorming,* a method used by military leaders to make important decisions by consensus. Those present would be asked to compile a list, on a chalkboard or flip chart, of all factors that might be involved in a decision, then rank them by order of importance, discuss them, and arrive at a recommended strategy. They learned it was important to write those ideas on the chalkboard or flip chart; their brains needed to *see* the ideas in order to examine them intelligently and arrive at a consensus that represented the best thoughts of the various experts present. The false start was the necessary first step.

In the 1970s, the term *clustering* began appearing—listing all the ideas in related clusters. The false start remains the first step in planning the order of the ideas, whether the writer chooses to arrange them into the inverted pyramid structure, cluster them, or draw a mind map. How each writer progresses beyond that, from random thoughts to a finished outline, is largely a matter of his or her own work habits.

THE DEVIL'S ADVOCACY

GURU

In classrooms, I like to advise people to use a sheet of paper with heel marks or coffee rings for the first "false start outline," the random list.

DEVIL'S ADVOCATE

Heel marks or coffee rings?

GURU

I recommend both, actually. Keep a good supply of throw-away paper for that *false start* work; those marks and stains serve as an important reminder: *If this doesn't end up in the wastebasket very soon, you're not using it correctly.* Remember, the first thing you put on paper is going to be a false start; you don't get the choice. We can't plan the best order of the ideas in our minds, so we need to put them down in some *wrong* order so we can *see* what should have been the *right* order, then make corrections. The choice we get is whether to correct early thoughts quickly in skeleton structure by drawing arrows back and forth, or by writing a whole report to see what was wrong, then correcting that. Repeat after me: FALSE START, six times.

DEVIL'S ADVOCATE

With computers, changing the order of large blocks of text is easy. So why not just start with a rough draft and make changes as I see the need? Computers are hot; outlines are not.

Avoid Clichés Like the Plague?

A cliché is a group of words used as a common expression, such as "like the plague." Writers usually enjoy them because clichés are colorful. (Ironically, they become clichés in the first place because they are so expressive.) For that same reason, they become overused and as inspiring as warm milk. Another objection is that the collective meaning usually does not agree with the individual meanings of the words, and there is no authorized definition of the cliché. How accurate are "*ball park figures*"? They can be as accurate or inaccurate as the author would like; readers have no way of knowing.

Still another objection is that in their eagerness to use clichés people often get the words wrong. "I could care less" should be "I *couldn't* care less." (You already care so little it would not be possible to care less.) Or: "Each one was better than the next." Now think. That really means each one was worse than the one before it; they got progressively worse. Is this what the author intended?

In spite of these shortcomings, writing without occasional clichés would probably be impossible and not worth the effort. You need not, therefore, avoid them "like the plague." But if you can avoid one as easily as saying "as carefully as you would avoid catching a deadly disease," you probably should. No one will mind the extra words.

GURU

Listen, if you want to be the guru, go ahead, but right now I am, so <u>no rough drafts</u>, please. Here's why: When you sit down to write with the attitude, "There's no sense trying very hard because the first version isn't going to be very good anyhow," it probably won't be. The order of the ideas will probably be wrong, or you may do less than your best in choosing words and building sentences. Or both. So you end up with a lot of—may I say—*junk*. Also remember, to rearrange the sections properly, and quickly, you need to see them all at once. Otherwise you can't sense how one change will affect other sections, and that's what is wrong with moving large blocks of text around by computer. The idea of the false start is to *reduce work,* not create more, but the rough draft deprives you of that advantage. And many grown people who move large blocks of text end up crying before they get it right. Okay?

DEVIL'S ADVOCATE

I suppose. . . .

GURU

Swear an oath.

DEVIL'S ADVOCATE

How long should it take?

GURU

The oath or the outline? Give up the pipe dream that outlining is a 5-minute job. Sometimes it may take just the few minutes most people envision, or it may take three-quarters of your total writing time. But remind yourself, if you're having fits arranging the ideas, how much worse it would be if you were trying to select the right words and build the right sentences at the same time.

DEVIL'S ADVOCATE

How about some rule of thumb?

GURU

In general, a 1:1 ratio may be reasonable; plan on spending as much time outlining as writing. For most novice writers that would mean rearranging their time—more time planning, less on writing. But the finished project would be better.

How detailed should it be?

The thing is, each writer has to decide that. Certainly, any useful outline has to include all of your *major* ideas—those that would have the Roman numerals in a traditional outline. And in proper order. How far the outline should be planned beyond that is mostly a matter of what makes you feel confident. One thing is certain: The more detail you put into the outline, the better organized and more clearly written the finished product will be. And the less time you'll need to write it.

CHAPTER 10   CLOSER LOOK: THE BLISSFUL "FALSE START"

Outlining is crucial to success; it is the most important single step in writing, and those who try to avoid it almost always end up going through the fundamental process anyhow, but with much rewriting rather than changing skeleton structures.

In the outline, far more than in the words and sentences, the writer determines how successful his or her work will be—or indeed, whether it is of value—because language arts skills alone will not win the day. Therefore, a random list of the ideas should be the first step in outlining. It is the blissful false start. (Most people unwittingly make their false start by writing the report in the wrong order, then rewriting it.)

A CASE STUDY: THE SLEEK AND MODERN OUTLINE

Imagine you are going to write a report on the subject of "flextime," a system many companies and government agencies use, which allows employees to choose their own working hours. You have just listed all the ideas you can think of on the subject, in random order as they came into your head. That list appears below; it is your false start:

Reduced absenteeism and tardiness	Many large users
Rules printed and distributed	Raises employee morale
Increased personal freedom	Hewlett-Packard
Objectives must be defined	Makes personnel recruiting more effective
The advantages	Employee briefing needed
The disadvantages	Reduces employee turnover

(continued)

Increases customer service hours

Hourly employees may complain

Scheduling may create conflicts

Steps to be taken in advance

Slows down communications

Metropolitan Life Insurance

Reduced parking lot congestion

Improves public image

Smith Kline Corporation

Reduced cafeteria congestion

Coordinator must be appointed

Department of Transportation

Flexible hours must be limited

U.S. Department of Agriculture

Management support needed

As the planning writer examines that random list of ideas related to flextime, he or she begins to *see* relationships that were not evident before. In the *flextime* outline the ideas clearly fall into four categories:

The Advantages of Flextime

Its Disadvantages

Major Corporate and Government Users

Things That Must Be Done in Advance

Now the steps become easier and more obvious; the planner may even begin feeling enthusiasm as each of the remaining (minor) ideas clearly belongs under one of the major ones. *The result:* An outline, the road map for the writer's trip through the paragraphs and pages:

I. THE ADVANTAGES OF FLEXTIME

Reduces absenteeism and tardiness

Increases personal freedom

Raises employee morale

Makes personnel recruiting more effective

Reduces employee turnover

Increases customer service hours

Reduces parking congestion

Improves public image

II. ITS DISADVANTAGES

Scheduling may create conflicts

Hourly employees may complain

Communication may slow down

III. MAJOR CORPORATE AND GOVERNMENT USERS

Hewlett-Packard

Metropolitan Life Insurance

Smith Kline Corporation

State Department of Transportation

U.S. Department of Agriculture

IV. STEPS TO BE TAKEN IN ADVANCE

Rules must be printed and distributed

Objectives must be defined

Employees must be briefed

Coordinator must be appointed

Flexible hours must be limited

And there it is. The conclusion or opening paragraph stares up from the page:

> Flextime work schedules for employees will benefit our company. There are a few disadvantages, but the advantages far outweigh them. Some of the largest corporations and government agencies use flextime and endorse it. If we are going to switch to such a plan, however, several important steps must be taken in advance.

Now, for the first time, the writer knows where he or she is going and is ready to write. expanding the ideas fully into words and sentences. The real-world writer would begin now to tell readers something important for every line item under each main (Roman numeral) heading. Hard work? Not really, *if the writer knows the subject.* And that is the important point here. People for whom writing is an important job skill are not called upon to create novels or poetry; being informed on the things they write about (content) is their everyday work, and so is conveying it to others. In their everyday activities, then, expository writers usually know all they need—and have all the information they need—when they sit down to write. Or they can get it quickly. In most cases they are simply unsure what to do with it.

And so there is not much about expository writing that is mysterious. It is mostly a matter of knowing the subject, knowing what you want to say about it, and knowing how to say it clearly and directly.

CHAPTER 11

The Elegant Finishing Touches

The great enemy of clear language is insecurity.

—George Orwell

When the writing is done, and the rewriting, the writer's work is not yet completed. Almost, but not quite. A few mechanical aids, easy to use, can help readers on their trip through the information from the first word they read to the last. Especially with computers, writers can do most of the elegant things that only professional publishers could do in the past; these touches are easy, and they are too important to overlook.

The writer new to these finishing touches learns quickly how much they add, especially to large reports and presentations. We get a lot for a little. They include headings, white space, reader-friendly paragraphs, bullets and other markers, special typefaces, and the special treatment of graphics. Letters, too, send a silent message of quality and courtesy when we know how to perform the procedural parts sensibly.

HEADINGS: JOY TO READERS *AND THE* WRITER

Probably the most important of mechanical aids are section headings. They are easy to use, and when properly used they add an astonishing look of professionalism. The longer the document, the more help headings provide readers. (But do not use them in letters; they give the appearance of a form letter, and readers resent that.)

Headings help several ways.   Readers feel comfortable just seeing them and knowing they are there. Those short phrases, standing out from the rest, break up the text and provide overviews along the way; headings announce each key point *before* its detailed discussion. (Remember, readers understand the details better and retain them longer when they know in advance the nature of the information they are going to receive.) Those little signposts along the way help the reader to read selectively—choosing to stop for a close look at some passages but not others. And they give readers places to pause, to regroup their thoughts or to rest.

The use of headings also helps the writer, by relieving the need for transition passages; headings provide all the transition readers need by announcing, "We're now going to the following topic." They allow the writer, as well as the reader, the pleasure of flowing smoothly and easily from the end of one major idea to the beginning of the next.

What should the headings be, and where should they go?   The writer who has outlined properly has already written them. They are those key word phrases from the finished, carefully planned outline; experienced writers simply transfer them into the text. Writers unaccustomed to using headings are pleasantly surprised how easily they fit and how effective they are—road signs that readers appreciate greatly, though subconsciously.

But caution: Too many headings may create a negative effect. If every page contains several of them, readers may form the impression at a glance that the writer gave each topic scant attention; they may be right.

THE POWER OF WHITE SPACE

The next way the writer can help readers, and send a silent message about his or her communicating skill, is to use white space generously. It is easy to use, inexpensive, and effective. Conscientious typists may tend to squeeze too much on a page, robbing both writer and reader of the white space they deserve. Experienced writers require the typist to leave at least 1 inch of white space around all four sides of every sheet that leaves the computer printer or typewriter; most secretarial manuals also advise this.

Experienced writers insist also on a noticeable gap at major headings, to make them stand out. Those signposts should not be buried; they should draw even the scanning reader's eye.

The typist should also skip a line between paragraphs, and if a letter or report is double-spaced, triple-spacing should be used between paragraphs; just as at the headings, there needs to be a visible gap at the paragraph breaks.

WHY THE MYSTERY ABOUT PARAGRAPHS?

Paragraphs help readers two ways. First, paragraphs present clusters of related sentences, which form the important building blocks in every writer's logic. A new paragraph suggests some break or shift in the logic, or a shift in time, place, or procedures. Less commonly known, paragraphs provide relief to the eye muscles; the breaks along the way allow readers to glance from the page for a split second, then find their place quickly and continue reading.

How long should paragraphs be? Generally, like sentences, they should be short. Thoughtful writers look for helpful places to break them. In most writing the paragraphs probably should average about 7 or 8 lines in length. Also as in building sentences, a good mixture of lengths is desirable: minimum 1 line, maximum 15. Generally the size and shape of the cluster of sentences should determine the size and shape of the paragraph, but if one goes much beyond 15 lines, the writer who is eager to help readers will look carefully for a place to stop.

Reading experts point out that comprehension begins to drop after about 10 typewritten lines and drops drastically after about 15 lines. (Curiously, this seems to be true regardless of the width of the lines.) If there is no logical breaking point after about 15 lines in a paragraph, break at the next convenient point.

Each paragraph does *not* require a topic sentence at the beginning; in fact, it is questionable whether most paragraphs need one at all. Topic sentences would convert each paragraph into a small inverted pyramid, but that is too rigid a discipline for writers and would bore readers.*

---

* This advice casts doubt upon the notion we can read quickly yet fully by concentrating on first sentences. Such a communication system could succeed only if all writers wrote topic sentences at the beginnings of all paragraphs, which is all but unthinkable.

It is also *not* true that a paragraph must contain more than one sentence. An effective way to emphasize an idea is to write it as a very short sentence and make it a separate paragraph. It practically jumps off the page, because that short idea stands out so singularly from the surrounding ones. Resist the temptation to do this very often, however; the text may begin looking like an outline instead of a carefully written collection of information. (For other common misbeliefs, see "The Three Taboos," on page 52, and "Changing Verb Tenses," on page 44.)

The page that follows is planned thoughtfully for the reader. It uses headings, there is white space at the paragraph breaks, and groups of ideas are divided into paragraphs of convenient lengths.

Summary

The "Be Proud, America" history course tested at Richard Whalen High School shows promise that television can provide new effective ways of teaching in the public schools. But much broader testing is needed, at schools throughout the U.S. and on all major subjects. Also needed is higher quality television than we could produce with our modest foundation grant.

The course, used in classrooms in the 1995–96 school year, combines the skill of the classroom teacher and the power of TV. Course materials consist of 16 videotaped sessions (one each week), student workbooks, and a teacher's guide. The lessons, a mixture of fact and historical theory, are entirely compatible with conventional courses. This course is intended to be taught *as part of,* not instead of, conventional ones; one lesson per week is provided.

"Be Proud, America" was given to half of the ninth and tenth grade students at Whalen in 1995–96. Records were kept both for the test group and for the students taking the prescribed course. Most of the test group enjoyed the educational experience. Almost all participating teachers felt their students learned more, as a result of the video enhancement, than the half who received only the conventional curriculum. Comparison records confirmed this.

Introduction

"Be Proud, America" was born in the fall of 1994. A group of English and History teachers from Whalen High School had seen a videotaped course called "The Amazing 20th Century," produced by Coldstream College and the National Educational Television network and designed to help adults studying for U.S. citizenship. The Whalen faculty and administration were excited by its new instructional methods. The school received a grant of $22,100 from the Mildred Holden Jackson Foundation

---

The Hippopotamus Joke

This zoo manager was about to be fired. The trouble was that the zoo needed two hippopotamuses, but he kept putting off ordering them because he didn't know whether to say *hippopotamuses* or *hippopotami*.

When you get desperate enough you often find a way, and he did. On the last desperate day he writes the hippopotamus company (or wherever you buy hippopotamuses) and says: "Gentlemen: Will you please send to the undersigned one healthy adult hippopotamus?" So he signs his name, then adds: "P.S.—As long as you're sending one, make it two."

Moral: There is a right way of saying anything, but you usually don't find it by piling more junk on the wrong way.

(Also see: "The Penguin Joke," page 77; "Salutations, Gentlemen," page 149; "The undersigned," page 45.)

in 1995. The goal: to test whether a part-video course could help students learn and appreciate American and world history.

In the summer of 1995 the Whalen High School auditorium was converted into a television studio. The lessons were designed as panel discussions. All TV technicians, and all actors except one history teacher, were high school students. Technical assistance was contributed by Sony Corporation, and in September, 1995, "Be Proud, America" began its pilot testing by ninth and tenth grade Whalen students.

Conclusion

Because these results are exciting but immensely inconclusive, I strongly recommend that the Oxford School Board seek funding through the Florida Department of Education for further research and testing.

Discussion

In Phase 1 pilot testing, "Be Proud, America" has proved beneficial to the students who took it. It presented pedagogies new to the teachers and helpful to the students. Some improvements were recommended; they are listed below. With them, the Whalen faculty and staff feel that the course could well provide an institutional change in education—a model curriculum for the teaching of history throughout the United States. All agreed such changes. . . . [Several pages follow, with subheadings further dividing the text.]

Here is that same passage—but with just a barely noticeable lead-in word where each heading was before, and little thought is given to convenient paragraph breaks:

SUMMARY: The "Be Proud, America" history course tested at Richard Whalen High School shows promise that television can provide new effective ways of teaching in the public schools. But much broader testing is needed, at schools throughout the U.S. and on all major subjects. Also needed is higher quality television than we could produce with our modest foundation grant. The course, used in classrooms in the 1995–96 school year, combines the skill of the classroom teacher and the power of TV. Course materials consist of 16 videotaped sessions (one each week), student workbooks, and a teacher's guide. The lessons, a mixture of fact and historical theory, are entirely compatible with conventional courses. This course is intended to be taught *as part of,* not instead of, conventional ones; one lesson per week is provided.

"Be Proud, America" was given to half of the ninth and tenth grade students at Whalen in 1995–96. Records were kept both for the test group and for the students taking the prescribed course. Most of the test group enjoyed the educational experience. Almost all participating teachers felt their students learned more, as a result of the video enhancement, than the half who received only the conventional curriculum. Comparison records confirmed this.

INTRODUCTION: "Be Proud, America" was born in the fall of 1994. A group of English and History teachers from Whalen High School had seen a videotaped course called "The Amazing 20th Century," produced by Coldstream College and the National Educational Television network and designed to help adults studying for U.S. citizenship. The Whalen faculty and administration were excited by its new instructional methods. The school received a grant of $22,100 from the Mildred Holden Jackson Foundation in 1995. The goal: to test whether a part-video course could help students learn and appreciate American and world history. In the summer of 1995 the Whalen High School auditorium was converted into a television studio. The lessons were designed as panel discussions. All TV technicians, and all actors except one history teacher, were high school students. Technical assistance was contributed by Sony Corporation, and in September, 1995, "Be Proud, America" began its pilot testing by ninth and tenth grade Whalen students.

CONCLUSION: Because these results are exciting but immensely inconclusive, I strongly recommend that the Oxford School Board seek funding through the Florida Department of Education for further research and testing.

DISCUSSION: In Phase 1 pilot testing, "Be Proud, America" has proved beneficial to the students who took it. It presented pedagogies new to the teachers and helpful to the students. Some improvements were recommended; they are listed below. With them, the Whalen faculty and staff feel that the course could well provide an institutional change in education—a model curriculum for the teaching of history throughout the United States. All agreed such changes. . . . [Several pages follow.]

THE TREATMENT OF GRAPHIC INFORMATION

Graphs, charts, tables, drawings, photographs, and other forms of graphic information are often important parts of a presentation, sometimes as important as the text itself—especially in reports. How they are presented makes a difference to readers, and *presentation software programs* for computers allow ordinary writers—even those unskilled in graphic arts—to create eyebrow-raising graphics that were unheard of a few years ago. These are discussed briefly in Chapter 8, but for full and understandable discussion many excellent books on the subject are available.

Even without computers, impressive graphic presentations can be produced by the various time-honored methods that carried most of the information to most of the world before cybernetics changed our lives. One of the most important questions writers must consider when using graphics of any kind is: *Where should they be placed?* As always in questions about writing, the answer is based on what is most helpful to the reader.

For documents with only a few pages of text, graphs, tables, drawings, photographs, and other forms of graphic information should be placed as attachments at the end, the same as for enclosures to a business letter.

But in long or complicated reports a merciful rule is: *Try to avoid sending the reader elsewhere to understand what he or she is reading.* Generally, each graph, table, and the like should appear in the body of the report—on the page where it is discussed if possible, or on the next page. Graphics should be grouped at the end (in an appendix) only when there are so many that interspersing them up front would interfere with the flow of information for the reader or when they are definitely unimportant (optional) reading.

Every piece of graphic information in the report, front or back, should be mentioned in the text; if it is important enough to be there it is important enough to be discussed, at least briefly.

Explain Those Graphics to Readers

Each one needs a full, detailed caption. The unsure writer may presume readers can examine those graphs, charts, tables, and photographs as intelligently as he or she can. The opposite is almost surely true. After all, *the writer* probably developed them and is intimately familiar with the information each one contains. Each caption acknowledges that the reader may benefit here from a little special help; each one should be an overview statement—a brief summary of what the writer hopes readers would learn if they studied the graphic in detail. It may be as long as 4 or 5 lines (rarely longer); a caption should tell enough that the reader learns the highlights without studying the graph, chart, or table carefully *and without reading its detailed discussion in the text.* This means some repeating, but only of key information. This kind of repetition is merci-

---

Should You Spell Numbers?
The basic rule is simple. Spell out one-digit numbers (one through nine); use numerals for all numbers having two or more digits. There are some exceptions, but they are logical and simple. Use numerals for all numbers in dates, for street addresses, for all units of measure (pounds, miles, degrees, etc.), and for enumerations (such as page and chapter numbers) no matter how low or high. Also, use numerals for all numbers in a sentence that contains both kinds (209 applicants for 5 jobs); the idea here is to be consistent within any sentence.

ful and adds little to the length. Each graphic and its caption should be capable of standing alone, fully self-explanatory.

BULLETS, SYMBOLS, AND SPECIAL TYPEFACES

Modern typography and the computer have given writers (so we can give to readers) the good life.

Skilled writers know many ways to help readers by singling out key words or short passages for attention. When we talk, we intuitively raise or lower our voices, gesture with our hands, or pause to emphasize key ideas to our listener. The developing writer should become familiar with a few simple tools that will achieve similar results with the written word. These are most useful for expository writing, however; they are rarely used in novels, short stories, or other narrative forms of discourse.

In the past, typewriters offered only <u>underlining</u> or CAPITAL LETTERS; writers envied commercial printers, who could use:

Italics

Boldface type

- Bullets (also ①, ②, ③, etc.)

✦ Symbols (also ☺, ☎, ♪, ➡, etc.)

Special effect typefaces (use sparingly if at all)

Today almost every word processing computer program gives writers those excellent tools.

Boldface type is commonly used for titles, subtitles, and section headings. It is a superb aid; it draws the reader to those very important signposts, which in turn provide overview information along the way.

Italicized type provides that same advantage *within the text,* to highlight an individual word or a short passage.

Bullets (dots at the beginning of lines or paragraphs) emphasize a list of items or ideas. Listing short phrases vertically gives much greater emphasis than on continuous lines separated by commas. For full paragraphs of information, the bullets and vertical listing allow the reader to pause between the ideas and to ponder them individually. (We used numbers for these purposes before bullets were available, but they command less attention. Unless the numbers are important, bullets are preferred.)

The first use of bullets in this book appears on page 12; the second is on page 35.

Most of these marvelously helpful tools are used throughout this book—and in other books and publications all of our lives. Surprisingly, however, many developing writers overlook them.

Do not overuse them, however, or the effect is lost.

FACT AND FANCY ABOUT LETTERS

All the advice on clarity and structure in this book applies to business letters as much as to any other kind of writing. Only a few things about letters are different, and those are procedural, based on the needs of the workplace. (See the College Park Industries sample letter on page 150; it is clearly written, well organized, and attractively laid out.)

The address block.   Include in this order: name; title*; department (if you include one); company; street address; city, state, and zip code. Notice that the name of the addressee ordinarily belongs on the first line, not in an attention line at the bottom of the address block. (Commonly, an attention line is used only when sending legal or financial documents; it carries the thought that the document is addressed to the company [or other organization], not the individual.)

The subject line.   Is one needed? It may be useful, but only if the *writer's* company (or organization) requires it for filing purposes, or if it serves some specific purpose for the reader. Two rules are important for subject lines if they are used at all:

1. Keep them short—subject *line,* not paragraph. If this line gets longer than a few words, the file clerk gets different choices of subjects or key words for filing.
2. Never refer to the subject line in the body of the letter; doing so would penalize the reader by making him or her look two different places to piece the information together. This means thoughtful writers should avoid referring to the "above subject customer," or the "above subject equipment," or the "above subject" anything.

The salutation.   Use the name of the addressee if you know it: *Dear Mr. Zielinski,* or *Dear Ms. Collins.* (*Gentlemen* and *Dear Sir* are, of course,

---

* Name and title may be on the same line or separate lines, usually depending on the length of the title.

COLLEGE PARK INDUSTRIES, INC.
160 East Campus Way   Hardin, MT 58104
Phone: (406) 891-1500 . Fax: (406) 891-1501 . email: colpark@aol.com

April 28, 1997

Mr. Hans W. Blake, Distribution Manager
CD Specialty Productions, Inc.
17162 Vermont Plaza
Brooklyn, NY 21409

Dear Hans,

Thanks for your April 22 letter and the accompanying audio specifications for your presentation at the Rock 'n Roll Hall of Fame. You'll be pleased with our test results. Yes, the Pentone Suppression System performed quite well; in fact, it exceeded your requirements by 22 percent. And the savings when you're ready to market this release should be exactly as you calculated them. Dealers will like that.

You will have one problem, however. Single-phase shipments are getting larger all the time. The reason? Today's engineers and designers have accepted the principle that one-piece construction costs less even if it means sectioning and reassembling. As a result, there may be complications getting the display to Cleveland, and you may have to ship it there by air freight. Bix Rosen thinks you should do that anyhow.

We measured the Pentone performance using both the ASA/IS specifications *and* the Harvard-May protocol. (That's pretty standard procedure, as you know.) The results were almost identical, well within standard variances. Computer printouts of both are attached. *You'll like this, Hans.* The UMontana lab people could hardly believe CD Specialty is going to market such quality music. (They understand, of course, that under our contract the research and its results are highly confidential.)

About your Hall of Fame sales meeting, yes, I'll be happy to co-chair the distributors' presentation with General Physics' Caitlin Farrow. We're both familiar enough with your company that I'm sure we can answer questions about the new strategy.

There is, however, the ever-present question about some of the low end products being imported. Within the next week I will send you a list of points Ms. Farrow and I would probably want someone to clarify for us well in advance.

Best regards,

Betsy

Betsy N. Nakamura
Vice president, Media Operations

A clear, well organized, and attractively designed business letter.

unthinkable.) When we must write to a person by title, name unknown (formerly the *Dear Sir* situation), his or her title forms the salutation: *Dear Sales Manager,* or *Dear Research Director.* When neither a name nor a title is available (formerly the *Gentlemen* situation), *Dear Reader* seems to be the best the experts have been able to recommend. *Dear Sir or Madam* or *Gentlepersons* just will not do. One easy solution: A phone call to a telephone operator or secretary will usually get the information needed for a more specific and courteous salutation.

The various salutations are not interchangeable; with a little thought, the right one is easy to find.

And what of the word *Dear* at the beginning of the salutation? Drop it if you like. Most readers will not even notice it is missing if the rest of the letter is warm and courteous, and, of course, if the letter is cold, *Dear* will not make it warmer.* But do not drop the entire salutation—just the word *Dear,* if you wish to be a little on the modern side. Also, avoid using off-beat salutations such as *Good morning Ms. Robinson,* etc.

What salutation should you use when unsure whether the person being written to is a man or woman? Find out. Again, a phone call will usually provide the information needed for an accurate and courteous salutation.

The opening sentence. Many people use a cliché opening. That is, some group of words used routinely to convey an implied meaning. Misguided writers often use clichés for convenience—as a substitute for thinking of an individual opening for each letter. Such openings have all the sparkle of a bureaucratic form letter, and they make any letter sound like one. (Indeed, these clichés are most common in form letters, where the motive is often to be as general as possible, so the same wording can fit as many situations as possible.)

Enlightened writers should avoid opening sentences containing such worn out clichés as *in response to, with reference to, in accordance with,* or *relative to.* They are badly overused and suggest that the writer did not put much work or thought into the opening. They are extraordinarily dull and project the image of a cold, uncaring bureaucrat. Here is an example of a typical cliché opening; the first sentence and part of the second contain three rubber stamp phrases:

---

* The author has not used "*Dear*" in a salutation in over two decades. When asked, most readers reported they did not notice its absence; those who did notice usually described the difference as unimportant.

The Case for Pronouns

To every person who ever paused, uncertain, not knowing whether to write *you and I* or *you and me,* similarly *he and she* or *him and her,* this advice: *Get your cases straight.*

Few people have trouble dealing with one pronoun at a time; nor is there likely to be trouble with two pronouns when they are subjects: *She and I discussed this with the doctor.* Only linguistic weaklings would say, *Her and me discussed. . . .* But adults who are otherwise capable and intelligent often collapse into whimpering heaps when confronted with two pronouns used together as *objects,* and we may see: *The doctor discussed this with she and I.*

Avoiding that kind of trouble is this simple; you do not even need to understand pronoun cases: *Use the same forms for two pronouns together as you would for either one alone.* If the doctor discussed this with *her* and also discussed it with *me,* then: *The doctor discussed this with her and me.*

Dear Jessica,

In response to your letter of February 19 *relative to* defective merchandise purchased at our store, the exact warranty terms on this matter are complex. *With regard to* the location of purchase, the manufacturer claims that. . . .

That creates the impression it was written by a rubber stamp with arms and legs. Here is the opening again, this time with thoughtful, original statements that apply specifically to this situation. Notice how much more they tell:

Dear Jessica,

Thank you for your letter of February 19 requesting that our store replace your defective television camera. The exact warranty terms on this matter are complex. Because you purchased the camera in Hong Kong, the manufacturer claims that. . . .

People who defend such cliché openings do so on the grounds that the beginning of a letter should serve as a summary. Yes, some kind of briefing may be useful (although it is not always necessary), but, in fact, writers who do want a briefing at the beginning should notice (as above) that the individually worded opening gives a far better, more informative one than the stereotyped opening in the first version of that letter. And the precise wording tells the reader this is a letter written specifically to her, as opposed to a form letter to be filled in with generalities that require little thought.

CHAPTER 12

When Writers Become Speakers

It's a terrible death, to be talked to death.

—*Mark Twain*

It is the same English language, and the communication principles remain the same. But when the sender will be *speaking* and the receiver *listening,* the roles of both change in important ways, and so do the rules. And if we understand these, even without silver-tongued oratorical skills we can captivate audiences; the right message and an ordinary speaking voice will get the job done. There is even a fool-proof butterfly repellant. Of course, a carefully planned message is the first requirement; without it, even a silver tongue will not save the day.

When Readers Become Listeners

Experienced speakers are aware of these fundamental differences:

Readers can receive at the speed most comfortable to them, but listeners must receive at the speed set by the sender. Nor can listeners do something important that readers take for granted and do regularly: stop for a moment to clarify some point, or even go back and reexamine a whole passage. The speaker has a heavy responsibility, then, to deliver his or her message successfully *the first and only time*. And so, in speaking as in writing, clear language and well-organized ideas will establish a tie between the sender and his or her receiver. They will carry the message the way it should be carried.

The speaker's main advantage: a captive audience.   We know that *readers* of expository information, in the privacy of their own surroundings, do not feel compelled to read carefully to the end. Or interruptions may prevent them from doing so. Listeners are the opposite; they rarely leave early, and for that reason the speaker gets a major gift he or she rarely enjoys as a writer: the almost certain knowledge that the receiver will be exposed to the whole story.

Speaker's disadvantage no. 1: the clock.   Rare indeed, and lucky, is the speaker who has enough time to cover the subject fully. Writers usually have the freedom to write as much (or as little) as they need in order to convey the message fully, but speakers are encased in a rigid block of time and cannot leave early or stay late. A new burden, then, is loaded upon the oral communicator: watching the clock, and adjusting accordingly. But the day is saved if the speaker employs the same tool that is a mainstay of expository *writing:* the inverted pyramid structure. (See Chapter 9.) This speaker can proceed without worry, knowing that as time runs down the information not yet covered keeps getting less important and can be shortened, or even dropped, if needed.

Speaker's disadvantage no. 2: a live audience.   Readers are never aware of the mistakes writers make and correct, or the awkward passages they nurse and massage later. But if the poor speaker, standing alone up there, makes a mistake, it shouts out and can never be hidden or taken back. How do speakers avoid displaying their mistakes in public? The same way writers do: by making and correcting them privately.

WRITE THE SPEECH?

Emphatically, yes. This will be the only opportunity to plan for perfection, to pave the way for success in front of the audience.

But there will be less time to write it as the date draws nearer, and countless inexperienced speakers can tell stories of horror and regret that ensued from the last-minute "*Oh well, I'll just work from an outline*" decision.

Talk about Ending with Prepositions . . .

The child asked the parent: What did you bring a book I didn't want to be read *to out of up for?*

An exact outline (see Chapter 10) is a must, but it is not enough. The speaker-to-be should write the *full* speech, as early as possible, for two reasons:

Up there before an audience, speakers do not have time to search for words and phrases to express each idea.   There is no time to examine one way, then another, until the best way is found to express each one. The speaker who has not chosen those *just right* words in advance is far less likely to reach for them and find them at the moment they are needed, and the resulting words are likely to be far less sparkling than his or her best.

Most speakers who capture audiences with just the right way of saying things, and are admired for it, plan that success in advance. They know they have to be *writers* before they can be the kinds of *speakers* who enthrall audiences and end with a feeling of deep satisfaction.

Writing the speech is the first rehearsal for giving it.   And it is probably the best rehearsal. Then, once the speaker-to-be has arrived at ideal ways to express each major idea, almost certainly he or she will read it at least once or twice to admire it and to look for shaky passages and correct them before the grand event. These repeated exposures become silent *rehearsals* for the grand event.

Gradually confidence, perhaps even a small amount of smugness, builds as the writer-speaker develops the attitude: *I know my subject, and I know that I know my subject, and I also know how to tell it.*

Connectives are even more important in speaking than they are in the writer-reader relationship.   (See Chapter 4.) They provide logical, smooth flow from idea to idea, and experienced, relaxed speakers look for key places to begin sentences with such convenient words as *And, But, Therefore, Next,* or *Nevertheless.* They are as important to listeners as to readers. Some gentle phrases can also carry an idea forward smoothly: *For this reason . . . You should understand that . . .* and *Even so. . . .* These and others like them are remarkably easy to use in writing and speaking, and the reward is great.

Memorize, and Deliver It from Memory?

This is excruciatingly hard for most people, and it is unnecessary and probably harmful. Delivering from memory risks creating a dull, monotonous style—as well as an image of insecurity. Monotonous because the speaker operating inside his or her memory may be too busy to think about vocal inflections. Insecure because there is the constant thought: "What if I forget those 'just right' words?"

But go up there unarmed? Only if the speaker is well rehearsed and extremely confident.

Some speakers deliver their presentation with a copy of the script in front of them. For occasional reference, and if it is used just for that purpose, audiences will not object. In this situation a few aids on the printed pages will help. The lines should be double-spaced (triple-spaced between paragraphs); the type should be large and dark but not glaring. Places suitable for brief pauses should be marked. Key ideas should be marked in color, so they can be found at a glance. The speaker will want to turn the pages in a way that attracts as little attention as possible, and so they should not be fastened.

Many speakers can deliver quite well this way, but turning the pages slowly, without attracting attention, is possible only if the speaker stands at a lectern; even then it may be tedious and require practice.

A better way is to reduce the full written text to a one-page outline. This may seem at first to be more risky than having the full text there for guidance; it is usually more helpful, however.* In either case we presume the speaker knows his or her subject thoroughly. The advantage of the outline, then, is that the entire plan is easy to see at all times. It not only provides the same section-by-section guidance as the full script; it does away with page turning. It also tells the speaker whether he or she is on schedule or needs to speed up or slow down. (Experienced speakers bring a small digital clock to the lectern to help stay on schedule.)

BUTTERFLY REPELLENT

Something remarkable happens in a room when a speaker knows the subject and has prepared reasonably to tell an audience about it. He or she exudes an aura, invisible but infectious to everyone involved. To the audience, it whispers: "This looks like it's going to be good." To the speaker, especially the inexperienced or nervous one, it is a steady reminder: "I'm the expert they came to hear, so this is going to be easy."

---

* But the speaker must resist the temptation to write the outline *instead of* writing the whole speech.

Butterflies will not approach this aura. It is called *confidence,* and in the absence of much speaking experience it is achieved by reasonable preparation.

THE THREE "TELL THEM" PARTS OF A SPEECH

Toastmasters, International and other speakers' groups traditionally advise: "*Tell* them what you're going to say—then *say* it—then *tell* them what you have said." This is almost identical to the recommended method of organizing expository writing; the difference is the summary restated at the end, not required in a report but important in a speech.

But: Like the expository writer, the thoughtful speaker may choose not to open with the conclusion if it will anger or alienate listeners and might cause them to leave. In these cases a thoughtful writer *or speaker* may be wise to present the supporting information first, leading inevitably to the unpopular conclusion. Here, the speaker has the advantage over the writer. He or she can build gradually to an unpopular conclusion without risk that the receiver will miss the supporting information.

How to end. If a written report is long, most *readers* will not (and should not need to) read to the end; the carefully planned summary (overview statement) at the beginning is the most important part, and the advice for ending reports is: When you have nothing more to say, just stop. But *listeners* will almost always be there at the end, and they usually want and expect a dramatic ending. The reason for this is little known: People enjoy applauding at the end of any performance; they feel the business is unfinished if there is no reason to say thank you as they leave. And so, wise speakers plan a fanfare at the end; hence, *tell them what you have said.* Speakers, too, enjoy the moment, but it is really planned to enhance the audience's feeling that the experience was worthwhile.

THAT PERSON AT THE LECTERN

What kind of image does the speaker project to the people out there? A well-prepared delivery is most important, of course, but much else can be done. Standing in front of his or her audience, the speaker is in a commanding position and has two important *special effects* available to enhance the delivery—advantages an invisible writer envies but can never enjoy quite as much.

None *Are* or None *Is* . . . ?

None began its Anglo-Saxon life as a contraction of *not one.* In that usage it is strictly singular and requires the verb *is* (*was, will be, etc.*). But through the centuries *none* gained broader usage, and today *none* often means *not any.* In that usage it took on the ability to be singular or plural—and to confound writers.

How to tell: First ask yourself whether your *none* is to mean *not one* or *not any.* If it serves as *not one* it is strictly singular: *Of all the mysteries about ships, none* (*not one*) *is more terrifying than the story of the Marie Celeste.* If it serves as *not any,* however, it may be singular or plural. Then ask yourself, "None (not any) of what?" The answer (a prepositional phrase beginning with *of*) will make clear whether you are in the singular or plural: *None* (*not any*) *of this food* (*singular*) *is fresh.* But: *None* (*not any*) *of us* (*plural*) *are going to touch it.*

The principle here is: The noun (or pronoun) in the prepositional phrases governs whether the verb is singular or plural. If you are unsure, most experts advise none *are* is usually safer than none *is.*

Special Effects of the Voice

Writers can use special typefaces (capital letters, italics, or boldface type) to add emphasis at key points. Speakers have more effective tools available to add emphasis *and variety,* and the speaker who fails to use them pays dearly.

Voice inflections. Speakers can raise or lower the voice for special emphasis, and the effect on listeners is dramatic, a welcome change of pace. It adds emotional impact that is much harder to achieve on a printed page. And, unlike special typefaces, which must be used sparingly, the raised or lowered voice may be used fairly often. Speakers should look for opportunities to deliver impact in this way, especially at key points.

The dramatic pause. How easy it is, and how effective. And the longer the pause, the more effective. But very long pauses (perhaps 7 or 8 seconds) deliver so much impact that wise speakers use them sparingly, and carefully. The long pause followed by a passage in a raised voice can have a blockbuster effect on the audience.*

Body Language

Most public speaking experts advise that occasional hand gestures enhance the speaker's image,† and a frequent first rule is *use only one hand, never both.* Keep the other hand motionless at all times, ideally holding the edge of the lectern platform. The *in motion* hand should spend most of its time resting at the other edge, but it may be called into action to punctuate words, phrases, or sentences (with mild gestures) from time to time along the way. This posture will create a calm, controlled mood. (On the other hand, the speaker who cannot keep that other hand stationary, out of trouble, will sacrifice an advantage never available to writers.)

VISUAL AIDS

The first rule for speakers using visual aids of any kind is: Check everything in advance. The speaker who discovers *in front of the audience* that

---

* Experienced speakers know also that pauses can serve as camouflage if they need a moment to think.
† The advice differs, however, for very formal speeches. Here, gestures of any kind are inappropriate; both hands should generally be out of sight.

something does not work loses credibility, and he or she may not regain it fully. Especially important: Using unfamiliar equipment is risky; experienced speakers always arrive early to ensure that the correct equipment is installed, that it works properly, *and that they know how to use it.*

Television and multimedia.   Only short segments should be shown, if any. Audiences do not come to watch TV, or to be impressed by production techniques, and experienced speakers use these only to deliver information that slides or transparencies or the speaker's own words cannot provide.

Slides and transparencies.   Their image is usually much larger and brighter than television, and they can be prepared quickly and inexpensively—especially with computers. Anyone today can produce remarkably attractive and impressive projections, using simple and inexpensive software programs. This solemn warning, to avoid looking like a novice: *Be sure the type is large enough that it can be read easily by everyone, including the people at the back of the room. DO NOT try to project typewritten material (or similar pages done by computer) or material copied from books or magazines.*

Flip charts.   A reliable tool of speakers in the past, these have largely given way to the more effective slides we can now produce on home computers. When is the old-fashioned paper chart still useful—and fashionable? When the information is fresh and cannot be prepared in advance. This is usually when the speaker wants to list information from members of the audience, especially if he or she will use that list to invite audience discussion. (But many speakers prefer overhead [transparency] projectors for this.)

THE SPEAKER'S VOICE SKILLS

Speakers new at this business who may be shaky about their speaking skills should relax with this knowledge: Audiences expect a competent speaking style, but not necessarily that you sound like a TV host. They care much more about the *message* than about fancy delivery skills. Careful planning, a well-written speech, and ordinary speaking skills will win the day. And if careful planning and good writing are not there, no amount of silver-tongued delivery—not even a dramatic ending—will bring much applause.

CHAPTER 13

Managing the Writing of Others

A watchdog that barks at every squirrel isn't very useful.

—*Elliot Ness*

Surveys have shown for decades that in most organizations writing is one of the most important employee skills, especially at the management level. Human resource departments often consider it the second most important, and most large corporations and government agencies conduct ongoing classes to improve writing skills; some train thousands of employees a year.

Like any other professional skill, employees' writing is certainly the manager's business. But writing is more difficult to evaluate than most other job skills, because there is no universal "right way" to say things, and there are no performance standards to measure quality. And, because the writing in an office environment is so visible, many bosses have strong feelings about it and seem to become self-appointed experts. They may not always be experts, however, and trouble can sometimes arise. Some guidelines, therefore, are important.

In reviewing and editing the writing of others,* one questionable habit is most common: Some managers may be tempted to think the best way to write anything is the way *they* would have written it. This attitude is sometimes questionable and may create poor employee relations. There may be several ways to write anything, all equally good. *Even though the manager may be the better writer, it is unreasonable to expect that someone else should write a thing the way he or she would have written it.*

Another questionable procedure when managing other people's writing is changing things just for change's sake. For example, why change *A large number of our stores . . .* to *Many of our stores . . .?* True, that change makes the writing a bit shorter, and it would be fine in one's own writing, but it is too minor a change to make in other people's. Again, it is poor employee relations, because it stifles initiative. Enlightened managers try never to give employees a chance to call them nitpickers about any subject, including writing. How many times in the corridors of the world of work have we heard, "They're going to change everything anyhow, so what's the sense of taking the time to do a good job in the first place?" Sometimes that accusation is justified.

When reviewing someone else's writing, a wise attitude seems to be: *I'm a watchdog; my job is to ensure that what goes out meets our standards.* A really wise watchdog should rejoice, however, if it is not necessary to bark. A wise manager should rejoice if an employee's work is so good it needs little or no supervision.

THE TROUBLE EVALUATING WRITING SKILLS

Still, there are some things a reviewer has a right to expect. This six-point checklist seems reasonable for evaluating someone else's writing:

✓ Is the content correct?
✓ Are the words clear and precise?
✓ Are the ideas divided properly into sentences?
✓ Is the conclusion at the beginning?
✓ Is the tone courteous?
✓ Are there headings to help the reader?

---

* *Reviewing* is generally for content (*what* is written), and *editing* for writing quality (*how* it is written). In most organizations the manager does both. Very large corporations and government agencies often have professional editors whose job is to read all important letters and reports and help the writer if help is needed.

If the answer to these questions is yes, the reviewer should rejoice. But what happens when we must honestly conclude that the writing is not good enough?

WHEN AND HOW TO GIVE HELP

Many managers or reviewers rewrite it themselves. This is unwise, for two reasons. First, if something is poorly written the reviewer may misinterpret and say the *wrong thing* in trying to clarify it. Second, rewriting his or her work does not help the weak writer. If the work needs rewriting, the reviewer can help most by pointing out exactly what is wrong and how to correct it. Are sentences too long? Words too complex? Is the organization weak? This kind of feedback—guidance from the manager—is necessary if the subordinate is to improve. Both will benefit; the subordinate will learn to improve an important professional skill, and the boss will need to spend less time editing and rewriting in the future.

Very minor editing and revising may not require discussion with the writer. But if changes are so extensive they reveal a basic writing deficiency, helping the writer improve may be one of the greatest favors a boss can do for an employee. Far more cruel would be to list this deficiency in a regularly scheduled performance review most employers require, without first trying to make help available. Employee training is one of the manager's responsibilities, in writing skills as much as in any other professional skill.

The outline review is most useful for major reports and presentations, and it is surprising that it is so often overlooked. Some companies call this the planning or *pre-editorial* review; it is a review of the content and the overall treatment the writer has in mind. Without it, a great deal of work can go wasted because an employee learns *after* writing that the approach taken was not what the manager wanted. How easily that wasted work could have been prevented.

Approving the outline should be as important as examining the fully written paragraphs and pages. Then, if managers can help improve the overall approach, or want some other approach, the writer learns of it in advance, and the finished paragraphs and pages need review only for editorial style—basic clarity and organization. And that is exactly the way it should be.

Always remember: Language is a communications tool—nothing more—a living tool of a living society. It is a means to an end, not an end in itself. The noble goal of the expository writer is to provide as much information as possible, as accurately and clearly as possible, in as little reading as possible. That is the only purpose for which cultures create language. For the expository writer, it is the only reason we write.

Simile: For Easy Description
A simile is a group of words that makes a direct comparison to something else, usually to create an image (You behaved *like a child*; The rear engine of the DC-10 is as large *as the entire body of the old DC-3*). Different from a metaphor, in which the comparison is indirect. (See page 38.)

PART 3

On Grammar

CHAPTER 14

What Is Grammar?

Sloppy writing instantly reveals the sloppy mind.

—James Kilpatrick

Grammar is a set of rules, really, for using a language. Its purpose is to help people understand each other by requiring them to follow the *same rules*—to use the language as closely as possible to the same way. You might compare grammar to traffic signals; everywhere in the world a green light means *go* and red means *stop*. Such rules exist only because people decided they would be useful and created them, and they are useful only to the extent people follow them.

Almost all these rules are based in the *sentence*. Indeed, in language as in traffic, the most important signs are *go* (capital letter) and *stop* (period). Few things in grammar go beyond a sentence; almost everything serves to regulate the arrangement of words and punctuation marks between one capital letter and its accompanying period. The noble purpose of it all: To broadcast a single idea one person is trying to convey to another so clearly that the reader (or listener) receives exactly that and only that idea. The person who can do that can write any thoughts his or her brain is capable of creating—whether a business report or a great novel.

HOW DO WE LEARN IT?

At first, by picking up language patterns from our home environment. Most of us learned some formal rules in school, but much of our knowledge of grammar comes to us intuitively, beginning in infancy. By the time the young child begins to talk, his or her brain has already recognized basic language patterns and learned to mimic them. (For example, even before they have learned to talk, babies in English-speaking cultures have learned to recognize the differences between *I, me,* and *my.* The youngest child says "*I* want . . . ," and "Give *me* . . . ," or "*my* doggie.")

Whatever language patterns the child is exposed to in the home environment he or she will learn as "correct," whether the Old English of *Beowulf,* the aristocratic English of *Oxford,* the nonstandard English or street talk of some American ethnic groups, or one of the many dialects of Sinhalese spoken in Sri Lanka.

WHAT MAKES GRAMMAR CORRECT?

Perhaps *correct* is the wrong word; most language scholars agree that *acceptance* of a language style is more relevant than whether one style of usage is *better* than another.

Whether you prefer "*He be's the coolest*" or "*Ontogeny recapitulates phylogeny,*" we really do not accomplish much by arguing which is better language usage. Each may be better *in its own environment,* and social or professional groups develop their own language styles and guard them jealously.

More important than which is better, then, is the question: "Which language style will get you where you want to be?"

WHO DECIDES WHAT IS "STANDARD"?

The public, really. That is, the people with clout. But they are not the authors, the television writers, the speech makers, or the many others who create the things we read and hear. Rather, the people who read and listen to them are the ones who have the real clout—who determine what is or is not acceptable. Whether for a scholarly dissertation or a beer commercial, the writer's choice of language style is influenced by those who must respond to it.

Linguists and scholars do identify a style they call "standard English." It is a moderate style, somewhere between academia and beer-macho, and it is the style used by newspapers, magazines, and television and radio stations. There is a reason for this: The style derives its solid foundation from the rules of grammar and usage as they have been collected and examined by such experts as H. W. Fowler, Otto Jespersen, and most recently such writers as William Safire and William and Mary Morris.

It's Feb**ru**ary, for Goodness Sake!

Let's start a national campaign to banish Febuary. This is a spoken nay-nay, never a written one, and those who squirm at its mention begin worrying each January that next month will have painful moments. We would like to think only klutzes say *Febuary,* but even some respected radio and television journalists have fallen to this heinous depravity. Males and females seem equally afflicted; nor have demographic variances been identified.

WHY DOES IT MATTER AS LONG AS PEOPLE UNDERSTAND YOU?

It matters for two reasons. First, the way we use language tells much more than just the word message being conveyed. Like clothing or hair style, a person's language style makes a strong unspoken statement. If the words and sentences do not quite follow the group's rules, people in that group will question his or her intelligence—or ability to do the job. They *shouldn't,* we may argue. But they *will*—whether they should or not. Likewise, if that person's language style does follow the group's standards, members of the group are likely to take a more kindly attitude and presume (at first, anyhow,) he or she is intelligent and capable—whether that is true or not. They will welcome his or her ideas with greater respect than if that language style does not comply with what they consider to be the "in" style. In the business and academic worlds, then, those whose language style follows the rules of standard English grammar always have a major advantage. *Remember: Whether it is fair or not, in any group we are judged as much on* HOW *we say things as on* WHAT *we say.*

Second, careful language is usually a sign of careful thinking. Obviously, the writer must *think* an idea clearly before he or she can express it clearly. Less obvious, however, is the opposite: Putting the ideas on paper also helps us think them out clearly. (See Chapter 10.)

Language skill, then, will first of all give others the impression the writer is a person of merit. It will also help the writer to think clearly and, therefore, to present his or her ideas in a clear, well-organized, hard-hitting way. Whether people say, "The dude is cool" or "This is a person whose ideas we should value," they are likely to be right.

For the Language Gourmet: What Is an Oxymoron?

It is a phrase, usually very short, made up of words that contain a built-in contradiction. (*Terribly* good, *pretty* ugly.) The term *oxymoron* describes the phrase, not the person using it. The contradiction must be in the literal meanings of the words; if it is figurative (as in *honest politicians, military intelligence*), whether there is a contradiction depends on the reader's point of view, and the phrase is not an oxymoron but just a sarcastic statement.

Ernest Hemingway, after being wounded as an ambulance driver in the Spanish Civil War, wrote: "It gives you an *awfully satisfactory* feeling. . . ." Undoubtedly he meant both.

CHAPTER 15

About English

I got into my bones the essential structure of the ordinary British sentence—which is a noble thing.

—Winston Churchill

Of the 4000 known languages, English is the native tongue of more people (approximately 650 million) than any other except Mandarin Chinese. In the number who employ it as their native or second language, it is by far the most widely used—and rapidly increasing its lead. English is truly the international language of politics (replacing French), science (replacing German), education (replacing Latin), commerce, and the arts.

English's emergence as the world's dominate language is due in part, of course, to recent world history; British and U.S. political interests, and U.S. business ingenuity, have carried English to every remote part of the world. But a large part of the credit must go to the language itself. English is a remarkable language with a fascinating history and an unlikely combination of diverse characteristics. Its vocabulary and structure offer a wide choice of images and rhythms to satisfy the poets; its efficiency provides scientists and engineers the precise expression they need; and, at the same time, its simple grammar and words (yes, they are) make it easy to learn—and the ideal language for plain talk in complex documents.

ITS REMARKABLE HISTORY

English is in the broad category of languages known as Indo-European. Its origin goes back about 2500 years, and probably the one influence that most contributed to its development was military occupation. Historians divide its development into four important periods: Pre-English (roughly 500 B.C. to 500 A.D.), Old English (500 to 1100 A.D.), Middle English (1100 to 1500), and Modern English (1500 to present). Dictionaries refer to these as PreE, OE, ME, and ModE.

Celtic Roots

The first inhabitants of Britain that historians know much about were the Celts, who migrated approximately 500 B.C. from the part of continental Europe called Gaul (later to become France). Historians generally refer to the people as Celtic and their language as Gaelic. This language does not at all resemble English or French, but it was the beginning of both. (It is still recognizable in the dialects of Scotland, Ireland, and Wales—and the French province of Brittany.)

The Romans invaded Britain in 43 A.D. and occupied it and influenced every facet of its culture for several centuries. Under Roman rule, the Celts (who now called themselves Britons) probably enjoyed greater security, freedom, and comfort than English peoples in any period until very recent history. But Roman soldiers apparently did not socialize much with the Britons; we assume this because the Gaelic language in Britain did not pickup many traces of Latin. (In Gaul it did; that is why French is one of the Romance languages and English is not.) Roman rulers did, however, impose their alphabet on the Britons. It was an unfortunate legacy, as the 26-letter Roman alphabet does not fit the 43 sounds of English very well.

The Celts produced no significant writers or poets. Greek and Roman authors of this period were creating works of such wisdom and beauty that they still endure as classical literature and probably will forever. But we know of no important Celtic writing or writers.

Old English (500 to 1100 A.D.)

"The cantons should take steps to defend themselves." With these words in the year 410, the Emperor Honorius issued warning of the decline and fall of the Roman Empire. Most of Europe would enter a 600-year period known as the Dark Ages, and the Anglo-Saxon (OE) period of British history was about to begin.

As Rome's economy weakened and its armies throughout Europe could no longer control the occupied lands, European tribes again dared to cross the English Channel, following the trek the Celts and

An Ongoing Controversy

In 1974 the Conference of College Composition and Communication, a branch of the National Council of Teachers of English, issued the policy statement: "We affirm the students' right to their own patterns and varieties of language—the dialects of their nurture or whatever dialects in which they find their own identity and style."

The well-meaning educators could hardly have issued a more troublesome statement. Most educators, including minority leaders, felt strongly that minority children *must* learn the language of the society in which they hope to share a slice of the pie, and that one of the most solemn obligations of our education system is to ensure they learn it.

The subject of standard English for African-American students is still controversial. In 1996 the Oakland, California Board of Education voted to treat *Ebonics*, a pattern of English often called *Black English,* as the primary language of many of its students and to teach them in that language. Again powerful voices in both races objected. But when the issue was clarified it became understood that Oakland's goal really was to use Ebonics as a shortcut to help its black students master standard English; students were not going to be taught Ebonics.

Romans had taken centuries earlier, and Britain was invaded again. This time the invaders were Vikings. They came up the rivers in their long boats first just to plunder and to take home gold and jewels from the churches. But gradually they learned that this warm, gentle island provided an easier life than their native lands of northern Europe, and they came to stay. The most durable of these were the Angles (who gave England its name), Saxons, Picts, Frisians, and Jutes. They were Teutonic peoples, from the area that is now northern Germany, Holland, and Denmark. Their languages were Germanic and would blend with the Gaelic of the native Britons, to form the beginning of English. Old English, then, is a mixture of Gaelic and Teutonic.

But the Viking marauders, after they became settlers, were interested mostly in farming; therefore, they did not pursue the native Britons who pulled back into the mountainous, less hospitable areas to the west (Wales) or north (Scotland), or across the straits to Ireland. In those areas, as a result, the two cultures and languages did not mix. That is why, today, Gaelic is still very evident in the Welsh, Scottish, and Irish languages (though not so evident in their spoken dialects today).

The Anglo-Saxon period is the period of King Arthur and the Knights of the Round Table. (Most historians believe they existed and fought fiercely against early Viking plunderers.) More notable kings were Alfred the Great, Aethelred the Unready, Canute (or Cnut), and Harthcanute. But the most famous of all was the last of the Anglo-Saxon kings, Edward the Confessor, who set the stage for the events that unfolded one October day of 1066 outside a village called Hastings.

The outstanding literary work of the Old English period is the epic poem *Beowulf,* an adventure story of heroes and dragons, written about 700 A.D. by Anglo-Saxon monks. It is not a particularly engaging story, but it is important because it tells us a great deal about life and beliefs in those times. The language is so different from Modern English, however, that an untrained reader could not possibly understand *Beowulf* without help from a specialist.

Middle English (1100 to 1500 A.D.)

The Norman period. British kings in the Old English (Anglo-Saxon) period reigned over a shaky empire. Powerful dukes and earls ruled large areas, commanding their own armies of feudal serfs, and they could usually influence the kings or ignore them. By the time of Edward the Confessor, however, the power structure was changing, and England had become, to a large extent, a unified nation. Edward was a beloved king, deeply religious. (He built Westminster Abbey and several other cathedrals.) But he and Queen Edith had no children. There was widespread fear that civil war would erupt among the noblemen to determine who would be king if he died without a successor, and so he was pressured to name one. Edward had strong ties to Normandy, a northern neighbor of France and today part of France. He had been raised there (in exile), and his mother was a Norman. In 1051 he named his cousin William, Duke of Normandy, to succeed him on his death as king of England. But before dying in January 1066, Edward named another cousin, Harold Godwin, to be king. Harold II, not Edward the Confessor, was actually the last of the Anglo-Saxon kings—but for such a short time that few people know of him. He was Edward's brother-in-law, son of the powerful Earl of Wessex (the "Kingmaker"), and it is likely that Wessex ruled for the dying king and made the appointment himself.

Poor Harold II (there has never been a Harold III). Evidence suggests he might have been an able king, but he did not live long enough to prove it. Two things prevented it: (1) the Vikings were restless again, and (2) the Duke of Normandy was, to say the least, unhappy at the appointment.

Vikings who stayed in Scandinavia (and now called themselves *Danes*) had never completely stopped their raids on the earlier Vikings who had migrated across the Channel (and now called themselves *Englishmen*). In fact, Anglo-Saxon kings often paid heavy ransoms of gold (called *Danegeld*) to buy peace. The death of Edward the Confessor was an invitation for the Danes to step up their harassment, to test the new king. They invaded from the north in the summer of 1066, and new King Harold considered them a serious threat.

But the second threat would prove more serious, and it too was of Viking origin.

During the social, political, and military turmoil of the Dark Ages, in the power vacuum created when Rome lost control, restless Vikings migrated on the European continent as well as across the English Channel. Some marauded and settled down the coast as far as the northern part of Gaul (France). Here they were called *Northmen,* or *Norman,* and the land they settled became Normandy.*

The Duke of Normandy, then, had ancient Viking ties. One way or the other, Harold could not escape his Viking end.

When Edward the Confessor died, his cousin William, Duke of Nor-

---

* In Gaul, as in Britain, Gaelic and Teutonic dialects met and combined to form a new language. Why then did English and French develop so differently? Largely because of Roman influence—or lack of it. In Gaul, Latin mixed with the local dialect *before* the Vikings added their linguistic influence; in Britain it did not (because the Romans conquered Britain a century later). That is why French is one of the Romance languages and English is not.

mandy, considered himself the rightful king of England. Edward had, after all, proclaimed him successor; William refused to acknowledge the later appointment of Harold Godwin and considered him a pretender. Furthermore, William was "born to the purple" (a blood relative), but Harold was related by marriage. In the autumn of 1066, the Norman armies crossed the English Channel from Calais and landed at Dover, 3 miles from their rendezvous with destiny.

Harold had just staged a major victory over the Danes; now he turned his armies southward, confident they would repel the Normans. The two forces met on Friday, October 13, at Hastings. The outcome still affects the shape of nations and cultures today.

Did Harold push his inexperienced armies too fast, and were they therefore unprepared for the disciplined and well-rested Normans? Maybe. Was the arrow that smashed Harold's brain (through the right eye-hole of his helmet) a lucky shot? Almost certainly. Military scholars believe, however, that the outcome of the Battle of Hastings had been determined before the armies met—by a technological breakthrough as significant then as nuclear weapons are today—the stirrup.

Both sides knew of these new leather straps with footloops, but the Normans were first to equip an army with them. Norman horsemen, then, had a major and unexpected advantage: They could hold their grip on the horse with their legs, freeing both hands in combat; this enabled them to wield a sword or ax and at the same time protect themselves with a shield. The battle lasted one day, and on that day William, Duke of Normandy, became known forever as William the Conqueror.

The Norman Conquest, however, was much more than just the Battle of Hastings. Large parts of England were under the rule of feudal lords who traditionally had little loyalty to the king, and the Conqueror was determined to bring all of England under his absolute rule. In the ensuing years, Norman knights rode through the land on a campaign to eliminate every possible source of uprising. All noble or otherwise prominent or influential families were stripped of power. Burning of villages, painful death by torture, cutting off hands, and burning out eyes with hot irons—these too were part of the Norman Conquest. (Still, historians generally consider William a fair ruler, in the sense of justice and morality.) When it was over, England was united politically but a country totally divided socially and linguistically. The ruling classes, from king to minor village officials, were Norman and spoke French; the ruled, mostly peasants and servants, were Anglo-Saxon and spoke (Old) English.

And that condition triggered the next major change in the English language, giving us Middle English.

Like the Viking invaders before them, the Norman invaders settled permanently in England and soon thought of themselves as English. In

What about Contractions?

They are never necessary in expository writing; we can easily achieve a relaxed, informal tone without them. An occasional one is acceptable, however, in all but the most formal writing; simply use the privilege sparingly. The first contraction in this book appears in the Preface, paragraph 7.

such situations throughout history, the cultures of the invader and the invaded (and their languages) blend to form a third. To a large extent that happened in the Norman Conquest of England. Just as Old English was a mixture of Gaelic and Teutonic, Middle English was a mixture of Old English and French.

But the two mixed in a curious way. Because the noble classes spoke French and the peasants Anglo-Saxon, the words likely to be used in upper-class life stayed French, and those common in peasant or servant life stayed English. Through the centuries they have still not blended completely, and today we have Oxford and Cockney English. Their difference was charmingly dramatized in George Bernard Shaw's *Pygmalion,* later set to music by Alan Jay Lerner and Frederick Loewe as the popular musical comedy *My Fair Lady.* The very proper, aristocratic English of Professor Henry Higgins was Norman, and the 'orrible 'owling of Eliza Doolittle was Anglo-Saxon.

That difference, too, shows in all of us every time our emotions demand quick, strong expression. Those pithy, energetic four-letter words that satisfy most of us in these situations are largely Anglo-Saxon. What determined which words are vulgar and which are acceptable in polite society? The battlefield, of course. The victors always declare themselves genteel and the vanquished to be slobs and louts. If Harold had defeated William at Hastings the slobs and louts might swear in words of French origin, and the genteel expressions might be those four-letter words that now cause the timid to blush. And why does the English-speaking world assign words of Latin origin to textbooks and relegate their exact English equivalents to pornography? Because Latin, even more than French, won its respectability on the battlefield. At two key points in the history of English, a people speaking a Latin-based language defeated and occupied a people speaking a Gaelic-based language: the Roman occupation of Gaul (creating French) and the Norman occupation of England (creating Middle English). This history also accounts for a large number of Latin-based words in the English vocabulary.

The most important writing of the Middle English period is the poetry of Geoffrey Chaucer. Then, as now, writers wrote the things readers like to read; *The Canterbury Tales* contains vivid romantic descriptions that shocked prudish readers in Chaucer's time. Although closer to today's English, the writing of Chaucer is still impossible to understand without the help of a specialist.

Modern English (1500 A.D. to present)

No military occupation, no infusion of foreign tongue at swordpoint, caused the final major change in English. Rather, the sudden shift to the

English of today was triggered by a combination of social and technological shakeups.

As Europe's kings strengthened their rule and "nations" emerged, invariably the new and powerful rulers took away the lands and the armies of the old feudal lords. The end of feudalism (in the eleventh and twelfth centuries) was the end of the Dark Ages. But in the new kind of society that was the Middle Ages, the people most affected were the serfs: No longer could they rely on a lord to provide their basic needs. A chandler, for example, under the old system lived and worked under the protection of a duke in exchange for food and lodging, and the duke would distribute the entire output of candles as he saw fit. Now circumstances forced the chandler to sell candles directly to those who used them, and to buy the goods and services needed directly from those who provided them. Commerce, unknown to Europe for a thousand years, developed, and with it, something else Europe had known much earlier: a middle class. Merchants and craftspeople emerged, and with them craft guilds, schools, and middle class participation in religion and the arts. And the Renaissance was under way.

Renaissance is the French word for "rebirth." But it was more than just the rebirth of the middle classes. The printing press was invented, and literacy and education expanded as books became more available. Equally important, the square-rigged sailing vessel was invented, and with it came exposure to, and influence from, other countries. The true Renaissance, then, was a rebirth of social and intellectual curiosity throughout Europe and England.

The English language by this time had grown used to changing at the drop of a hat (especially if the hat belonged to an invading swordsman). Adaptability, in fact, had already become a major trait of English. Now, with the vast exposure to the languages of the Continent, English began picking up some of their stronger traits—especially in sentence structure, which until now had remained largely Teutonic (verb at the end). And in a relatively short time English underwent what linguists consider its last major change.

For all these reasons, the English language of Shakespeare (who lived early in the Modern English period) was quite different from that of authors only slightly before him. Our language continues to change. (Indeed, unedited Shakespeare is extremely hard to understand today without the help of a specialist.)

LATIN'S INFLUENCE

English is not one of the Romance (or Roman) languages. (They are Italian, Spanish, French, Portuguese, and Rumanian.) It is of Teutonic origin and is more directly related to German, Dutch, and the Scandinavian languages. True, we have many Latin-based words. But most of them came from Roman Catholic liturgy, from French (which is Latin-based) during the Norman Conquest, or from translators of ancient literature who had greater respect for the classical languages than for their native English. (After all, Latin was the language of the church—and the universities.) In general, Latin has had little effect on English. Their grammatical structures are very different. Attempts to apply Latin rules to English almost always fail.

Latin grammar is in the category called "influential." That is, the endings of words, not their positions in the sentence, tell their grammatical roles in the action being described. In the Latin-like sentence, "Dogus bit personum," the *us* ending (for subject) and *um* (for object) tell clearly which is "bitor" and which is "bitee." The relationship of the dog and the person is the same regardless of the order of the words. In fact, any order of the words is acceptable; the meaning stays unchanged.

English grammar, however, is "syntactical." This means the positions of the words in the sentence (syntax), not their endings, determines their roles in the sentence and the action it describes. "Dog bit person" and "person bit dog" use identical words, but there can be no doubt, from their positions, who did what to whom. Furthermore, we can sense these relationships even if we have never seen or heard the words before and don't know what they mean. (For example: *Brithels glape onargs.*)

ITS CHARACTERISTICS

Vocabulary is changeable, cosmopolitan.   A hodgepodge, really. From its beginning, English has never hesitated to take useful words and grammatical traits from other languages. At first it was forced to do so by foreign armies, but the habit stayed. It is for this reason we often have the choice of several words to express the same idea—a trait especially useful for controlling poetic rhythm. Most languages do not accept outside influence so easily. German, our first cousin, almost refuses to do so; it is quite the opposite of English in this respect.

Grammar is simple.   It really is. Compared to most other major languages, English grammar is a joy. Our nouns and adjectives do not have gender (masculine, feminine, or neuter). Noun endings do not change for different uses. Our verbs have very few different forms. Yet, though relatively uncomplicated, the language is remarkably efficient.

Spelling and pronunciation are nightmares.   Here is the real madness of English. No other language is so inconsistent. By what rules do we

---

**Different *From*
or Different *Than?***

Different *from* is always
correct.

The logic: Than expresses
degrees of comparison—larger
than, faster *than,* more expensive *than.* But *different* does not
allow degrees of comparison;
either something is different or
it isn't. (Unless you are saying
something is *more different*
than something else. Even then,
more is the comparative adjective, not *different.*)

Some writers argue that *different than* occasionally fits better:
*Linebackers require different
skill than defensive backs.*
Granted, that is slightly less
wordy than: *Linebackers
require skills different from
those of defensive backs.* But it
is also grammatically wrong,
though ever so slightly, and
when we use *different than* we
should do so with the attitude
that it is incorrect but may be
accepted anyhow. (But in
British English: *different to.*)

explain *half-staff-laugh-graph,* or *enough-bluff,* or *ocean-motion?* Scholars don't even try.

English is undemocratic.   Because our spelling and pronunciation are so illogical, more formal education is likely to be needed than for most other languages. And English appeals to snobbish users because so many levels of vocabulary are possible. For these reasons experts generally consider it a somewhat undemocratic language.

No more sudden changes.   Mass media tend to speed up vocabulary changes (especially in English, where change has been a fundamental trait). But mass media and mass education have slowed down changes in the structure of our language. It will probably never undergo sudden changes that would create a new English "period" in future centuries.

Words (the Parts of Speech)

It took me fifteen years to discover I had no talent for writing, but I couldn't give it up because by that time I was too famous.

—Robert Benchley

There are only eight parts of speech, but every writer *must* know what they are and how to use them correctly. Nothing less will do. Readers lose confidence in the writing and the writer when they find grammar flaws; the writer is expected to have mastered the basic skills of his or her craft.

The key words are:

- Adjective
- Adverb
- Conjunction (or connective)
- Interjection
- Noun
- Preposition
- Pronoun
- Verb

But: the same word can serve as different parts of speech. *Following*, for example, can be a noun (they have a large *following*), verb (we are *following* you), adjective (the *following* day), or preposition (*following* the election). The part of speech of any word depends on how it is used in the sentence containing it.

ADJECTIVES, VERBS . . . AND EVERYTHING IN BETWEEN

Adjective. An adjective modifies (adds to the meaning of) a noun or pronoun by describing it or limiting its meaning in a sentence (*favorable* decision; *blue* paint; the *tallest* player). Several adjectives may modify the same noun (the *brilliant, efficient, new* technician). Note, however, that adjectives are not always found next to the noun they modify (the *new* technician has proved to be *brilliant*). *A, an,* and *the* are the most commonly used adjectives. They are articles (see page 233).

Adverb. An adverb modifies, or adds to, a verb (*ad verb*) by telling *when* (*recently* announced), *where* (arriving *here*), or *how* (trying *desperately*). An adverb can also modify an adjective (*badly* damaged merchandise) or another adverb (*very quickly* realized). Adverbs usually end with *-ly* (*easily*), but not always (*soon*). Like adjectives, several may modify the same word, and they are not necessarily next to the word they modify.

Conjunction. Also called a *connective*, the conjunction connects words or complete ideas. These little words are more important than most writers realize because they *bridge* our ideas; they help the reader see some relationship the writer can *feel*. There are three kinds: (1) Coordinate conjunctions (*and, but, or, nor, for, so, yet*) join two or more words or ideas (the chairman *and* the president; I gathered the data, *but* she wrote the report). (2) Subordinate conjunctions (*although, as, because, if, unless, etc.*) connect a phrase or subordinate clause to a main clause by showing some relationship between them (*if* you go, don't come back; there are fewer errors *because* we changed the procedure). (3) Correlative conjunctions (*either-or, neither-nor, whether-or, both-and, not only-but*) connect pairs and must always appear in the sentence as pairs. Conjunctions are little gems in building logical relationships between ideas.

Connective. *Connective* is a more modern word for conjunction.

Interjection. An interjection is an exclamation, usually at the beginning of a sentence, serving no grammatical function (*Oh*, that's not true; *Well,* I see you're late again). It may be a sentence of its own requiring neither subject nor verb (*For goodness sake!*). Interjections usually express emotion.

Noun. A noun is the name for a thing (*airplane*), idea (*truth*), process (*cooking*), or condition (*illness*). Nouns always serve as the subject of

For the Language Gourmet

What is the difference between a *gourmet* and a *gourmand?* A *gourmet* is a judge of good food; a *gourmand* is a person who overeats.

clauses, or as objects. In many languages, the form or ending of the noun changes to show its grammatical function. In English the form does not change; the function a noun serves is shown by its position in the sentence (*person* bit *dog; dog* bit *person*). Largely for this reason, grammar is simpler in English than in most other major languages. (That may seem surprising, but it is true.) In languages that do use changing noun forms to show function, these forms are called *declensions*. Proper nouns are the capitalized names of people, places, organizations, and products. Adding *-s* or *-es* to most nouns makes them plural. (Exceptions: Nouns ending with *-y* use *-ies* for the plural, although these, too, have exceptions: *attorney/attorneys*. There are also some irregular nouns: *man/men, mouse/mice.* Adding *'s* to most nouns makes them possessive.)

Nouns and verbs are the most basic parts of speech. (But they are not necessarily the ones used most often; articles are: *The* [*definite article*] is used far more often than any other word in the English language.)

Preposition.   A preposition connects a noun (or word functioning as a noun) with some other part of the same sentence. Usually, a preposition describes place (*on* the desk; *to* our office) or time (*before* the audit *in* 1984), but not always (*for* lunch, *with* my brother).

Pronoun.   A pronoun substitutes for a noun (*pro noun*), or for a phrase or clause serving as a noun (he mailed *it* to *them*). There are eight kinds: **(1)** personal pronouns, which may stand for first person (*I, we*), second person (*you*), or third person (*he, she, it,* or *they*); **(2)** relative pronouns (*who, which, that,* etc.), which relate a subordinate part of a sentence to the main clause (as here); **(3)** demonstrative pronouns (*this, that, these, those*), which point out a specific person or thing; **(4)** indefinite pronouns, which refer to people or things generally rather than specifically (*all, some,* etc.); **(5)** interrogative pronouns, which ask a question (*who, what, which,* etc.)—these may be the same words as relative pronouns (of subordinate clauses), but they are part of the main clause (*which regulation is the most recent?*); **(6)** numerical pronouns, which are numbers standing for nouns (the *second* play was the least interesting one); **(7)** reflexive pronouns, which are formed by adding *-self* or *-selves* to a personal pronoun; **(8)** reciprocal pronouns, which stand for two or more people or things interacting—the verb tells the interaction between them (these statements contradict *each other*).

In English, the form of the pronoun usually (but not always) changes to describe three other things about the noun it stands for: **(1)** number, which tells whether the noun is singular or plural (*me, us*); **(2)** gender, which tells whether the noun is masculine, feminine, or neuter (*he, she, it*); and **(3)** case, which tells whether the noun is the subject of the verb (nominative case), object of a verb or preposition (objective case), or pos-

Infamous Quotation 2

Education in the United States has been under severe criticism since the 1970s for failing to teach basic skills. English teachers have been particularly singled out, as writing skills have declined steadily. But not all English teachers agree they should teach writing. At a conference in Columbus, Ohio, in 1995, an assistant school board superintendent said (and his colleagues agreed): "Corporations want us to teach writing so they can improve their profit margins, but parents aren't paying us to produce cannon fodder for big business. They're paying us to teach global citizenship . . . and creative thinking." That attitude is expressed often in education journals. (Also see: "Infamous Quotation 1," page 60.)

sessor of another noun (possessive case). Example of all three: *He* (nominative) said that *my* (possessive) check was sent to *you* (objective).

As with nouns, the various forms of pronouns that show different relationships are called *declensions*.

Verb.   The verb is the action word. Every sentence or clause must have at least one. It tells what the subject (a noun or pronoun) is or does. The verb may be transitive (requiring an object), intransitive (complete without an object), or linking (requiring more information). Examples: Transitive—*Perkins* (subject) *collects* (transitive verb) *coins* (direct object). Intransitive—*She* (subject) *snores* (complete verb). Linking—*Geldings* (subject) *are* (linking verb) *neutered male* (predicate adjectives) *horses* (predicate nominative). A simple test to tell whether a word is a verb: Ask yourself, "Can it be done?" Be sure, without fail, to read the comments on predicate adjective and predicate nominative, page 238.

In English, the form of the verb usually (but not always) changes to tell five other things about the action it describes: **(1)** number, which tells whether the subject is singular or plural (it *turns;* they *turn*); **(2)** person, which tells whether the subject is *I, you, he, she, it,* or *they* (I *am;* you *are;* he, she, or it *is;* they *are*); **(3)** tense, which tells whether the action is in the past, present, or future (*constructed, constructs, will construct*); **(4)** voice, which tells whether the subject performs the action (active) or receives it (passive) (The IBM multimedia group *gathered* [active voice] the information; the information *was gathered* [passive voice] by the IBM multimedia group); **(5)** mood, which tells whether the action is fact (indicative mood, the most commonly used), command (imperative mood), or contrary to fact (subjunctive mood) (you *are* here; *be* here; if you *were* here). These varying forms of a verb are called its *conjugations*.

Verbs and nouns are the two most basic parts of speech.

CHAPTER 16   CLOSER LOOK: GRAMMAR BASICS

These eight kinds of words, and the differences between them, are so basic you must know them.

ADJECTIVE (Modifies Nouns or Pronouns)

. . . *lean, juicy* meat. (*Lean* and *juicy* tell more about the noun *meat.*)

. . . *loud* music. (*Loud* tells more about the noun *music.*)

. . . *two new* ones. (*Two* and *new* tell more about the pronoun *ones.*)

ADVERB (Modifies Verbs, Adjectives, or Other Adverbs)

. . . arrived *late.* (*Late* tells more about the verb *arrived.*)

. . . *perfectly adjusted* instrument. (*Perfectly* tells more about the adjective *adjusted*, which tells more about the noun *instrument.* But wait! Isn't *adjusted* a verb? Normally yes, but in this case it modifies a noun, *instrument,* so it is an adjective.)

. . . *very* slowly. (*Very* tells more about the adverb *slowly.*)

CONJUNCTION (Also Called "Connective," Connects Words or Ideas)

. . . labor *and* management. (coordinate conjunction)

. . . *if* prices come down. (subordinate conjunction)

. . . *whether* you go *or* not. (correlative conjunctions—always in pairs)

INTERJECTION (Short, Emotional Statement)

Look, this job is so difficult. . . .

Good grief, if you didn't think surgery was necessary. . . .

NOUN (The Name of Something, Always a Subject or Object)

Our voter survey *report* (subject) is ready.

. . . on the other *side* of the computer *printout.* (*side* and *printout* are indirect objects of the prepositions *on* and *other.* But wait! Isn't *computer* a noun? Normally yes, but here it modifies the noun *printout,* so it is an adjective.)

They wear special *uniforms.* (*uniforms* is the direct object of the transitive verb *wear.*)

PREPOSITION (Connects a Noun with Another Idea— Usually in Time or Place)

. . . *with* our help, they will be able to finish.

. . . *until* tomorrow.

. . . *by* the customer *from* Nigeria who left her umbrella *under* the table.

. . . what they were talking *about*.

These samples are all prepositional phrases.

PRONOUN (Stands for a Noun, Hence Its Name. That Noun Is Its "Antecedent")

. . . listening to *her* yesterday. (personal pronoun)

. . . *which* arrived late. (relative pronoun)

. . . cut *myself* slightly. (reflexive pronoun)

These are the most common, but there are others; see page 183.

VERB (The Action Word, or Words, of a Sentence)

Cyd *hates* (transitive verb, present tense, active voice) martinis.

The parts *will be shipped* (future tense, passive voice) tomorrow.

Your request *was* (past tense, linking [auxiliary]) unreasonable because the committee *handles* (present tense, active voice) these matters, so I *will ignore* (future tense, active voice) it.

WHY ALL THE FUSS ABOUT MODIFIERS?

We cannot avoid using modifiers, and precise grammar requires understanding how they work. Think of a modifier as something that changes something. In grammar, modifiers change the meaning of (more accurately, *add some meaning to*) the words they modify, making them more exact.

There are only two kinds—*adjectives* (*laptop* computers) and *adverbs* (speak *clearly*).

To appreciate the importance of modifiers, consider the sentence: "Pipelines carry oil." That sentence structure is the backbone of the English language—subject, transitive verb, direct object.

But "Pipelines carry oil" is not a very exciting sentence. More important, it is not very accurate. "*Some* (adjective) pipelines carry oil" tells more. "Some pipelines carry oil *inefficiently*" (adverb) is an entirely different statement. The modifiers *some* and *inefficiently* make the difference.

Phrases and clauses (discussed in the next chapter) also serve as modifiers—but, like single words, always as adjectives or adverbs.

ABOUT EMBEDDING*

Of all the fleas that ever flew
(And flying fleas are rather few
((Because for proper flying you
(((Whether you are a flea or not)))
Need wings and things fleas have not got)))—

(I make the further point that fleas
Are thick as these parentheses
((An illustration (((you'll agree)))
Both apt and pleasing to a flea)))—

Now then where were we? Let me see—
Ah, yes—We said to fly you ought
(Whether you are a flea or not)
To have some wings (yes, at least two
((At least no less than two will do
(((And fleas have something less than one
((((One less, in fact (((((or, frankly, none,
Which ((((((as once more you will agree))))))
Limits the flying of a flea))))))))))))))).

And let me add that fleas that fly
Are known as Flears. (You can see why.)
All I have said thus far is true.
(If it's not clear, that's up to you.
((You'll have to learn sometime, my dear,
That what is true may not be clear
(((While what is clear may not be true
((((And you'll be wiser when you do.))))))))))

—Saturday Review

* See page 204.

Phrases and Clauses

From Words to Ideas

> *The key words are* phrase, clause, restrictive, nonrestrictive, dependent, *and* independent. Writers need to understand these in order to use commas correctly.

These two paragraphs contain exactly the same information:

> Kovall, traded to the Brewers by the Red Sox in 1997, was American League rookie of the year in 1992, when he batted .294 with 23 home runs and 91 runs batted in, but he suffered a spinal disk injury his second year and has seen limited duty since.

And:

> Kovall was traded to the Brewers. The Red Sox traded him. The year was 1997. Earlier he had been rookie of the year. That was in the American League. The year was 1992. He batted .294 then. He also hit 23 home runs. He also batted in 91 runs. But he suffered an injury. It was to a spinal disk. This happened his second year. He has seen limited duty since.

The difference between those two passages is the use of phrases and clauses. They make the first passage seem reasonable and readable, causing the ideas to flow in a smooth, easy way from the writer to the reader. In the second passage there are none but bare essential clauses, and these contain only a few modifying phrases (it would be impossible to write without any); as a result the ideas seem childlike and the flow awkward.

But note: Stylish writers would argue that the first passage (above) contains too much information for one sentence, and they are right. Though it is vastly better than the childlike second passage, it would be still better as two sentences. We can make a dramatic improvement simply by changing *batted in, but* . . . to *batted in. But.* . . . (Yes, ending sentences with prepositions is permissible. See Chapter 4.) The related but separate ideas are now easier to read. Equally important, they both gain added emphasis. Dividing ideas properly into sentences is one of the most important skills in writing.

All of us have been using phrases and clauses all our lives, or at least since early childhood, whether we knew it or not. Probably we use them intuitively, and so their correct usage cannot be too difficult—in most cases. But intuition is not always correct. Being able to recognize these groups of words, and understanding what they do, helps us write accurately, easily, and, if you wish, stylishly.

These subjects may have been distasteful to most of us earlier in life, in that period when we hated brussels sprouts because kids are supposed to. Phrases and clauses are not particularly hard to understand, however, and writers really must know them if they are to use English correctly—for example, to recognize the subject and verb of a sentence and make sure they agree with each other, and to put commas where they belong (and avoid them where they do not belong).

A Phrase Is . . .

A *phrase* is a group of words working together. Not just any cluster of two or more, however; a group of words becomes a phrase when they serve collectively as one of the parts of speech, and when the group does not contain a subject and verb. A phrase can have a subject *or* verb, or neither, but it cannot contain both. (If it has a subject and verb it is a clause.)

This is not nearly as complicated as it sounds. Phrases are usually a few words serving as a *noun:* You can fool *most of the people;* as a *verb:* We *have been working* all night; as an *adjective:* The *large and heavy* machinery; or as an *adverb:* We failed, *like those before us.* But some can be quite long: *During the years between Richard Nixon's humiliating political defeat in the California congressional election and the stunning victory of his election as President of the United States . . .* (There is not a verb in sight so far) . . . *his career took. . . .*

Two things cause confusion about phrases. *First,* a phrase can contain other phrases. (The long one about Richard Nixon, above, is all one phrase, serving as an adverb modifying the verb *took.* [The phrase tells when.] Yet it contains seven smaller embedded phrases, and these in turn can be recombined to create many others.) This point can be shown more clearly with a shorter phrase: *During his presidency,* John F. Kennedy was. . . . The words *During his presidency* form one phrase, modifying the verb *was.* (The phrase tells when.) But within the phrase, *his presidency* is also a phrase—in this case serving as a noun, the object of the preposition *during.* So phrases can overlap.

Second, the most common phrases and the ones most mentioned, prepositional phrases, do not really exist. Well, let's put that another way. Of course they exist—but as something else. Countless phrases begin with prepositions, and these are loosely called prepositional phrases. But they never *serve* as prepositions. A prepositional phrase always serves as an adjective or adverb. The following are some phrases serving as adjectives (modifying nouns or pronouns): it's the house *on the corner* (tells what house); investments *in movies and plays* made Mizrachi rich (tells what investments); those containers *under the lights* need larger shields (tells which containers). And these are some phrases serving as adverbs (modifying verbs): *in 1997,* Congress reacted to this quickly (tells when they reacted); birds fly *over the rainbow* (tells where they fly); We approved *by e-mail* (tells how we approved).

Nonrestrictive or Restrictive Phrases

(You must know this, for proper punctuation.) A phrase is *nonrestrictive* if its thought does not change the basic meaning of the *main clause* of the sentence: The grandfather clock, *at the top of the stairs,* needs to be wound every week. (There is one grandfather clock, and it needs to be wound every week; by the way, it's at the top of the stairs.) The phrase here is prepositional, serving as an adjective modifying the noun *clock.* It does not restrict the main idea; if you remove it the main idea remains the same. Note that nonrestrictive phrases are surrounded by commas. Always use two commas, unless the phrase begins or ends the sentence. (All the advice in this paragraph applies also to clauses, in the next section.)

A phrase is *restrictive* if the thought it expresses limits (restricts), or adds to, or changes the meaning of the sentence containing it: The grandfather clock *at the top of the stairs* needs to be wound every week. (There are two or more grandfather clocks, and one needs to be wound every week; it's the one at the top of the stairs.) The phrase here, like the nonrestrictive one in the paragraph above, is prepositional/adjectival. This phrase definitely *restricts* the main idea of the sentence; if you remove it the intended meaning becomes incomplete. *Note* that restrictive phrases are not separated from the rest of the sentence by commas. (As with nonrestrictive phrases, the advice in this paragraph applies also to clauses, in the next section.)

A Clause Is . . .

A *clause* is a group of words that has a subject (noun or pronoun) and a verb acting with that subject. It may be a whole sentence (*They arrived.*) or part of a sentence (*When they arrived,*).

A clause differs from a phrase in two ways. *First,* a phrase does not have both a subject and a verb; a clause must have both. *Second,* a phrase always serves as some part of speech in the sentence containing it (noun, verb, adjective, or adverb); a clause may or may not. This will become clear in the next few paragraphs.

Every sentence must have at least one clause: its main clause. Some sentences have nothing else: *Your Pocahantas statue was shipped yesterday.*

Independent or Dependent Clauses

An *independent* clause is one that can stand alone; as its name implies, it does not depend on the rest of the sentence to make sense: *Smedley is going to Toronto.* Every sentence must have a main clause, and it is always independent.

But note: Although the basic clause is usually just a few words, any number of embellishments can be added through phrases and other modifiers, and, therefore, the whole statement conveyed by one short clause can end up quite long: *Because of the rush, and the long delay obtaining customs clearance by mail,* Smedley is going to Toronto *and will discuss the changes with the Freedom of Religion Committee.* It becomes clear, when the many phrases are brushed aside, that *Smedley is going to Toronto* is still the only clause. The phrase *Because of the rush* has no subject or verb; neither have *and the long delay, by mail,* or *with the Freedom of Religion Committee. Obtaining customs clearance* has a subject (*obtaining*) but no verb, and *will discuss the changes* has a verb (*will discuss*) but no subject.

Writers can add one independent clause to another, stretching out a sentence: *Smedley is in Toronto, and the Nomura Group has informed us the statistics are ready.* You can even embed one independent clause within another: *Smedley, it was decided yesterday, is going to Toronto.*

Also note: Stylish writers warn against very much of that kind of embedding. It quickly becomes clumsy, hard to understand, too much for one sentence.

Now examine this clause: *although Smedley is going to Toronto.* Now the clause is no longer independent; it does not make sense alone. It is *dependent;* it depends on something else to give it sense, and that something else must be another clause. A phrase will not work; an independent clause is needed, to make a sentence: Although Smedley is going to Toronto, *her work* (subject) *must not fall* (verb) *behind.* The second one is the independent or main clause: *her work must not fall behind* can stand alone and make sense. *Although Smedley is going to Toronto* cannot.

A shorter example: People *who live in glass houses* shouldn't throw stones.

Any writer can add any number of dependent clauses to a main clause, stretching out a sentence. It is possible (though not usually very artistic) to embed one dependent clause within another: Because Smedley, whose work *the Freedom of Religion Committee has assured me* will be approved, is going to Toronto, we have asked the Nomura Group to analyze the statistics while she is gone.*

As with independent clauses, stylish writers warn against very much of that kind of embedding.

Another name for dependent clauses is *subordinate*. By its nature, the main (independent) clause usually contains the dominant idea of the sentence; the idea conveyed in the dependent clause, then, seems less important, or subordinated.

Nonrestrictive or Restrictive Clauses

Dependent clauses are further broken down into the same subcategories used for phrases: *nonrestrictive* and *restrictive*. This explanation will sound very much like that for phrases, because the conditions are the same.

A dependent or subordinate clause is *nonrestrictive* if the thought it expresses does not change the meaning of the main clause; its thought is not essential to the main thought and could be omitted: The third couple, *who ordered fish,* won the prize. The third couple won the prize; by the way, they ordered fish. Note that nonrestrictive clauses are surrounded by commas. Always use two commas, unless the clause begins or ends the sentence.

A subordinate clause is *restrictive* if the thought it expresses limits (restricts) or adds to the meaning of the main clause. If you omit it you change the meaning: The third couple *who ordered fish* won the prize. Many couples were there, and some of them ordered fish; the third couple who did won the prize. Note that restrictive clauses are not set off from the rest by commas.

Be sure to punctuate every clause correctly, to let your reader know whether its information is nonrestrictive or restrictive. There is a vast difference between:

Sales representatives who can't answer customers' questions are a nuisance.

Acronyms: Mercy to All Readers

An *acronym* is a word made of the initials of a group of words, usually of a name or a specialized term: National Aeronautics and Space Administration (NASA); Mothers Against Drunk Driving (MADD); United Nations Children's Emergency Fund (UNICEF). Used properly, acronyms are gifts of kindness to readers; they replace long or difficult terms with simple ones.

Always spell out the full term the first time it appears in any piece of writing, then follow it immediately by the acronym in parentheses, almost as if saying, ". . . hereinafter referred to as . . .": Mothers Against Drunk Driving (MADD).

Caution: Avoid overuse of acronyms. If a sentence looks like a bowl of alphabet soup (*when the CFPM reading on the CRT reaches the DRG level, the SNRF needs to be recalculated and checked for an ASV condition*), you are being inconsiderate, not merciful, to your reader. (For other advice on abbreviations, see page 95.)

* This is a hard-to-read structure, even though it is grammatically correct. (See Syntax, page 202.)

and

Sales representatives, *who can't answer customers' questions,* are a nuisance.

As stated earlier, a clause may or may not serve as a part of speech in the sentence containing it; a phrase always does. This needs clarification. An independent (main) clause, because it can stand alone and make complete sense, could not possibly serve as one part of speech. A dependent (subordinate) clause can—in fact, always does. Every dependent clause, whether nonrestrictive or restrictive, serves as an adjective, adverb, or noun. You can see this clearly by finding the word the clause *modifies* in the main clause. Remember, adjectives modify nouns or pronouns; adverbs modify verbs, adjectives, or other adverbs. (Noun clauses are a little different; they may serve as the subject of the main clause *or as the object of a verb or preposition in the main clause.* In that usage the dependent clause is actually part of the main clause.)

CHAPTER 17   CLOSER LOOK: SELF-TEST ON PHRASES AND CLAUSES (ANSWERS ON PAGES 195–196.)

1. **What part of speech is the italicized phrase?**
   The Solon Road Bridge will be reopened *on October 17th.*

2. **Is the punctuation correct in the sentence below?**
   The netboats, with their capacity for enormous catches are depleting the stock of shrimp in the bay.

3. **Is the italicized passage a phrase or clause? Restrictive or nonrestrictive?**
   Some 50 cats, *all descendants of cats raised by Ernest Hemingway,* still live in his house on Key West.

4. **Is the italicized clause dependent or independent?**
   Politicians *who speak at professional meetings* often get $15,000 for an hour or less.

5. **Is the italicized passage a phrase or a clause?**
   The Hunchback of Notre Dame *is a famous heroic character in French literature.*

6. **What part of speech is the italicized clause?**
   Personal computer programs *that correct grammar* haven't been very successful.

7. **Is the italicized clause restrictive or nonrestrictive?**

   People *who play the flute* are called flautists.

8. **True or false:**

   A phrase always serves as one of the parts of speech.

9. **Is the italicized passage a phrase or a clause?**

   Benjamin Franklin invented many things *but is not recognized as a great scientist.*

10. **What is the error in the sentence below?**

    According to Barbara Payne who is a noted entomologist, the housefly serves no purpose in the world's ecology.

11. **Is the italicized passage a phrase or a clause? What part of speech is it?**

    I don't know *what you should do.*

12. **Is the italicized passage a phrase or clause? What part of speech is it?**

    John Minoprio, my old and dear friend in Shopshire, whom I owe so much, loves *to photograph horses and fashion models.*

13. **True or false?**

    A clause can be as short as two words.

14. **Is the italicized clause dependent or independent? Restrictive or nonrestrictive?**

    I was surprised, *because I thought you were out of town.*

15. **What is the grammatical name of the italicized words?**

    Dominic DiMaggio, *Joe's brother,* was also an all-star baseball player and also a center fielder.

THE ANSWERS

1. ADVERB, modifying the verb *will be reopened.*

2. NO. The phrase *with their capacity for enormous catches* is nonrestrictive and, therefore, must be separated from the rest by commas *at both ends.*

3. PHRASE. It has a subject (*all*) but no verb. The commas at both ends tell readers it is NONRESTRICTIVE; it could be lifted out without changing the meaning or accuracy of the rest.

4. DEPENDENT. It cannot stand alone; it has meaning only as part of the independent clause that contains it.

5. PHRASE. It has no subject; it is the predicate of *The Hunchback of Notre Dame,* and together they form a sentence clause.

6. ADJECTIVE, modifying the noun *programs.*

7. RESTRICTIVE. The clause restricts the statement containing it; the meaning is very different if you take it out or surround it by commas.

8. TRUE.

9. It has no subject, so it is a PHRASE.

10. The clause *who is a noted entomologist* cannot stand alone grammatically, and so it is *dependent.* Because it does not alter the meaning of the rest, it is *nonrestrictive* and should be surrounded by commas.

11. It is a dependent CLAUSE, serving as a noun (direct object of the transitive verb *know*).

12. It is a prepositional PHRASE, serving as a noun (direct object of the transitive verb *loves*).

13. TRUE, regardless of whether it is an independent or dependent clause. Independent: "Camels bite." Dependent (restrictive): "The marines *who remained* had the privilege of. . . ."

14. It is DEPENDENT; it cannot stand alone but depends on the *independent* clause before it. It is also NONRESTRICTIVE; it can be lifted out without changing the meaning or accuracy of the rest.

15. They form an APPOSITIVE. As a group they do not modify anything, and so they do not serve as a part of speech (phrase).

CHAPTER 18

The Noble English Sentence

Grasp the subject; the words will follow.

—Marcus Porcius Cato (Cato the Elder)

It was Winston Churchill who called the simple English sentence "noble." And if sentences can be noble, the use of language to simplify ideas—to convey as much knowledge as possible to as many people as possible—is divine.

All the rules of grammar, including punctuation, serve one purpose: to help writers construct individual sentences, one at a time, that are clear to the reader. If you can do that, you can write any thoughts your brain is capable of creating.

Mastery of basic grammar will make your writing acceptable. Mastery of syntax, which is the part of grammar that deals with the arrangement of words within sentences (discussed later in this chapter), can make it outstanding—even artistic.

There are four basic kinds of sentences: simple, compound, complex, and compound/complex. Writers need to understand these, as well as the different kinds of phrases and clauses, to use punctuation correctly.

THE SIMPLE SENTENCE

A simple sentence is one that consists of one independent clause and has no dependent clauses. *The waiter* (subject) *poured* (verb) *the coffee* (direct object). *The baby* (subject) *is crying* (complete verb). But this is also a simple sentence: *A majority of House members* (subject), *lobbied with understandable but simplistic ferocity by American labor and management groups, that week began* (verb) *seeking to pass a bill requiring foreign governments to open their markets further to U.S. products or suffer the consequences of much-tightened import quotas* (object). That terribly complicated sentence is grammatically a simple sentence. It contains just one independent clause; all the rest consists of phrases and other modifiers. (And, although it is grammatically correct, it is an awkward sentence for reasons of *syntax.* See page 202.)

About Predicates

The two most basic parts of every sentence are a subject and an action. Usually (but not always) the subject performs that action. (When the verb is in the passive voice the subject receives the action. See Chapter 3.) The subject is always a noun or a pronoun (standing for a noun). The action is carried to the reader by a verb. The basic parts of any sentence, then, are its subject and verb. But each of those in turn can consist of several smaller parts: *Levitt and the people he represents* (subject, noun phrase) *demand* (verb) *a cleanup by next year* (object) *and will be satisfied only upon approval of funding for it* (adverb phrase, not part of the subject or verb). That is still a simple sentence; there is still only one clause.

Because so many variations of subject and verb are possible, it is useful to think in terms of subject and *predicate.* The person, thing, or place performing the act is the subject. The predicate contains the verb but usually includes more; it tells you what the action is (or was, or will be).

Skip Horowitz, the manager of our accounts receivable department (subject), *received his Ph.D. in Business Administration last week, after four years of study* (predicate). In that sentence, the simple subject is *Skip Horowitz,* and the simple verb is *received.* But everything from *received* to the end of the sentence is the predicate; it is all part of the action performed by the subject.

Breaking Predicates Down a Little Further

Because *subject, transitive verb, direct object* is the backbone of English sentence structure, most English-speaking people learned those terms (or should have) early in their educations. *Transitive* comes from the Latin *trans* or across; the transitive verb, then, takes the action across from the subject to the object.

Leah (*subject*) raises (*transitive verb*) Siamese cats (*direct object*).

I Feel *Good* or I Feel *Well*?

If you are describing your health, *good* (predicate adjective) is correct. You feel *well* (adverb) only when talking about the efficiency with which you feel something.

Note that you cannot stop at the verb when it is transitive; the verb needs to be directed somewhere. You cannot say *Leah raises;* a listener would ask, "Yes? Go on." The sentence demands a direct object, something to which the verb *trans*fers its action—in this case, something that is raised.

Complements.   A *complement,* when a sentence contains one, completes the action of the verb; like the verb, it is part of the predicate. In the subject-transitive verb-direct object structure, the direct object is usually the complement; it completes the action of the transitive verb: Skip Horowitz, the manager of our accounts receivable department, received (*transitive verb*) his Ph.D. in Business Administration (*direct object–complement*) last week.

But not all verbs need a complement.   Some verbs are intransitive—that is, nothing needs to receive the action. There are two kinds of intransitive verbs. *Complete* verbs need nothing more (*She snores,* or *I lied*). The verb is the whole predicate; no complement is needed. *Linking* verbs do need a complement, but that complement is not a direct object. For example: *The potato salad tasted. . . .* You cannot stop there; a listener would ask, "Yes? Go on." We know that the potato salad did not taste something, so the verb *taste* will not have a direct object. In this case it is a linking (intransitive) verb, and our computer brain tells us intuitively as we read that the rest of the sentence (complement) must tell us not *what* the potato salad tasted but *how* it tasted. The types of complements that do this for linking verbs are called *predicate adjectives* or *predicate nominatives:* The potato salad tasted *terrible* (*predicate adjective*). But if the linking verb requires a what, not a how, the complement will be a noun called *predicate nominative:* The potato salad was *the main course.*

COMPOUND, COMPLEX, AND COMPOUND/COMPLEX SENTENCES

A compound sentence contains two or more independent clauses, and they are separated by a comma then joined by one of the coordinate conjunctions (*and, but, or, nor, for, so, yet*). Because they are independent, each of the separate clauses is capable of standing alone as a separate sentence:

We got there late, but the program hadn't started yet.

Try using the alphanumeric code, and be sure to fill out the forms completely.

but not:

Try using the alphanumeric code, being sure to fill out the forms completely.

In that one the second part is a phrase (no subject), not a clause.

A complex sentence contains two (or more) clauses—one independent clause and at least one dependent (or subordinate) clause:

We're going to run the entire test again when the adjustments are completed.

Note that *We're going to run the entire test again* can stand alone; *when the adjustments are completed* cannot.

Because Kevin's big game is Tuesday night, we've postponed the meeting.

Because Kevin's big game is Tuesday night cannot stand alone; *we've postponed the meeting* can.

A compound/complex sentence, as its name implies, combines both. It contains two or more independent clauses, making it compound, and at least one of them has a dependent or subordinate clause, making it complex.

Dimethyl sulfoxide, when it is used with medical supervision, is often effective in relieving arthritic pain, but it is a highly controversial substance.

Note that the division between the compound parts occurs at the conjunction *but*. In the first (complex) part, *when it is used with medical supervision* is a nonrestrictive dependent clause (and therefore surrounded by commas). The second part, *but it is a highly controversial substance*, is a simple independent clause.

MORE ABOUT OBJECTS

Direct objects (of transitive verbs) are not the only kind. You will need to know about two others if you are to choose the correct pronouns in key situations: indirect objects and objects of prepositions.

Indirect Objects

Not all sentences contain indirect objects. Think of an indirect object as a secondary object—always secondary to the direct object. In the famed

Pennsylvania Dutch construction, *Throw Momma from the train a kiss,* "*Momma*" isn't being thrown; *a kiss* is. That *kiss* is the direct object (of the transitive verb *throw*), and *Momma* is the indirect object (of the implied preposition *to*). (The subject is *you*, also implied.) The relationships would be the same, but not as funny, if the sentence were in the more natural construction: *Throw Momma a kiss from the train.*

The same is true of an ordinary, everyday sentence such as: *I sent Alexis the toys by Express Mail.* Here we have the basic subject-transitive verb-direct object structure. The subject and verb are obvious: *I sent.* But watch out, now. What is the direct object? Surely Alexis was not sent by express mail; the toys were, and they are the direct object. Alexis is the indirect object (again of the implied preposition *to*).

> The Review Committee (*subject*) studied (*transitive verb*) the proposal (*direct object*).

but:

> The Review Committee (*subject*) gave (*transitive verb*) the proposal (*indirect object*) careful study (*direct object*).

> Sara (*subject*) showed us (*indirect object*) their evaluation (*direct object*) yesterday.

Objects of Prepositions

A prepositional phrase always contains (at least) a preposition and its object. That object is always a noun or pronoun; there may also be modifiers.

> We got sheet music from the band department. (*From* is the preposition; *department* is its object; *the* and *band* are adjectives modifying the noun *department.*)

> That book on your desk contains all the answers. (*On* is a preposition; and *desk* is its object.)

Why should you care?   No writer can succeed without being able to recognize whether something (or someone) is a subject or object. This skill will help you select pronouns correctly and avoid some embarrassments. For example, *He and I talked to Smedley* is perfectly correct grammar, but *Smedley talked to he and I* is an unforgivable error. How do you

---

You May Coin a Phrase, but It's Not Likely.

Misguided people trying to impress with quotations often make this kind of mistake: "To coin a phrase, 'There's something rotten in Denmark.' "

To *coin* (transitive verb) means to invent or produce. The person who made the statement above then, should have said: "To copy a badly over-used phrase. . . ."

Use words correctly. And, if you are going to take credit for someone else's work, for goodness sake don't pick Shakespeare. Further advice: Writers who are going to quote anyone should take the trouble to find out the exact wording and quote it accurately. As Hamlet followed the ghost, Marcellus commented to Horatio: "Something is rotten in the state of Denmark."

tell which is which? One way is correct for subjects, the other for objects.

The same is true for *who* or *whom*.

SYNTAX: THE ART OF MAKING SENTENCES BEHAVE

> The network of four gas chromatographs, which will be controlled by the SR-4100 System, and which was designed and assembled at our lab under the direction of Dr. Anne Greenglass, who last year won the Granville Award for her work on radioisotopic conversion even though her analysis had been only partially tested, includes two dual-channel instruments, of which the first features an automated sample selection system coupled to an injection and backflush system, and the second utilizes standard injection techniques but features automated backflush valving and senses when the sample is in the ready condition.

Even though it is grammatically correct in every way, that is a terrible sentence, and it demonstrates an important point: Good grammar alone does not make good writing; it does not even ensure basic clarity.

The weaknesses are in syntax—the arrangement of the words, phrases, and clauses within the sentence.

Only a part of syntax involves grammar; the rest is a matter of common sense and understanding what goes on in the reader's brain as he or she receives those words, phrases, clauses, and sentences. Remember, everything the thoughtful writer does should be for the benefit of that communications partner at the receiving end—the reader.

Two important things are wrong with that monstrous sentence above: It is much too long (95 words and several major ideas), and some important words are badly separated from the words they modify. These are common flaws among inexperienced writers—especially those who are highly educated. (Less educated people probably could not keep the grammar straight in a sentence that long and complicated, and they probably would not try.)

Now examine those same ideas again. We needn't be scientists or engineers to understand. This is how to win friends and influence readers:

> The network of four gas chromatographs includes two dual-channel instruments. The first features an automated sample selection system coupled to an injection and backflush system. The second utilizes standard injection techniques but features automated backflush valving and senses when the sample is in the ready condition. This network will be controlled by the SR-4100 system. It was designed and assembled at our lab under the direction of Dr.

Anne Greenglass, who last year won the Granville Award for her work on radioisotopic conversion (even though her analysis had been only partially tested).

Note that the two versions contain exactly the same information. Not even the slightest detail is sacrificed in the second (simpler) one.

Keep Most Sentences Short and Simple

The most obvious difference between the two versions of the passage above is that the first was one monstrously long sentence of 95 words, and the second was five sentences, averaging 18.4 words and totaling 92 words. The first example consisted of one main clause interwoven with five dependent clauses; the second contained four independent clauses (simple sentences) and one complex sentence containing an independent and two dependent clauses.

Note, too, that the clearer version ended up slightly shorter; 95 words became 92. Brevity is not one of the most important considerations in writing, and if the writer needs more words to be clear he or she should take them (see Chapter 2). But it is enlightening to note that so often the clearer way is also the shorter way of saying something.

Working within reasonable limits any writer can find all the freedom for artistry and self-expression that any writer needs.

Short sentences give emphasis. The shorter they are, the harder they hit. They also create the feeling of action. This is because shorter sentences mean more sentences and therefore more verbs. Verbs are the action words, and skilled writers deliberately use short sentences to create the tense, fast-moving mood appropriate for action passages. *(That passage contained 11 words per sentence—acceptable for brief passages but too short for sustained reading for adults.)*

Long sentences, however, are generally useful for the slower pace necessary in descriptive passages, which are as important for proper balance as the action. They meander along, like peaceful stretches of a river, at the relaxed speed best suited for detailed viewing, slowly, deliberately unfolding information about the people, places, and things that provide the background for the actions. Although an important part of most writing, such sentences tend to subordinate the ideas they contain and therefore are generally ineffective for presenting major ideas. *(That passage contained 29 words per sentence—much too long for sustained reading. The shortest sentence had 25 words, and the longest, 35 words.)*

It is the combination of those two techniques that causes readers to say, "I enjoyed reading this."

Keep Related Words Close Together

Adjectives and adverbs should be close to the words they modify. So should prepositional phrases. Pronouns should be close to the nouns they stand for (their antecedents). Especially, subjects and their verbs should be close together. Never separate a subject from its verb by very much other information; the reader may not be able to match the two, and the result is verbal derailment. In the 95-word passage on page 202, the subject of the main clause (*network*) is separated from its verb (*includes*) by three other clauses—three other subjects and verbs—50 words. Such constructions are put on paper by klutzes, not writers.

This is not to say writers should avoid using subordinate clauses; such advice would be unthinkable. Subordinate (dependent) clauses are marvelously useful because they do exactly what their name implies: They signal to readers that some facts are subordinate to (less important than) others. The trouble is that some developing writers, perhaps trying to appear literary by using long sentences, put vital information into subordinate clauses. *Buried information.* That simply does not make sense. Writers are not being reasonable if they expect readers to know an idea is important when the person who wrote it sends signals it is unimportant.

Putting a clause or phrase into another is called *embedding*. It is not always wrong, but it is an invitation to trouble:

> The report, which was prepared by a panel of prominent educators appointed by the President, shocked Americans by stating we would view it as an act of war if a foreign power had attempted to impose on America the mediocre education performance that exists today. (45 words)

That construction invites readers to pass quickly by the information between the commas, or to ignore it. The writer treated as incidental the idea that the report was prepared by a panel of prominent educators and that they were appointed by the President; why, then, should the reader not also consider it unimportant? The two major ideas compete for the reader's attention. One dominates, and the other goes partly unnoticed; or they share equally, neither getting the full attention it deserves.

Try:

> The report shocked Americans by stating we would view it as an act of war if a foreign power had attempted to impose on America the mediocre educational performance that exists today. It was prepared by a panel of prominent educators appointed by the President. (Still 45 words)

Should You Split Infinitives?

Well, not usually. The infinitive is the *to be* form of a verb (*to examine, to walk*); you split it by putting another word between *to* and the rest of the verb (*to carefully examine, to slowly walk*). You can almost always unsplit it easily by just switching two words (*to examine carefully, to walk slowly*). And when you can do this, you should. Occasionally, however, unsplitting may create awkwardness (*To really understand differential equations . . .*). In such cases, but only in such cases, even the strictest grammarians will concede that a split infinitive may be useful.

Perhaps a century too late, in 1995 the Oxford University Press announced it agrees with this slightly relaxed attitude toward splitting, dismissing the total ban as "schoolroom mythology." It cited "To boldly go. . . . ," the introduction to the television series *Star Trek*. A few newspaper editorial writers groaned, however—in the United Kingdom and the United States.

or:

> The report was prepared by a panel of prominent educators appointed by the President. It shocked Americans by stating we would view it as an act of war if a foreign power had attempted to impose on America the mediocre education performance that exists today. (Still 45 words)

The sentence structure Winston Churchill described as "noble" (see page 197) contains a subject, transitive verb, and direct object. It may contain much more, but that structure is the foundation of all the rest.

THE SIMPLE SENTENCE

It need not always be simple in the sense of *easy,* or even *short,* but grammatically a simple sentence comprises* one independent clause. It needs no more than a subject and verb:

> Pavarotti sang.

Clauses that simple are occasionally useful, but they are inflexible, and most writers use them sparingly. The *subject–transitive verb–direct object* structure is far more widely used:

> Daisy chases squirrels.

This too is a simple sentence (only one clause):

> The new optical fiber (*subject*), with a core only one-sixth the thickness of a human hair (*phrase*), will improve (*transitive verb*) video quality (*direct object*).

This too:

> Despite Libya's intervention in Chad and the public furor over the conviction of a former CIA agent for smuggling secret information to Libya (*phrase*), for years agents (*subject*) of the Kadaffi regime continued (*transitive verb*) to seek the aid of U.S. business executives in acquiring American military equipment (*direct object* [from "to seek" to the end]).

---

*Yes, *comprises* is correct here. The whole comprises the parts. (See page 92.)

COMPOUND SENTENCES

Daisy chases squirrels, but she has never caught one.

Two (or more) independent clauses are joined by conjunctions; each has its own subject, transitive verb, and direct object.
These also are compound sentences:

An aspirin a day can keep heart attack away, according to research reports from several sources recently, and growing numbers of doctors are recommending this regimen, now approved by the Department of Veterans Affairs, to patients of middle age or older.

No one here has the authority to tell you what to do, but if you're sensible you will listen to good advice and decide on the basis of what is best for the organization, not for you.

In each one, two independent clauses are joined by a conjunction (*and* . . . / *but* . . . ,) and each one is adorned by several phrases. (No other clauses, not even subordinate ones.) Compound sentences rarely get more complicated than these. As more information is added, one of the many phrases may take on a subject and verb, making it a clause; the sentence is then *complex,* or *compound/complex.*

COMPLEX

As writers pack more information into compound sentences, grammar relationships often change and they tend to become *complex.* These sentences combine one independent and at least one minor (dependent or subordinate) clause. Complex need not always be complicated, however:

The sexy actress failed her screen audition by the National Committee, which plans to edit her out of this year's Memorial Day National Telethon.

Then there are complex sentences with the dependent clause sandwiched in the middle of the independent one:

This new document, which defines the terms of your insurance coverage in plain English, now becomes part of the policy and should be kept in your files as part of the policy.

COMPOUND/COMPLEX SENTENCES

Compound/complex sentences are exactly what the name implies. Although their name sounds menacing, they can be as natural and as welcome as sunshine:

I failed, but others *who follow me* (*dependent clause*) will succeed.

Even long ones can be reader friendly when composed by writers who understand the effect sentence structure has on readability.

Trouble comes, however, when writers let ideas just pile up, concerned only with finishing the job, indifferent to the person (victim) at the other end. The content may be accurate and the grammar correct, but those qualities alone do not ensure good writing:

Although ecologists, conservationists, and resource planners have been predicting for decades that a water shortage in the near future will hinder future industrial and population growth in the Southwest, the results of research studies are inconclusive and have in fact raised newer controversies, encouraging some state and city planners in the Great Lakes area of the United States, where fresh water is a plentiful commodity, to conduct preliminary studies, hopeful that the shift in national growth will reverse itself in the next 15 to 20 years and that business activities (if not populations) will return, at least somewhat, to the demographic patterns of the post-World War II period. (108 words)

Long before it gets that overpacked, it almost invariably becomes compound/complex, but few people would care.

What a Difference Punctuation Makes

Your manuscript is both good and original; but the part that is good is not original, and the part that is original is not good.

—Samuel Johnson

If grammar may be compared to a set of traffic rules, punctuation marks are like traffic signals. They guide readers; they tell readers when to go and when to stop, and when to turn, and in what direction.

The modern tendency is to use as little punctuation as possible, and that is probably a wholesome attitude. But the question is: How much is enough? We would not want a traffic light at every street corner, but with none at all driving would be a survival sport. Likewise, reading would be tedious with a comma after every phrase but impossible with none at all. Those little black marks had better be where they are needed.

Punctuation marks can be divided into two categories.

Bread-and-butter punctuation marks are the ones every writer *must* use regularly: the period and the comma. You could not write much without both of them. Elegant punctuation marks are all the others, and most nonprofessional writers do not use them very often—but should.

To use punctuation correctly, and to understand fully the advice in this section, the writer needs to understand what phrases and clauses are, and the differences between them. Also the meanings of the terms *restrictive, nonrestrictive, dependent,* and *independent.* (See Chapter 17.)

THE BREAD AND BUTTER MARKS

Everything in writing begins with a capital letter and ends with a period. The sense of what is in between depends as much on those little black marks as on the words themselves.

The Period

Just as a capital letter signals the beginning of a sentence, a period signals the end of one. No problem here. Use periods at the ends of sentences (except when ending with a question mark or exclamation point). The period denotes a full stop. (In fact, the English call it a "*full stop.*") Because it signals the end of a sentence, a period can never show its face in the middle of a sentence for any reason (except abbreviations).

Use periods after most, but not all, abbreviations. How to tell which? If the term is normally pronounced in its abbreviated form, no periods are necessary. Acronyms (words made of the initials of a compound term) usually fall into this category. We usually pronounce *NASA* as "Nas-sah"; the periods are not necessary (though they are acceptable). But with *Dr.*, we say "Doctor," not "Der." Here the period is necessary. (But not in England.)

The Comma

If the period is a full stop, the comma ranges from a half to a quarter stop. The comma tells readers to pause, helping them relate the words in their minds the way the writer intended, to ensure that each little piece of information is received the way the writer intended.

What a difference a comma makes! There is a vast gulf of misunderstanding, for example, between:

> I hereby bequeath all of my worldly possessions to the first of my offspring, who lives a good life. (*The first one is a nice kid.*)

and:

> I hereby bequeath all of my worldly possessions to the first of my offspring who lives a good life. (*One of them may turn out nice, but it's too early to tell which one.*)

Capital Letter after a Colon?

No, in most cases. Yes, when the passage that follows is a full sentence and is longer than just a few words. *We can't grow peppers for one reason: rabbits love the young plants.* Or: *The committee must find solutions to two problems: poor visibility and irregular harvest schedules.* But: *One fact about American automobiles should not go unnoticed: They are uniquely designed for transportation needs in a country larger than all of Europe.*

And between:

> After studying the plans, I feel sure, Smedley will approve them. *(Smedley will study and approve them.)*

and:

> After studying the plans, I feel sure Smedley will approve them. *(I have studied them and feel sure Smedley will approve them.)*

In each of these examples, both versions are grammatically correct. But in each case only one is what the writer intended to say. Which one the reader chooses is a matter the careful writer should not be willing to leave to chance.

Use commas in the following seven situations:

To separate independent clauses in a compound sentence. Remember, both halves of the sentence must be able grammatically to stand alone, and they must be connected by one of the coordinating conjunctions: *and, but, or, nor, for, so,* and *yet.*

> The food coloring is suspected of causing cancer in test animals and cancer and birth defects in humans, and the FDA does not allow its use in soft drinks.

Some writers argue that this comma is unnecessary if the two clauses are short. But how short? Setting a limit would be hard, and doing so is not necessary. A safer attitude: Use a comma between the independent clauses of all compound sentences, no matter how short:

> I'm going *now,* but I'll be back soon.

To separate a conjunctive adverb from the main clause of a sentence. Introductory words such as *therefore, however, incidentally, furthermore* need a slight pause (unlike conjunctions):

> *Nevertheless,* the result may not be known for years.

Because they are adverbs, you can also place these gems in the middle, next to the verb:

> We decided, *therefore,* not to return to Alaska this year. *(Note that the conjunctive adverb requires two commas when placed in the middle of the sentence.)*

or at the end:

> The Wimbledon judges disagreed, *however.*

To separate an introductory phrase or clause from the main clause of a sentence.   With phrases you get some freedom of choice. For a very short phrase (such as that one) you may omit the comma.

> A year later those same students organized a campaign to. . . .

But if the introductory phrase is long enough (such as this one) to cause readers trouble sensing its end and the beginning of the main clause, this comma provides an important pause and should be used:

> A year after volunteering to fight the forest fires spreading rapidly throughout the nearby Hocking Valley National Park, those same students organized a campaign to. . . .

When it is an introductory *clause* (such as these two), no matter how long or short it is, the comma will help your reader and should be used.

To isolate *nonrestrictive* phrases, clauses, or appositives from the rest of a sentence.   These commas make an important statement. They tell readers the information between them is optional (nonrestrictive); it could be removed or ignored without changing the essential meaning of the part that remains. Be sure to use a pair:

> George Gershwin, *one of America's greatest composers,* had an equally famous brother named Ira.

But if that parenthetical passage begins or ends the sentence containing it, of course you need only one comma rather than a pair:

> *One of American's greatest composers,* George Gershwin died at age 39 of a brain tumor.

> Nowhere was baseball more exciting to watch than in Yankee Stadium, *the house that Ruth built.*

To separate the items in a series.   Write: The colors are *red, white, and blue.* For a brief time the *U.S. Government Printing Office Style Manual* decreed that the last of these commas (before the *and*) was optional. Many writing experts objected, pointing out that confusion can often result from its omission, and the government's style authorities restored it in the next edition of the *Manual.* Most careful writers today do use this comma. It is called the "serial comma."

To separate a quoted passage from the words used to introduce it.

Julian Krebsbach said, "I don't think this will really solve the problem."

or:

"I don't think," Julian Krebsbach said, "this will really solve the problem."

In some cases you may want to use a colon to introduce a quotation with more emphasis than the comma conveys:

Bailey Herrington told the employees: "We have surpassed last year's sales, and each of you deserves part of the credit."

But not:

Gregory said: "I'll phone you tomorrow." (*In that one the colon overstates the point; a comma is more appropriate. Use a colon also to introduce any quotation of two or more sentences.*)

To provide a pause in any group of words if the absence of a comma might cause readers to misread. Time after time writing demands that we watch carefully for situations in which readers might turn the wrong direction if the writer fails to provide signals:

For the opening, segments of the play were cut out.

Traditional grammar says the comma is optional after a short introductory phrase. But then readers might begin receiving:

For the opening segments of the play. . . .

After going that far most careful readers would realize the rest does not fit, and would readjust the idea and continue reading correctly; although the punctuation is awkward, no great harm is done. But how about:

For the opening, segments of the play that contained really torrid sex scenes or that seemed draggy in final rehearsals were cut out.

Who or Whom?

To tell, you need to be able to recognize whether the word is being used as a subject or an object. *Who* is nominative (for subjects), and *whom* is objective (for objects). Sometimes deciding is easy: *Who* (subject) took that photograph? I'm not sure *whom* (object) to call about this.

But other times you may have to examine carefully: "The report must be signed by (*whoever* or *whomever?*) made the arrest." Answer: *whoever,* because it is the subject of the dependent clause, *whoever made the arrest.* (The entire clause is the object of the preposition *by.*)

By the way, the possessive of *who* is *whose,* not *who's.* Use *who's* only as the contraction of *who is.*

Further by the way: "Who's Who?" is correct, not "Who's Whom?"

Now if that comma is removed, a reader who makes the wrong turn at that point has a long way to go (to *rehearsals*) before realizing he or she misread. Readers will not—perhaps cannot—tolerate such klutzlike workmanship for long.

In such situations, knowledge of the rules cannot substitute for alert thinking. Good writers need both.

THE ELEGANT PUNCTUATION MARKS

Periods and commas are, of course, the most widely used punctuation marks. But there are many other marvelously useful ones that most writers seldom, if ever, use. Examine any computer or typewriter keyboard. Every punctuation mark there is useful, and every writer ought to know how to use them all.

The Semicolon

The semicolon is a truly elegant tool, but it is badly misunderstood and underused. Perhaps the misunderstanding comes from it name. A semicolon is not a half colon; in fact a semicolon has nothing to do with a colon, and therefore the name is misleading. It is always used as either a semiperiod or a supercomma.

Use the semicolon as a semiperiod (*half stop*) when you feel that a period (full stop) would create too large a break between the ideas. Typically this occurs when the ideas are intimately related:

> A hen can lay eggs without a rooster; they're simply not fertile and won't hatch into chicks.

Note that in this example both the clauses are independent; each is capable of standing alone as a full sentence. The author could just as easily have written ". . . without a rooster. They're simply . . . ," but the passage would be less stylish. Also note there is no conjunction between the two independent clauses when the semicolon replaces a comma (and a conjunction) to join independent clauses.

Use a semicolon as a supercomma to separate items which themselves contain commas—the writer has already used the ordinary comma and now needs a slightly larger pause. For example, a series in which each part itself contains a smaller series:

> The colors were red, white, and blue; green, white, and orange; and red, yellow, and black.

Parentheses

Parentheses flash to the reader that the information contained (whether a word, phrase, or clause) is optional reading. That information must be *nonrestrictive;* the writer must be able to lift it and close the gap without destroying the unity or meaning of the sentence:

> Most of us believe that Klipinger (although right now she is emphatic) will change her mind before June 30th.

Always use parentheses in pairs. There are no exceptions. Whenever opening a passage with one, the writer should *without fail* check and double-check that its closing mate appears where it belongs. Also remember: Parentheses signal to the reader that the information they contain is optional. Do not, therefore, use them for important information; that would be self-defeating.

Use brackets for parentheses within parentheses (again [as here], always in pairs). All computer keyboards and most modern typewriters have them.

The Dash

Use dashes to mark a sudden break in thought, or to give some information added emphasis:

> Many states—New York was the first—have passed laws requiring that consumer contracts be written in plain English, so the ordinary consumer can understand.

Notice this usage is exactly the same as parenthesis, but the separated information gets far greater emphasis; readers no longer treat it as optional reading. The information may be a phrase or a clause, but it is *nonrestrictive.* Also notice that when used this way *in the middle of a sentence* the dashes must appear in pairs, the same as parentheses.

A slightly different use of the dash is to provide dramatic separation for an idea immediately after a main clause:

> We tried everything we could—but nothing worked.

In that example, the second idea is an independent clause joined to the first by a dash (serving as a conjunction). The regular rule calls for a comma here, but the dash gives greater emphasis—and style. It even gives the writer freedom to drop the conjunction:

We tried everything we could—nothing worked.

Furthermore, the added idea need not be a clause; it can be a phrase:

Pierpont is the hardest worker in the company—on Mondays.

But note: Do not use dashes very often. Their overuse interferes with the smooth flow of ideas and may annoy readers.

Neither computer keyboards nor typewriters have a key for the dash. For computers, most word processing programs provide one in the menu bar *insert→character set* selection box. On a typewriter we create a dash by typing two consecutive hyphens.

The Colon

Think of the colon as a trumpet blast. It announces: Stop what you're doing, and pay attention to what follows.

The terminals that must be replaced immediately are:

And that is the major way the colon is used. It is certainly a valuable signal to give readers.

(Many writers say: "The terminals that must be replaced are *as follows*:. . . ." Not a serious flaw, but the words *as follows* are wasted here; the colon says the same thing.)

Use a colon also to introduce a quotation if you want the quoted passage to have greater emphasis than a comma (ordinarily used for this purpose) would give it. Also use a colon to introduce a quotation of two or more sentences.

The Apostrophe

Use the apostrophe to form the possessive case of nouns: *The real estate agent's commission,* or *everybody's business,* or *Claudette Vachon's monkey.*

If a singular noun ends with *s,* use the apostrophe but the *s* after it is optional: The Atlas's pages. . . . or the Atlas' pages. . . . (Note, however, that this question can be avoided by changing the wording slightly: *the pages of the Atlas.* For plural nouns ending with *s,* add only the apostrophe—no *s* after it: *The players' decision,* or *the babies' mothers.*

Use the apostrophe also to replace missing letters in a contraction: It's (it is), we're (we are), aren't (are not), etc.

Pratt's Law

In large organizations such as government agencies, several people may have to approve everything you write, and this can cause trouble because they may not agree on what is or is not good writing. In fact, they may sometimes contradict each other. Disagreement about the amount of detail the writer should include is especially common. The poor public servant may try to please the boss by including as much supporting information as possible in a report. That boss may be pleased, but the next one up the line often says, "Too much detail—burdens the reader—the chief will never approve this." The poor public servant, then, removes the details, and the next boss up says, "Conclusions are unsupported—add details." The poor writer is bounced back and forth like a ping-pong ball.

At the U.S. Central Intelligence Agency, writers developed Pratt's Law as a guideline: "Whether you should include a large or small amount of details depends on whether there will be an even or odd number of reviewers." (See: "Managing the Writing of Others," page 161.)

Use the apostrophe also to form the plural of a number or a letter: In the 1970's and '80's. . . . or Your *R*'s look like *N*'s. For the plural form of abbreviations, follow this rule: Use 's if the letters of the abbreviation are lowercase; omit the apostrophe if they are all uppercase (capital) letters.

The Question Mark

No problem here. Most people know how to use question marks properly; we end questions with them, as we end sentences with periods.

The trouble is, most writers rarely if ever use questions in their writing. Why not? Questions are as useful in writing as in speech, and there is little reason to deprive oneself of them.

The Exclamation Point

Most writers should not need the exclamation point very often. But when we need it, how marvelously it performs! An exclamation point is a period with a bang. Not much of a bang, but enough that it signals to the reader that the writer wanted special emphasis here.

Quotation Marks

Generally speaking, use quotation marks only for quotations. Do not use them unless you are repeating the *exact* words of the person being quoted. Always use them in pairs; there is no situation in which a quotation mark can be used singly (except as a symbol for inches).

We say *generally speaking* because some writers use quotation marks another way—not for quotations but to notify the reader that a word or phrase is being used in some unusual way: The air seemed "stuffy" after the storm. The writer seems almost to be apologizing for the word. This usage of quotation marks is controversial, but most language authorities tolerate it. A wise attitude might be: A writer who feels the need to apologize very often for using words is probably not choosing them very well.

To set off a quotation within a quotation, use single quotation marks.

The Hyphen

Use this valuable little mark to divide a word that will not fit at the end of a line. Computers will hyphenate automatically if you tell them to. If you divide manually, do so only between syllables (indicated in dictionaries by a dot between letters).

Use a hyphen also to connect the words of a compound adjective if its absence could cause misunderstanding:

> Model VT8100 comes with four-channel indicators. (Its indicators have four channels.)

There is an important difference between that and and:

> Model VT8100 comes with four channel indicators. (It has four indicators of channels.)

Compound adjectives may be more than two words: *Ready-to-wear clothing, faster-than-average production rate, seventy-six-year-old marathon runner.*

Ellipsis

Three spaced dots in a quotation tell readers that the writer has deliberately left out some words:

> Abraham Lincoln said, "My paramount objective . . . is to save the union, and is not either to save or destroy slavery."

A little-known fact about ellipses: Three dots indicate the omission of words in the middle of a sentence. Four dots indicate that the omission continues to the end of a sentence; the fourth dot stands for the period. Be sure to put spaces between the dots.

Also see the Interrobang (page 122).

CHAPTER 19   CLOSER LOOK: COUNT THE PUNCTUATION ERRORS

> Humphrey Bogart, never said "Play it again Sam"; he said "You played it for her, you can play it for me. If she can stand it, I can. Play it". "Sam" is not mentioned.*

---

*Casablanca, Warner Bros. Pictures, Inc. Other famous lines from this film: "Of all the gin joints in all the towns in all the world, she [Ingrid Bergman] walks into mine," and "Here's looking at you, kid."

THE BOGIE ERRORS

1. There is no reason for a comma before *never*.

2. Use a comma to introduce most quotations; use a colon for greater emphasis.

3. Use a colon to introduce a quotation of two or more sentences.

4. The period after *Sam* seems a better choice than a semicolon because the comma a few words later between *her* and *you* needs to be a semicolon, and two of then in the sentence would be inappropriate. Without that semicolon Bogie would have had to say "for her, and you."

5. The comma after the dependent clause, *If she can stand it,* is optional (because it is a short introductory passage to the independent clause *I can*). In the film Bogie does not pause at that point, and so it should be deleted in the quote.

6. Periods and commas always go inside quotation marks. The closing punctuation must be "Play it."

7. Sam's name in the last sentence is not part of a quotation, and so no quotation marks should be used.

THE CORRECTLY PUNCTUATED PASSAGE

Humphrey Bogart never said, "Play it again, Sam." He said: "You played it for her; you can play it for me. If she can stand it I can. Play it." Sam is not mentioned.

The Five Most Common Mistakes

*There is always a comforting thought in time of trouble
when it is not our trouble.*

—Don Marquis*

Most people who write things of importance very often are likely to have passed life's basic grammar tests. They may not be quite able to quote the rules, but they are unlikely to let distasteful grammatical blips into their sentences and paragraphs, however brief. But less glaring mistakes are common among ordinary, educated adults who must write things—even the highly educated. From a zoo curator: *"Being a baboon who grew up wild in the jungle, I was aware Wiki had special nutritional needs."*

Although the creative aspect of writing is an art, the part of the job that deals with putting our ideas onto paper (after we have created them) is a craft. And, as with any other craft, certain principles need to be understood and mastered if we are to join the truly skilled. Mistakes always lurk over the writer's shoulder, and the skilled know how to avoid them.

The most common problems are: dangling participle, subject-verb disagreement, noun-pronoun disagreement, false series, and the missing second comma.

---

* *The Lives and Times of Archie and Mehitabel,* Doubleday and Company, Inc.

This axiom of the craft helps writers avoid such errors: *In grammar, related parts must match.*

If the parts do not match, or if they match in a way the writer could not envision, a sentence can end up saying something the writer never intended.

DANGLING PARTICIPLE

Of course the zoo curator was not a baboon who grew up wild in the jungle. Why did that writer make a statement he or she never intended? For the same reason business executives write such statements as:

After *discussing* the things that could go wrong, the outdated machines worried the engineers.

As *reconstructed* by officials, the terrorists blew up the ship around midnight.

All three of these danglers are participles (verb forms) in phrases that have no subjects. (They have objects.)

The fault is that in each case that participle (*italicized*) has no noun to make a proper connection. Something else (the subject of the main clause) lurks nearby, however, and that something else ends up receiving a modifier the writer certainly never envisioned: *Being a baboon . . . , I realized . . . ; After discussing . . . , the machines worried . . . ; As reconstructed by officials . . . , the terrorists. . . .* Those tricky little orphans dangle, or wander around, like barnacles ready to latch onto the first big thing that bumps into them.

It's significant that danglers usually live in phrases. If the subject of the main clauses comes along immediately, a troublesome (often outrageous) statement awaits the reader. *Note* that if the phrase were a clause it would have its own subject, and the mistake would not be possible:

Because *she* is a baboon . . . *I* realized Wiki had. . . .

After *the engineers* discussed the things . . . the outdated machines. . . .

As *the tragedy* was reconstructed by officials, the terrorists. . . .

Now the actions and conditions match their sources as the writers intended.

But there can be other kinds of danglers, beside participles:

Vital to all U.S. wildlife, the President is pressing for passage of the Bill.

Is any president that popular? This writer obviously intended the introductory phrase to serve as an adjective modifying *the Bill*. It has neither a subject nor a verb; it just hangs there waiting for something to modify. And the wrong thing comes along.

SUBJECT-VERB DISAGREEMENT

Singular subjects take singular verbs; plural subjects take plural verbs. There are no exceptions, and violators will be mistreated.

No thinking person would write, *The solution are easy*. But one wrote: *The solution to these problems, and to similar problems faced by millions of travelers between cities in eastern states, especially those that are airline hubs,* are *easy*.

The structure of that errant sentence was an invitation to trouble. Its subject is *solution* (singular); the verb *of the main clause* belongs to that subject, and therefore it too *must* be singular: *is*. But it is too far away. Embedded between them, surrounded by commas, is a string of nonrestrictive phrases (too many combinations to count), containing nine plural pronouns, and that is the invitation to trouble. Perhaps the writer carelessly thought the subject was *problems* (plural) because it is closer to the verb.

Remember, whether it is a simple sentence or the most complicated one you can construct, every clause consists basically of a subject and verb. It may also have in it several modifying words, phrases, or even other clauses, embedded between the subject and verb of the main clause. Take care, writer. That separation is a trap waiting to spring. The writer may be unsure, when the verb finally comes along: *what was the subject, anyhow?* And that is why writing stylists so often advise, on syntax: Do not embed very much other information between a subject and its verb. A better place for such embellishments, still in the same sentence, is *after* the main subject and verb.

Might This Advice Limit the Writer's Freedom of Style?

This question is asked often. Surely we need phrases and subordinate clauses—for subordinate ideas. If every small idea were a separate sentence, major and minor ideas would be treated alike; readers would have great difficulty telling them apart. Surely too, an occasional writer can construct extremely long sentences containing large chunks of embedded information, some of those having further embeddings, and keep all the parts matching. But can readers absorb all the information? A more useful question regarding freedom of style, then, seems to be: *Should writers want to exercise the freedom to erect barriers between themselves and readers?* English always leaves us an infinite variety of styles—without sacrifice.

Skilled writers are able to identify subjects and verbs and keep their relationships correct, perhaps intuitively. The less skilled, who may be shaky on this, should be aware: *The longer the sentence, the greater the care that must be taken to ensure that all the parts match.*

Sometimes a particular group of words may cause the writer fits trying to decide the singular/plural question.

Either the manager or the two lab chiefs revise (?) the database every day.

Or should that be revises? Both are half right, because each agrees with half of the subject. But both are also half wrong. Smart writers will not allow themselves to be snared in that kind of trap. Reword the idea:

Either the manager revises the data base every day, or the two lab chiefs do.

The compound sentence gives us two subjects, each comfortably matched with the verb it needs.

There is *always* a way to keep the parts matching, and it should be easy if the writer is alert.

NOUN-PRONOUN DISAGREEMENT

The trouble with reading to check the accuracy, or clarity, of our own writing is that the writer has an advantage no other reader can ever have. Every honest writer knows what he or she is trying to say *and is not relying on those little black marks on the page to find out.*

In an important sense this is a also a major disadvantage to every writer. Each of us is the least typical reader in the world of our own writing. If something is wrong down there, we tend to see not what we wrote but what we *intended* to write. With its privileged information, the writer's brain (but no one else's) tends to fill any gaps.* (This is the main reason the serious writer should never, never proofread his or her own work.)

* See "Blind spots," page 41.

Pronouns are especially dangerous in this respect.

Their trouble, of course, is that pronouns usually stand for something else nearby (*pro-noun,* for a noun). That something else is called the *antecedent,* and a pronoun and its antecedent must match each other.

Loose Antecedent (Dangling Pronoun)

The writer of this sentence knew what it meant, but can readers tell? Only if they already know:

> The two Hemsley mountain bikes were preferred for prolonged use in humid terrain, according to the Italian test results. Because these tests were limited, however, experts are unwilling to give *them* high marks.

The trouble here is obvious: Are the two Hemsley mountain bikes or the Italian test results the antecedent of the pronoun *them?*

Grammar tells us a pronoun tends to stand for the last noun before it. Ah, if life were that simple. *Tends to?* That may be statistically reliable, but the sentences do not take statistics very seriously. Further trouble arises because real-world readers are not likely to analyze such a mistake as carefully as people reading books about writing. In fact, most readers would not notice anything wrong in a sentence such as the one above; they are likely to read one interpretation or the other, unaware they had a choice.

> The President has decided to veto the measure, and minority leaders consider the decision outrageous. Most Americans, according to network surveys conducted over the weekend, agree with *this* point of view.

Which point of view? the President's, or that of the minority leaders? The antecedent of the pronoun was obvious to the writer, but readers can't tell.

How do writers ensure that their pronouns have obvious antecedents? This is probably one of the most difficult problems—even for skilled, experienced writers. Not even an understanding of the problem is a guarantee of accuracy. We can advise only: Be careful. Be sensitive. Be kind to your pronouns, but be suspicious of them. And make sure each one has a proper mate.

Singular Noun and Plural Pronoun (or Vice Versa)

A midwestern disc jockey signs off each day saying:

> When you see someone without a smile, be sure to give *them* yours.

Pronouns must agree with their antecedents in gender (sex) and number. In the old days, before nonsexist writing became important, most of us would have said or written "be sure to give *him* yours," and few people would have cared or even noticed anything wrong.

Today, generic use of the pronoun *he* causes women *and men* who care about sexual equality to frown. But singular pronouns with plural antecedents cause people who care about correct grammar to frown.

That nondiscriminating disc jockey, trying to do the right thing, could have satisfied both sides if he or she had read some sensible Guidelines for Nonsexist Writing. (See Chapter 6.)

It is true English does not have neutral third-person *personal* pronouns in the singular. (*It* is third person but impersonal.) So, nonsexist guidelines advise: Switch to the plural. *But we must do so for both the pronoun and its antecedent.* We lose nothing at all by saying:

> When you see *people* without a smile, be sure to give *them* yours.

This is not to suggest, however, that the problem of mismatched pronouns and antecedents is unique to nonsexist writing. In any writing, antecedent and pronoun, like subject and verb, must agree in number: singular-to-singular (he, she, it, . . . him, her, it) and plural-to-plural (they . . . them). They must also agree in gender: male-to-male, female-to-female, and neutral-to-neutral.

Then there is the problem of pronoun case (unrelated to antecedents). Which is correct: *he and I* . . . or *him and me?* Both, depending upon how they are used.

In English, the form of a pronoun depends also on whether it is a subject or an object. If the pronoun is a subject it takes the *nominative* case: *I* like red wine. If the pronoun is an object, it takes the *objective* case: But red wine doesn't like *me.* Two kinds of objects are most common: direct objects of transitive verbs (we notified [transitive verb] *her*) and objects of prepositions (we sent the notice to [preposition] *her*).

Which is correct, then: . . . between *he and I* or . . . between *him and me?*

> *He and I* sat between the two kids. (The pronouns are subjects and, therefore, must be in the *nominative* case.)

But:

> The two kids sat between *him and me.* (The pronouns are objects—of the preposition *between*—and, therefore, must be in the *objective* case.)

Exception: the verb *to be*. If the main verb of the sentence is a form of *to be* (*was, is, will be, am*, etc.), use nominative pronouns, not objective. It is *I* (not *me*) who must make the decision. In this construction, the pronoun is actually a predicate nominative, not an object.*

FALSE SERIES

A normal series follows the pattern: *one, two, and three*. A false one follows the pattern: *one, two, and C.*

> The new cartridges save time, money, and improve employee morale.

> Mastroianni's last effort is well acted, well directed, and will be remembered for the sensitivity of the aging actor's performance.

Related parts *must* match! In both the examples above, a writer declares the intention to build three thoughts on a word they share in common.

The new cartridges *save*. . . . That is a transitive verb, and it requires a direct object. The author started out to give us three of them but got careless. Direct objects must be nouns (or pronouns). The first two, *time* and *money*, are; then for the third item of the series we are set up for another noun but receive a verb (*improve*) instead. You cannot do that to us, author. Readers require all the parts to match.

Mastroianni's latest effort *is*. . . . That is a linking verb, and it needs something to link to. The author gives us two predicate adjectives (*well acted* and *well directed*), then throws us off balance by slipping us a verb (*will be remembered*). We will have none of it, author. Get your parts to match.

Correcting such errant passages will be easy, as the writer sits working, if he or she gives the matter a little thought. Only slight rewording is needed in these two examples. The first one should be a series of verbs:

> The new cartridges save time, save money, and improve employee morale.

or no series:

> The new cartridges save time and money, and they improve employee morale.

What's ". . . is, is . . ." Doing Here, Anyhow?

Language watchers first spotted this odd usage soaring across the skies in the mid-1980s, barely noticeable at first. It is alleged a young secretary in Cleveland told her boss, "The trouble is, is that the accountants won't finish the report until Monday." Other spotters reported similar incidents shortly later, some attributed to older perpetrators; this was clearly not a youth thing or a regional quirk. You can hear it fairly often now, even on television and radio, but we never see it in print (except in books about writing).

The "is-is" has no explanation in grammar or in the history of English. The only correct usage of *is* (twice consecutively) might be a statement such as, "The important question facing us now is: Is the public ready for Is-is-ism?"

Listen for it. Report it to us.

---

* This example of linguistic purity (pronoun cases) from The Holy Bible: "He that is without sin among you, let him first cast a stone at her." —*John, 8:7.*

And the second example:

> Mastroianni's latest effort is well acted, is well directed, and will be remembered for the sensitivity of the aging actor's performance.

or:

> Mastroianni's latest effort is well acted and well directed, and it will be remembered for the sensitivity of the aging actor's performance.

The same mistake in a different form occurs when the writer presents a series of items vertically but gets thoughtless.

> These are the steps we must take in order to update the system:
> A. Replace all existing disks.
> B. Modify the terminals.
> C. The operators must be retrained.

Nothing doing, writer!

Use parallel structures for parallel ideas. If A and B begin with verbs (or any other part of speech), so must C. This is easy, and it is important. Only slight rewording is needed:

> C. Retrain the operators.

Then all the parts match.

THE MISSING SECOND COMMA

Earlier we emphasized that a nonrestrictive phrase or clause is set off from the rest of the sentence by a pair of commas *when it is in the middle of a sentence*. Those commas signal something important as the receiver receives the sender's words and sentences and reconstructs them into ideas. A *pair* of commas. But many writers omit the second one.

> The only parts of the body capable of feeling heat, the doctor explained are the skin and the inside of the mouth.

That should be:

> . . . capable of feeling heat, the doctor explained, are. . . .

And:

> We will, if necessary instruct the airline to return the shipment to us.

must be:

> We will, if necessary, instruct. . . .

Those commas tell the reader that the information between them is optional (nonrestrictive). It should be possible to lift out that information and close the gap without changing the meaning of the parts that remain. And the reader must be able to tell quickly and easily where the nonessential information begins and ends. Hence, the two commas. The parts then match.

Sentences containing the five most common mistakes are shown below, followed by the corrected versions.

CHAPTER 20   CLOSER LOOK: DANGLING PARTICIPLE

> Delaney was found guilty, but instead of going to jail the judge placed her on probation.

> After spending 20 minutes in the icy water, rescuers finally arrived and pulled the child to safety.

should be:

> Delaney was found guilty, but instead of *sentencing her* to jail the judge placed her on probation. (The judge did not go to jail.)

> After *the child spent* 20 minutes in the icy water, rescuers finally arrived and pulled *him* to safety. (The rescuers were not in the water.)

SUBJECT-VERB AGREEMENT

> This particular group of veterans want to achieve a goal that seems entirely reasonable to me.

> The young, slick-fielding second baseman and shortstop, both products of a minor league development program that is the creation of general manager Henry Weiss and the envy of the baseball world, receives a large part of the credit for the team's resurgence.

should be:

> This particular group of veterans *wants* to achieve. . . . (The subject is *group* [singular]. Or: "*These* particular veterans *want*. . . .")

> The young, slick-fielding second baseman and shortstop, both products of . . . *receive* a large part. . . . (The subject is *second baseman and short-stop* [plural], not *Henry Weiss.*)

NOUN-PRONOUN AGREEMENT

The Klondike entries led the competition in price and reliability, according to this year's ASWS survey, but its default settings feature was judged less convenient than most others.

You'll never find a tiger in Africa; they live only in Asia.

should be:

> . . . but *their* default reset *features were judged* less convenient than most others. (The pronoun reflects back to *entries* [plural]. Note that this error triggered similar ones in the subject [*feature*] and verb [*was judged*] of the second clause; they too should be plural.)

> You'll never find *tigers* in Africa; they live. . . .

FALSE SERIES

Bianca can play flute, piano, guitar, and sing second soprano.

I'm tired, angry that we're in this mess, concerned we may not finish on time, and P&W hasn't sent the totals I requested.

should be:

> Bianca can play flute, piano, and guitar. She can also. . . . (*Singing* is not one of the things she can play.)

> I'm tired, angry that we're in this mess, and concerned we may not finish on time. And P&W hasn't. . . . (*I'm* [*I am*] is followed by a series of things about the writer; the P&W problem is not one of them.)

THE MISSING SECOND COMMA

The American goldfinch, unlike most other birds lays eggs and has chicks in late summer.

Christine Blair, the bank's loan officer told us this was a good idea.

How ironic that Alfred Nobel, the Swedish industrialist who invented dynamite established the Nobel prizes, including the Peace Prize.

should be:

The American goldfinch, unlike most other birds, lays eggs and. . . .

Christine Blair, the bank's loan officer, told us. . . .

How ironic that Alfred Nobel, the Swedish industrialist who invented dynamite, established. . . .

(In both examples the part between the commas is a *nonrestrictive clause;* the pair of commas signals to readers that this information is optional.)

Glossary of Grammar Terms

Accusative.   Synonym for *objective.*

Active Voice.   The verb form in which the subject performs the action rather than receiving it.

Adjective.   Modifies (adds to the meaning of) a noun or pronoun by describing it or limiting its meaning in a sentence.

Adverb.   Modifies (adds to the meaning of) a verb (*ad verb*) by telling when, where, or how. An adverb can also modify an adjective or another adverb.

Antecedent.   The word, usually a noun, that a pronoun stands for in a sentence. An antecedent may also be a phrase or clause (serving as a noun or pronoun).

Article.   There are only three articles in English: *a* and *an* (indefinite articles), and *the* (definite article). Because they modify nouns, they are adjectives.

Auxiliary Verb.   (Also called *helping verb.*) Some form of the verb *to be* in front of another verb. The main verb may take several auxiliaries: (The painting *should have been* completed by now).

Case.   The form of a pronoun that tells whether it's used in a sentence as the subject (*nominative*), an object (*objective,* sometimes called *accusative*), or a possessor (*possessive,* sometimes called *genitive*). Nouns in English change form only for the possessive (by adding *'s*).

Clause.   A group of words that has a subject and predicate (*verb*). A clause may be a whole sentence or part of a sentence. There are two kinds: (1) An independent clause can stand alone and be a complete sentence without the help of another clause (All employees received raises). (2) A dependent clause (often called *subordinate*) limits or enlarges the idea of an independent clause and depends on it for meaning (although less than half belong to the union).

233

Dependent clauses are further divided into two kinds: (A) Nonrestrictive clause—does not change the meaning of the main clause (The red brick building, *which contains the nuclear reactor,* is closed to the public). Nonrestrictive clauses are set off by commas. (B) Restrictive clause changes or qualifies the meaning of the main clause (The red brick building *that contains the nuclear reactor* is closed to the public.) Restrictive clauses are not set off by commas.

Writers really must know how to recognize these clauses if they are to use punctuation correctly.

Cliché.   A group of words used as a common expression. Writers like to use them because clichés are usually colorful or impressive. But they are generally looked upon unfavorably in serious writing; their meaning is often imprecise, and they are overused and become trite. They are never necessary.

Colloquial Language.   Common, informal language that carries neither the heaviness of formal vocabulary nor the undignified tone of slang. Colloquial language is between the two and is probably the best kind of language for most writing and all speeches. (This book is written in colloquial English.)

Complement.   A word or phrase that completes (complements) the main verb of a sentence. A complement is part of the predicate and usually appears after the main verb: (DeTocqueville, a French nobleman, wrote *an amazingly accurate study of American democracy.*) In this case, *study* is the direct object of the transitive verb wrote.

Complex Sentence.   A sentence containing one independent clause and one or more dependent (*subordinate*) clauses.

Compound-Complex Sentence.   Just as its name implies, this sentence contains both compound and complex clauses. It has two or more independent clauses (making it compound), and one of them has a dependent clause (making it complex).

Compound Sentence.   A sentence containing two or more independent clauses. Because they are independent, they must be joined by a comma and a coordinate conjunction (*and, but, or, nor, for, yet*).

Conjugation.   The changing forms of a verb to show its function (number, person, tense, voice, and mood) in a given sentence.

Conjunction.   A word (usually small) used to connect ideas. They provide logical flow from the end of one to the beginning of the next, and by so doing they help readers understand the relationships between the ideas.

Conjunctive Adverb.   (*However, therefore, nevertheless, for example,* etc.) These connect independent clauses; therefore they serve as conjunctions. But conjunctive adverbs modify the verb in the clause; therefore they are technically adverbs. Like conjunctions, they are important to writing because they connect ideas—some relationship the writer can feel—such as cause and effect (I think; *therefore* I am). Unlike conjunctions, however, they can appear either at the beginning of the clause (as in the last sentence) or in the middle, close to the verb (as in this one), or at the end. That choice gives writers choices of rhythm, variety, and emphasis.

Coordinate Clauses. The two independent clauses of a compound sentence, joined by a comma and a conjunction (*and, but, or, nor, for, yet*).

Dangling Modifier. A word or phrase that does not properly modify the part of the sentence the writer intended. Most common is the dangling participle: (*Being* the most experienced student present, the control panel was operated by Gregory.) (Strange control panel!)

Declension. The changing forms of a noun, pronoun, or adjective in many languages, to show its exact function (number, gender, and case) in a given sentence. English has no noun or adjective declensions; a noun's function is shown by its position, and adjectives do not change.

Definite Article. *The* is the only definite article in English. So called because it specifies a particular thing (*the* quarterback), as opposed to an indefinite article, which does not specify a particular thing (*a* quarterback).

Dependent Clause. A clause not capable of standing alone as a sentence (When you finish the report,. . . .); it depends on an independent clause to give it full meaning.

Direct Object. The noun or pronoun that receives the action of a transitive verb: (Our secretary [subject] answered [transitive verb] *the phone* [direct object]). The direct object may also be a phrase or clause acting as a noun: (We [subject] are trying [transitive verb] *to find a solution to this problem* [direct object]).

Gender. The form of a pronoun which tells the sex of the person that pronoun stands for (*he, she, it*). Nouns also have gender in many languages, but in English almost all nouns are neuter. (Exceptions: actor-*actress*, widow-*widower*, etc.) Adjectives, too, have gender in many languages, but not in English In French, for example, something cannot be described simply as *large*. It is *grand* if the thing we are describing is masculine (the table) and *grande* if it is feminine (the house). How do we know whether a noun is masculine or feminine? French infants have no trouble learning. But English-speaking people, used to simpler patterns, have fits memorizing these things when learning Romance languages as adults.

Genitive. Synonym for *possessive*.

Gerund. A verb used as a noun, always ending with *-ing*. A gerund may be a subject (*Swimming* is the best of exercises), or an object (We attended the *opening*). Verb phrases, too, can be gerunds (People learn better by *seeing and hearing* than by either one alone).

Helping Verb.   Another term for *auxiliary verb.*

Idiom.   A commonly accepted term that does not follow the rules of the language—in fact may even violate them: (Passenger trains have *all but* vanished from the American way of life). Idioms occur in all languages and are a curse to people learning a new language. We say "Hurry *up,*" but "Slow *down.*" Although the literal meanings of up and down are opposites, their idiomatic meanings here are almost identical; yet, we dare not switch them. Conversely, "*up* the street" and "*down* the street" mean the same thing. Who can tell why? In English, prepositions are most often used idiomatically, and they cause fits to people learning English as a second language. No logic can explain why we say: *Agreed on, hurry up, going over to, chasing after,* or *down to the corner.*

Imperative.   The form (mood) of a verb that denotes command: (Be here promptly at ten). The subject (you) is omitted, implied.

Indefinite Article.   *A* and *an.* These are the only indefinite articles in English. So called because they do not specify a particular thing (*a* computer program), as opposed to *definite article,* which does specify a particular thing (*the* computer program).

Independent Clause.   A clause capable of standing alone as a sentence without the help of any other words. Every sentence must have one.

Indicative.   The most common form (mood) of verbs, denoting that the action is fact: (My left-handed son *wants* to be a pitcher).

Indirect Object.   A second object of some transitive verbs, other than its direct object. This kind of object usually denotes the person or thing indirectly affected by the action of that verb: (We [subject] sent [transitive verb] *them* [indirect object] flowers [direct object].) Note that the preposition *to* is implied.

Infinitive.   The *to be* form of any verb (*to speak, to travel,* etc.). This is the basic verb form.

Interjection.   An exclamation, usually a word or phrase at the beginning of a sentence, serving no grammatical purpose but used to add emotion.

Intransitive Verb.   A verb that does not need an object to complete its meaning (my back *hurts*). All passive voice verbs are intransitive (the instructions *were ignored*); the subject of that structure (*instructions*) would be the direct object of a transitive verb if the same statement were in the active voice. Note, however, that not all intransitive verbs are passive voice.

Jargon.   The specialized language of a particular profession. It is a kind of shorthand, sometimes expressing complex ideas in a few words. But it is generally considered undesirable because only people in that profession can understand it. Jargon often complicates writing unnecessarily; avoid it if possible.

Linking Verb. Every sentence must have a verb to give its subject a predicate. Usually the verb is active (the action is done by the subject to the object) or passive (the action is received by [done to] the subject). But occasionally the verb is neither active nor passive, it just links the subject to something else. That something else is either a predicate adjective (caviar is *expensive*) or predicate nominative (caviar is *fish eggs*). Another name for linking verbs is *copulative*.

Modify. To further describe the meaning of another word. (In the statement just finished, *further* modifies *describe*.) In English, adjectives modify nouns (a *modern* office) or pronouns (an *old-fashioned* one). Adverbs modify verbs (*strongly* objected), adjectives (*always* too hot), or other adverbs (*when carefully* controlled).

Mood. The form of a verb that tells whether the action it describes is fact (*indicative* mood), command (*imperative* mood), or condition contrary to fact (*subjective* mood).

Nominative Case. The form of a pronoun that denotes it is the subject of its sentence: (*We* [subject] demanded [transitive verb] a refund [direct object]).

Nonrestrictive Clause. A dependent (*subordinate*) clause that adds to the meaning of the main clause to which it is attached. It is separated from the main clause by commas: (The increase in crime, *which is everybody's concern,* has many causes). A good test: If a clause can be removed without causing the meaning of the remaining part to be inaccurate, it is nonrestrictive.

Noun. The word for a thing (*car*), idea (*truth*), process (*cooking*), or condition (*illness*). Nouns always serve as subjects of clauses or as objects. Nouns and verbs are the two most basic parts of speech.

Object. The noun or pronoun that receives the action of a verb, or that is linked to a preposition. (An object may also be a noun phrase or clause.) See: *direct object* and *indirect object*.

Objective Case. The form of a pronoun that denotes it is an object in its sentence: (They [subject] asked *me* [indirect object] to mail *it* [direct object] to *them* [object of preposition]). Also called *accusative*.

Participle. A word derived from a verb but used as an adjective (so named because it participates as both). Commonly used as a simple adjective (the *nominating* committee; *being* a retired army officer).

Also, the latter part of a verb constructed with some form of *to be*. A few of the possible forms: (he has *asked* [past participle, active voice]; he is *asking* [present participle, active voice]; he will *ask* [future participle, active voice]; he had *asked* [past perfect participle, active voice]; he had been *asked* [past perfect participle, passive voice]; he will have been *asked* [future perfect participle, passive voice]). All these participles are technically adjectives, because they modify the subject of the *to be* part of the verb.

Passive Voice. The intransitive verb form in which the subject receives the action of the verb rather than performing the action. In passive constructions, the object (of a preposition) performs the action: (The battalion *will be inspected* by the base commander). Or, there may be no object and hence no stated source of the action: (The battalion *will be* inspected).

Perfect. The verb form which denotes that the action reported by the verb was complete at the time of being reported: (She *had finished* her speech before I arrived.)

Phrase. A group of words lacking a subject or a verb, or both, but serving as some part of speech in a sentence. A phrase is distinguished from a clause, which must have a subject and a verb. Phrases may serve as a noun (*giving to charity* is a solemn obligation), adjective (*higher-than-average earnings*), verb (the lab *has been working* on this all year), or adverb (we failed, *like those before us*). Note that the noun phrase above is a gerund (verb serving as a subject). Most common are prepositional phrases (*at* each location; *before* buying). These, however, always serve in sentences as adjectives or adverbs. Many prepositional phrases are badly overused in business writing and are often called *rubber stamp phrases* (*prior to, in accordance with, in response to*). Phrases may be nonrestrictive or restrictive.

As with clauses, the writer really must understand and know how to recognize phrases to use punctuation correctly.

Possessive. The form (case) of a noun or pronoun that denotes ownership. In English, nouns are made possessive simply by adding 's. Pronouns change form entirely: (I feel as though *my* [possessive-nominative] thoughts are not really *mine* [possessive-objective]). Also called *genitive*.

Predicate. The part of a sentence or clause containing the main verb, which makes some statement about its subject: (The hovercraft ride from Dover to Calais *was the most interesting part of the trip.* René Descartes, a French philosopher, *made the simple but profound statement, "I think; therefore, I am."*)

Predicate Adjective. An adjective used to complete a linking verb. This is grammar at its trickiest. (Rush hour traffic is *heavy*.) Although *heavy* is part of the sentence's predicate, or verb statement, it is an adjective modifying the noun *traffic*. A person could live 100 years and not need to know this.

Predicate Nominative. Like a predicate adjective, a predicate nominative is used to complete a linking verb. (She is the *chairwoman*.) Although *chairwoman* is part of the predicate, or verb statement, it is a noun (hence *nominative*) modifying the pronoun *she*. This is tricky. But anyone boasting to friends about predicate adjectives probably ought to know this too.

Preposition. Used to connect a noun (or word serving as a noun) with some other part of the same sentence. That other part is its *object*.

Pronoun. A word substituting for a noun (*pro noun*), or a phrase or clause serving as a noun, usually as a subject or object.

Restrictive Clause. A dependent (subordinate) clause that limits (restricts) the meaning of the main clause. A restrictive clause is not set off by commas. (All employees *who have been with the company ten years or longer* were invited to the dinner.) A good test: If it cannot be removed without causing the meaning of the remaining part to be inaccurate, it is restrictive.

Sentence. A group of words expressing a complete thought. A sentence must contain at least one independent clause, and it must begin with a capital letter and end with a period (or other ending punctuation). A sentence contains a subject (usually a noun or pronoun) and a predicate (some statement about that subject, containing the verb). All the rules of grammar, including punctuation, serve one purpose: to help writers construct individual sentences, one at a time, that are clear to the reader.

Sentence Fragment. A partial sentence standing as a complete one (as here). Even the strictest grammarians approve the use of an occasional sentence fragment. Two rules should limit their use, however: (1) Keep them short, so the reader can tell that the omission is deliberate rather than the result of carelessness. (2) Use them only occasionally; readers feel uncomfortable if we break conventional patterns very often.

Simple Sentence. A sentence containing one independent clause and no dependent clauses: (*They passed the test*). In spite of its title, a simple sentence may be complicated. It may contain phrases, compound subject or verb, and several modifiers: (*The newly appointed adoptive parents and the natural parents, though openly hostile, need to find ways to work together and with the court representative and above all to respect the needs of the children in this most difficult of situations*).

Slang. Informal language, usually considered undignified except in writing to close friends or loved ones, or writing dialogue. (Differs from colloquial language, which is informal but dignified enough for all but the most formal writing.) In English, slang often gains dignity gradually, through common usage, and becomes colloquial. Slang is also considered less dignified than idiom, which is commonly accepted language that does not follow rules or literal definitions.

Subject. The part of a sentence or clause that connects with the main verb (predicate), by either performing or receiving the action of that verb. The subject names the person, place, or thing about which that sentence makes a statement. It is usually a noun or pronoun, but it may also be a gerund (*walking* is good exercise), a phrase (*to succeed in* *business* is not every person's goal), or a clause (*whoever lost the flash attachment* should pay to replace it).

Subjunctive.   The form (mood) of a verb which denotes that the action or condition described by that verb is contrary to fact (if I *were* a rich man).

Subordinate Clause.   Another name for dependent clause. So called because the information it contains is less important than (subordinate to) the idea in the main clause on which it depends.

Syntax.   Sentence structure; the order or relationship of the words in a sentence.

Tense.   The form of a verb that denotes whether the action it describes is in the past, present, or future.

Transitive Verb.   A verb that needs an object (direct object) to complete its meaning. In English, by far the most commonly used sentence structure is subject, transitive verb, direct object: (A rolling stone [subject] gathers [transitive verb] no moss [direct object]). There can be no sensible meaning to *A rolling stone gathers.*

Verb.   The action word. Every sentence or clause must have one; it tells what the subject does or is. Verbs and nouns are the two most baisc parts of speech.

Verbal.   A word formed from a verb but used as something else. The three common types are gerunds, infinitives, and participles.

Voice.   The form of a verb that tells whether the subject performs the action that the verb describes (active voice), or receives it (passive voice).

Index

Abbreviations, 95
Abstract (of reports), 121
Accusative case, pronouns, 233
Acronyms, 193, 210
Action, and simple sentences, 203
Active voice verbs, 36, 46, 184,
  233, 237
  (*See also* Passive voice verbs)
Address block, of letters, 149
Adjective, 182
  dependent clauses used as, 194
  phrases used as, 190
  predicate, 238
Adverb, 182
  comma used with conjunctive,
    211
  conjunctive, 222
  dependent clauses used as, 194
  phrases used as, 190
Agreement
  noun-pronoun, 224
  subject-verb, 223
American English, 4
And/but, beginning a sentence
    with, 52
Anglo-Saxon, 172
Antecedent, 183, 225, 233
Apostrophe, 216
Appendix (of reports), 122, 127

Arthur, King, 173
Article, 233
Auxiliary verb, 36

Benchley, Robert, 181
Beowulf, 168, 173
Blind spots, 41, 224
Body (of report), 122
Bogart, Humphrey, 218
Boldface type, 148
Brackets, 215
Brevity, how important, 58
British English, 4, 8
Bullets, 148 (*See also* Computers;
    Symbols)
Bureaucratic writing style, 151
But, beginning sentences with, 52
By whom information, and passive
    voice verbs, 37

Capitalization, after colon, 210
Carter, Jimmy, 60
Case, of pronouns:
  determining, 151
  nominative, objective, posses-
    sive, 183
Cato the Elder, 197

Celts, 172
Chairman, sexist nature of title, 86, 90
Charts, and appendixes, 146
Chaucer, Geoffrey, 14, 176
Chicago Manual of Style, 22
Chinese, Mandarin, 171
Churchill, Winston, 14, 36, 55, 56, 171
Clarity, principles of, 1–50
  and brevity, 58
  and references to people, 42
  and sentence length, 18–26, 69
Clause:
  defined, 191
  dependent/independent, 192
  comma use, 211
  coordinate, 235
  independent, 192, 233
    and semicolons, 214
    use of comma with, 206, 211
  nonrestrictive/restrictive, 193
  subordinate, 24, 239
Cliché, 135, 150, 234
Clustering, 135
Coin a phrase, 201
Coleridge, Samuel Taylor, 12
Colloquial language, 234
Colon, 210, 216
Comma:
  missing second, 228
  and quotation marks, 110
  uses of, 210–214
Common mistakes, grammar, the five, 221
Commonly misused words, 91–98
Communicating, xiv, 3–7, 13, 20, 39, 66, 76, 110, 153, 163, 202
Complement, 234
  in sentences, 199
Complex sentences, 200, 234

Compound adjective, hyphen used with, 218
Compound sentence, 199, 234
  use of comma in, 211
Compound/complex sentence, 200, 234
Comprise, 117
Computers, writing with, 99–104
Conclusion (of reports):
  also called *overview statement*, 112
  at the end, not needed, 114
  start with, 109
  what it should contain, 122
Conclusion (of speeches), 157
Conjugation, of verbs, 184
Conjunction, 182:
  beginning sentences with, 52
  vs. conjunctive adverbs, 60, 222
Conjunctive adverbs, use of comma with, 211
Connective (*see* Conjunction)
Contractions, 175
Conversational style, 39
Correct, who decides, 168

Dangling modifier, 235
Dangling participle, 80, 122, 222, 229
Dark Ages, 172
Dash, 215
Data are/is, 92
Deadlines, and planning, 130
Declension, of nouns, 235
Definite article, 235
Demonstrative pronoun, 162, 183
Dependent clause, 235
Descartes, René, 4
Detail, amount to include, 216
Dialects, 173
Different from/than, 178

Direct object, 235
Discussion section (of reports), 122
Disney, Walt, Studios, 17
Double negatives, 68
Double-Is-Ism, 227

Ebonics (*see* English, Black)
Editing other people's writing, 162
Edward the Confessor, 173
e.g., use of, 93
Ego satisfaction, and language, 8
Einstein, Albert, 65
Elevator door statement, 110
Elizabeth I, Queen, 5
Ellipsis, 218
Elongated Yellow Fruit Sickness, 55
Embedding, 187, 192, 204
"Emperor's New Clothes, The," 9
Emphasis, control of:
   by paragraph length, 144
   by sentence length, 22
English:
   Black, Ebonics, 172
   characteristics of, 178
   correct, 22, 168
   differences between American and British, 4
   history of, 171
   how it changes, 8
   illogic of, 52
   standard, 168, 172
Exclamation point, 217
Expletive, 92
Expository writing, organizing:
   five Ws of journalism, 111
   format for reports, 120
   goals of, 107
   inverted pyramid structure, 110

False series, 227, 230
False start:
   importance of, 131
   method of outlining, 132, 137
February/Febuary, 168
Fiore, Quentin, xiv
First-choice words, 56
Fisherman Who Had Nobody to Go Out in His Boat with Him, The (Maxwell), 16
Five Ws of journalism, 111
Formal language, 4
Format, reports, 120
Formulas, readability, 68–75, 78, 81
Fowler, Gene, 129
Fowler, H. W., 168
Fragments, sentence, 27
French connection, 171–176
Freud, Sigmund, 35
Full stop, 210
   (*See also* Period)

Gaelic, 172
Gender, of English words, 84, 86, 178, 183
Genitive case, 235
Gerund, 235
Girl, referring to a grown woman as, 86
Good/well, 198
Gourmet/gourmand, 182
Grammar:
   checking by computer, 101
   common mistakes, the five, 221
   importance of, 169
   inflectional/syntactical, 178
   rules of, 181–206
   standard, 168, 172
   what makes it correct, 168

Graphics:
  captions for, 147
  where to locate, 146
Gunning, Robert, 70

Hamlet, 92, 201
Harold II, King, 174
Hastings, Battle of, 175
He, generic use of, 84
  (*See also* Nonsexist writing)
Headings (in reports):
  as part of checklist, 124
  joy to readers, 141
  what they should say and where
    they should go, 142
Helping verb, 235
  in passive voice verbs, 36
Hemingway, Ernest, 102, 132
Hippocrates, 3
Hippopotamus joke, 144
Hopefully, 96
Huxley, Aldous, 83
Hyphen, 217
  and prefixes, 42

I and *we,* interchanging, 43
Iambic pentameter, 17
Ideas:
  arranging the order of, 111
  buried (subordinated), 24
  dividing into sentences, 21
  multiple, in long sentences, 202
Idiom, 235
i.e., use of, 93
Image, 6
Imagery, 15
Imperative mood, 184, 236
Impersonal style, 29, 42
Impressing others, 8
Indefinite article, 235

Indefinite pronouns, 183
Indicative mood, 184, 236
Indirect object, 200, 236
Indo-European languages, 171
Infamous quotation no. 1, 60
Infamous quotation no. 2, 183
Infinitive, 236
  split, 204
Inflectional grammar, 178
Information clusters, 18
  size of, 19
Interjection, 182, 236
Interrobang, 122
Interrogative pronouns, 183
Intransitive verb, 36, 184, 236
Introduction (of reports), 122
  when to write, 123
Introductory clauses/phrases, use
  of comma with, 212
Inverted pyramid structure:
  comprehension increased by,
    110
  novice writers' objections to,
    115
  opening paragraph of, 111
    elevator door statement,
    110
  and readers' needs, 111
  when conveying bad news, 118
"Is-is-ism," 227
It, used as expletive, 92
Italics, 100, 148, 158
Its, it's, and *its',* 94

Jargon, 14, 84, 236
Jefferson, Thomas, 99
Jespersen, Otto, 168
Job descriptions, sexism in, 85
Job titles, sexism in, 86
Johnson, Samuel, 209
Journalism, five Ws of, 111, 126

Key word phrases, outlining with, 133, 134
Kilpatrick, James, 167

Lady, referring to a woman as, 87
Language:
    changes in, 8, 51
    purpose of, xiv
    rules of grammar, 181, 219
    special, 14, 84
Language workload, 68
Large words:
    and clarity, 12, 18
    and resistance to understanding, 69
Latin, influences on English, 55, 172, 177
Lazy thinking, and overcomplicated language, 7
Leadership, image created by writing, 7
Legal writing, 75
Lengthening sentences, 25
Letters, fact and fancy about, 149–152
Lincoln, Abraham, 58
Linking verb, 184, 199, 236

McLuhan, Marshall, xiv
Man words, 84
Marquis, Don, 221
Maxwell, William, 16
Meat cleaver technique, 23
Melville, Herman, xiv, 71
Metaphor, 38 (*See also* Mixed metaphor)
Middle English, 173
Mind dump, 113
Mind mapping, 134
Missing second comma, 228, 231

Misunderstanding that had to happen, 14
Mixed metaphor, 30
Moby Dick (Melville), 71
Modern English, 176
Modifiers, 186, 222
    placement of, in sentences, 204
Modify, 204, 237
Mood:
    created by sentence length, 20
    of verbs, 184, 237, 239
    subjunctive, 162
Morris, Mary/William, 168
Ms., 87 (*See also* Nonsexist writing)
My Fair Lady, 176

Narrative writing, 109
National Council of Teachers of English, v, 78, 86, 92, 172
Negatives, double, 68
Ness, Elliot, 161
Noble English Sentence, 197–206
Nominative case, 237
    and pronoun agreement, 151
    of pronouns, 183
Nominative, predicate, 238
None are/is, 157
Nonrestrictive clause, 193, 233, 237
    use of commas with, 212
Nonrestrictive phrase, 191, 237
    use of commas with, 212
Nonsexist writing, guidelines for, 83–90
Normandy, Duke of, 174
Normans, 173
Noun, 182, 237
    dependent clauses used as, 193
    phrases used as, 190
    and pronoun disagreement, 224, 230

Number:
  and pronouns, 183
  and verbs, 184
Numbers, spelling of, 147

Objective case, 237
  and pronoun agreement, 151
  of pronouns, 183
Objectivity, style and, 42
Objects, 237
  in active and passive voice, 36
  direct, 197, 235
  indirect, 200, 236
  of prepositions, 201
Old English, 172
Only, position of, 57
Opening sentence, letters, 151
Organizing the information,
    110–128
  checklist for, 123
  five Ws of journalism, 111
  format, for reports, 120
  inverted pyramid structure,
    110
  narrative/expository style, 109
Orwell, George, 141
Outline, review of, by manager,
    163
Outlining, 129–139
  beating the deadline, 130
  the "false start" method, 131
  heel marks and coffee rings,
    135
  key word phrases, 133
  mind mapping, 134
  Roman numerals and, 132
  time required for, 136
  and word/sentence skill, 134
Overcomplicated language, mis-
    guidance and, 4
Oversimplified writing, 5, 25

Oxford English Dictionary, 53
Oxymoron, 169

Paradigms, 13
Paragraphs:
  lengths of, structuring, topic
    sentences of, 143
  of one sentence, 58
Parallel structure, 86, 227, 230
Parentheses, 103, 215
Participle, 237
  dangling, 80, 222, 229
Parts of speech, 181–186
Passive voice verbs, 36–39, 46–48,
    237
  appropriate use of, 37
  changing to active, 38
  concealed information, 38, 47
  concealing personal opinion,
    43
  and dull writing, 38
  past tense compared to, 38,
    44
  recognizing, 38
  and the writing of procedures,
    37
Pause:
  in public speaking, 158
  use of comma to create, 213
Penguin joke, the, 77
Pentameter, iambic, 17
People, referring to, 42
Perfect, 237
Period, 210
  called *full stop* in Britain, 4
  in legal writing, 75
  where placed with quotation
    marks, 110
Person, and verbs, 42, 184
Persuasion, 7, 58
Philosopher, grammar, 190

Phrase, 190, 238
  comma use with introductory,
    212
  nonrestrictive/restrictive, 191
  prepositional, 191
Planning, 130–140
  and deadlines, 130
  false start, importance of, 131
  outlines, 132, 137
Plurals, avoiding sexist writing by
    switching to, 84
Poe, Edgar Allan, 17
Polysyllables, 69
  in measuring readability, 70
Pope, Alexander, 11
Possessive case, pronouns, 151,
    183, 238
Possessive form of nouns, apostro-
    phe to show, 216
Pratt's Law, 216
Predicate, of sentences, 198, 238
  adjective/nominative, 238
Pre-editorial review, 163
Pre-English, 172
Prefixes, hyphenation of, 42
Preliminary sections of reports, 120
Preposition, 183, 238
  ending a sentence with, 55,
    154
Prepositional phrases, 191
Prewriting (see Planning)
Principles of Clear Writing, the
    Five, 11–50
Professional words (see Jargon)
Pronoun, 183, 238
  antecedents of, 21, 225
  case, 151
  and noun disagreement, 224
  syntax and, 204
Pronunciation, British vs.
    American, 5
Public speaking, 153

Punctuation, 209–219
  bread and butter, 210
  elegant, 214
  inside/outside quotation
    marks, 110

Quotation marks, 217
  punctuation inside or outside,
    110
Quotations, comma or colon
    before, 213

Readability, 65–82
  index, figuring, 70
    by computer, 102
  limitations of, 73
  sentence difficulty and, 69
  strengths/weaknesses,
    analyzing with, 72
  word difficulty and, 69
Readerbrain/writerbrain relation-
    ship, xiv, 112
Readers:
  knowing, 11
  understanding the needs and
    habits of, 108
Reading process, 66
Reagan, Ronald, 162
Recommendations (of reports),
    122
Renaissance, The, 177
Repetition of key words, 55
Reports:
  format for, 120
  headings, 141
  how to end, 114
  opening statement, or overview,
    112
Reviewing other people's writing,
    162

Revising one's own writing, 40
Rhythm, words creating, 17
Romance languages, 177
Romans, 172
Romeo and Juliet (Shakespeare), 8, 17

Safire, William, 168
Salutation, of letters, 149
Saturday Review, 187
Scientific writing, 76
Second comma, missing, 228, 231
Sections of a report, 120–123
    length of, 121
    when to write, 123
    (*See also* Abstract; Appendix; Body; Conclusion; Introduction; Recommendations; Summary; Title)
-sede, -ceed, or -cede, 117
Semicolon, elegant, 214
Sentence(s):
    beginning with *and/but*, 52
    buried ideas in, 22
    compound, complex, compound/complex, 199
    dividing ideas into, 21
    ending with preposition, 55
    fragments, 27, 239
    length of, and clarity, 18–26
    long:
        difficulty of reading, 69
        legal writing and, 75
        meat cleaver technique, 23
        multiple ideas in, 62
    noble English, the, 197
    readability and, 69
    short:
        combining when too short, 24
        impact of, 22
    simple, 197, 239
    subordinate clauses and, 204

syntax and, 202, 239
and words, combined workload of, 66
Series:
    false, 227, 230
    use of commas with, 212
    use of semicolons with, 214
Sexism (*see* Nonsexist writing, guidelines for)
Shakespeare, William, 5, 8, 14, 17, 92, 201
Shaw, George Bernard, 51
Simile, 163
Slang, 239
Smith, Alexander, 18
Snow job, concealing weak material with overcomplicated language, 8
Speeches (*see* Public speaking)
Speed of communication process, 6
Spelling:
    British vs. American, 5
    checking by computer, 100
Street talk, 4
Students, special writing needs of, 32
Style:
    children's, 5
    conversational, 39
    difficulty of, vs. content, 14
    overcomplicated/oversimplified, 5
    third person, 42
    of writing, 4
Style manuals, 22
Subject:
    in active and passive voice verbs, 36
    of clause, 191
    and simple sentences, 197
    syntax and, 204
    and verb disagreement, 223, 229

Subject line, of letters, 149
Subjunctive mood, 162, 184, 239
Summary (of reports), 121
Summary statement, or conclusion, importance to reader, 110
Symbols, 148 (*See also* Computers)
Synonyms, 57, 63
Syntactical grammar, 178

Taboos, the three, 52
Teacher, writer as a, 8
Tetrameter, 17
Teutonic, languages, 17, 173–176
That/which, 87
There, used as expletive, 92
Thesaurus, and word choices, 57
Third person:
  pronouns, for nonsexist writing, 84, 87
  style (impersonal), 42
Time, saved by efficient writing, 6
Title (of reports), 121
To be (*see* Verb, infinitive)
Tone:
  impersonal vs. personal, 43
  and objectivity, 43
Topic sentences, of paragraphs, 143
Twain, Mark, 91, 153
Typefaces, 148 (*See also* Computers)

Unit, as a universal synonym, 57

Verb, 184, 240
  action words, 184
  active and passive voice, 36
  close to subject, syntax, 204
  infinitive, 204, 236

mixing tenses of, 57
phrase used as, 190
and subject disagreement, 223
transitive, 36, 240
Verbal, 240
Very, banish? 100
Vikings, 173
Villon, François, 162
Vocabulary:
  attitude toward, 13
  and legal writing, 75
  and scientific writing, 75
Voice, 240 (*See also* Active voice verbs; Passive voice verbs)

Wall Street Journal, 54
Wayne, John, 107
We and *I*, interchanging, 43
Weak material, concealing with overcomplicated language, 8
Which vs. *that*, 87
Which hunt, 87
White space, the power of, 142
Who Decides What Is Correct? 22
Who vs. *whom*, 213
Who, What, Where, When, Why, 111
William the Conqueror, 175
Words:
  beauty of, 15
  choosing, 12
  clarity of, 14, 18
  difficulty of, and readability, 69
  large, created for new concepts, 14
  nonsexist, 84
  professional (jargon), 14
  repeating first choice, 55
  and sentences, combined reader workload of, 31, 66
  short ones are the most specific, 14

Workload:
  reader, 65
  word/sentence relationship,
    66–70
Writerbrain/readerbrain relation-
    ship, xiv, 112
Writing:
  academic, 77
  analyzing strengths and weak-
    nesses, 72
  bureaucratic, 151
  the first, xv
  expository, 107–109
  legal, 75

  managing other people's,
    161
  narrative, 107, 109
  nonsexist, 83–90
  oversimplified, 5, 25
  quickly and productively, 6
  reasons for, xvi, 58, 102, 124,
    163
  revising, 40
  scientific, 76
  styles of others, learning from,
    18
Writing process, xii, 6, 7, 41, 66,
    133

About the Author

Albert M. Joseph is president of International Writing Institute and is recognized worldwide as a consultant in the field of corporate education. Earlier editions of *Put It in Writing* were designed as texts for his audiovisual training programs, used by leading companies and government agencies such as AT&T, General Motors Corporation, IBM Corporation, Travelers Insurance Companies, National Aeronautics and Space Administration, and the U.S. Treasury Department. His other publications include the college textbooks *Writing Process 2000*, *English 2000*, and *Executive Guide to Grammar*.

Earlier in his career Mr. Joseph was editor-in-chief of a national business magazine, a member of the faculty of Case Western Reserve University, and guest lecturer at several other universities. For 11 years he was writing consultant to the U.S. Central Intelligence Agency.